JAZZ REFERENCE AND RESEARCH MATERIALS

CRITICAL STUDIES ON
BLACK LIFE AND CULTURE
(Vol. 22)

GARLAND REFERENCE LIBRARY
OF THE HUMANITIES
(Vol. 251)

Volume 22

Critical Studies on
Black Life and Culture

Advisory Editor
Professor Charles T. Davis, Chairman
Afro-American Studies, Yale University

Assistant Advisory Editor
Professor Henry-Louis Gates
Afro-American Studies, Yale University

JAZZ REFERENCE AND RESEARCH MATERIALS
A Bibliography

Eddie S. Meadows

GARLAND PUBLISHING, INC. • NEW YORK & LONDON
1981

Library of Congress Cataloging in Publication Data

Meadows, Eddie S.
  Jazz reference and research materials.

  (Critical studies on Black life and culture ;
v. 22) (Garland reference library of the humanities ;
v. 251)
    1. Jazz music—Bibliography. I. Title.
ML128.J3M33   016.781′57   80-8521
ISBN 0-8240-9463-8   AACR2

Printed on acid-free, 250-year-life paper
Manufactured in the United States of America

For
Eddie, Jr.

CONTENTS

II. Reference Materials

INTRODUCTION

A bibliography is one of the best means of gaining an in-depth view of a particular subject area. It can indicate what work has been completed as well as what work needs to be done. The need for a comprehensive bibliography of jazz reference and research materials is both genuine and immediate because more and more scholars throughout the world are becoming interested in the teaching of and research into jazz. This bibliography is intended to fulfill that need. In particular, it has been my purpose to compile a selected list of materials, primarily those published in the United States, that will help to improve the quality of jazz research. It has also been my purpose to provide a representative list of reference materials for music librarians' use in helping others to find the information they require.

While this bibliography is not complete, it is intended to provide a thorough survey of books, articles, and theses and dissertations written on or about specific jazz styles and jazz musicians from the turn of the century through 1978. Those materials considered most significant in and appropriate to the study of jazz subjects and individual jazz artists were the ones selected for inclusion.

The bibliography is divided into two major sections—Jazz and Its Genres and Reference Materials—with one numbering sequence throughout to simplify access. The first section contains alphabetical listings of books, articles, and theses and dissertations arranged according to several style categories. These style categories are defined and limited as follows:

General—Includes information on jazz analysis and appreciation, criticism, fiction, history, influence, and jazz and the classics. In essence, this category gathers together a range of materials to provide an overall perspective on jazz, its development, and its significance.

Pre-Swing—Includes information on performers and on

characteristics of the styles generally known as "Dixieland," "New Orleans," and "Chicago."

Swing—Includes information on Big Band arrangers, composers, conductors, and performers as well as on other jazz musicians who lived and performed during the thirties and forties.

Bop—Contains information on a select number of performers generally associated with Bop and some material on the development, influence, and criticism of Bop.

Modern—Includes information on a select number of jazz arrangers, composers, and performers as well as on jazz styles since Bop. Items on John Coltrane, Miles Davis, and Charles Mingus are listed in this category, although these musicans also performed during the Bop era.

The bibliography includes a seperate index for each section. The index for the first section includes several classifications that may require some explanation. Among them are:

Appreciation—Identifies materials with primarily positive comments on the need for or appeal of jazz for jazz's sake. The entries in this section build a case for appreciating jazz.

Critics and criticism—Identifies materials with primarily negative views on jazz.

Jazz: classics—Lists items containing primarily negative comments by classical musicians on jazz.

Jazz: effects and influence of—Lists those entries dealing with the effect of jazz on people and on other music.

Jazz: sociology—Cites entries that address issues of social change and their relationship to jazz or jazz musicians.

To assist researchers in grouping information under single research categories, some index entries, such as those for saxophonists, trumpeters, and clarinetists, have been cross-listed.

The second section of the bibliography consists of reference materials. This fully annotated section is designed to help librarians and researchers quickly identify materials they might need in investigating topics related to jazz. It contains listings of bibliographies – dictionaries – encyclopedias; biographies – auto-biographies; discographies; histories–surveys; technical materials (including improvisation); and selected anthologies–collec-

tions (recordings). The entries for biographies–autobiographies
and discographies are divided into collective and individual.
Items listed under the collective heading treat several composers
or performers while those listed under the individual heading
deal with a single jazz figure.

The materials on improvisation are also organized by
categories, with entries listed according to instrumental families,
i.e., brass, reeds, and rhythm. These families are further broken
down by instrument in the index to this section, thereby allowing
for quick identification of materials on improvisation for specific
instruments. For example, by referring to headings such as
chord studies, scales, or solos in this index, the researcher will be
able to locate related materials for such specific instruments as
guitar, piano, or saxophone.

To locate citations in this bibliography on individual jazz
musicians or jazz styles, the user is urged to consult both sections
as well as both indexes. By so doing, the librarian or researcher
will be able to identify all materials relevant to his or her particular area of inquiry.

In the process of compiling this bibliography many sources
were consulted. In addition to surveying the bibliographies of
Benford, Kennington, Gregor, Horn, and Merriam, the author
consulted *The Black Perspective in Music*, *Jazz Journal*, *Journal of
Jazz Studies*, *Record Changer*, *Metronome*, *Down Beat*, the *RILM
Abstracts*, and *Dissertation Abstracts* as well as the libraries at
Michigan State University, UCLA, the University of California
at Berkeley, and the New York Public Library. Horn's *The Literature of American Music* was particularly helpful in supplying information on a few books that were either out of print or un-
available to this writer.

This bibliography differs from the works of Benford, Kennington, Gregory, Horn, and Merriam in several ways. It is more
comprehensive than any of these previous works in that it covers
early jazz through 1978. In addition, it is arranged to meet
wide-ranging research needs; that is, the style categories in the
first part bring together a broad range of information under
single headings while treating books, articles, and theses and
dissertations separately in each category. The annotated list of
reference materials will prove particularly helpful in identifying

both jazz performance and research materials, and the two indexes will facilitate the user's access to desired materials both in the bibliography and, ultimately, in the music or general library.

A special note of thanks is due several people who helped directly or indirectly in the compilation of this bibliography. They are David and Margaret Cobbs, Samuel and Joyce Brown, and Iva LaKota.

There may be disagreement about the organization and grouping of materials in this bibliography, as there might be with any work of this scope in which the author must individually determine how best to present the material. However, it is my hope that despite any such disagreements this bibliography will be beneficial both to its users and to jazz research in general. For any errors in this work, the author accepts full responsibility.

I
Jazz and Its Genres

A. GENERAL

This category contains general information on
analysis and appreciation, criticism, fiction,
history, influence, jazz, and the classics.

BOOKS

1. Baker, David N. *Jazz Improvisation: A Comprehensive
   Method of Study for All Players*. Chicago: Maher,
   1969.

   "For the school teacher, student, amateur and professional musician. Various aspects of jazz improvisations
   are treated. Content ranges from nomenclature through
   fundamental exercises in improvisation techniques to
   advanced concepts of jazz playing. Bibliographies and
   discographies are included." (Standifer and Reeder)

2. Baker, Dorothy. *Young Man with a Horn*. New York:
   Houghton Mifflin, 1938.

3. Balliett, Whitney. *Sounds of Surprise*. New York: E.P.
   Dutton, 1959.

   Primarily concerned with important jazzmen of the
   1954-1959 era.

4. Berendt, Joachim Ernest. *The New Jazz Book: A History
   and Guide*. New York: Hill & Wang, 1962.

5. Blackstone, Orin. *Index to Jazz*. New Orleans: Gordon
   Gullickson, 1947.

6. Blesh, Rudy. *Shining Trumpets*. New York: Knopf, 1946.

   A history of jazz.

7. Coevroy, André, and André Schaeffner. *Le jazz*. Paris:
   Aveline, 1926.

8. Condon, Eddie. *Treasury of Jazz*. New York: Dial, 1956.

3

9. ————, and Thomas Sugrue. *We Called It Music.* New York: Henry Holt, 1947.

10. Dance, Stanley. *Jazz Notebook.* Newark, Nottinghamshire, England, 1945.

11. Dankworth, Avril. *Jazz: An Introduction to Its Musical Basis.* London: Oxford University Press, 1968.

12. Delaunay, Charles. *Hot Jazz.* New York: Criterion, 1950.

13. ————. *De la vie, et du jazz.* Lausanne: Editions de l'échiquier, 1939.

14. DeVita, A. Ray, comp. *Musicians' Handbook: Standard Dance Music Guide.* Brooklyn: DeVita, 1958.

15. Dexter, Dave. *Jazz Cavalcade.* New York: Criterion, 1946.

16. ————. *The Jazz Story.* New York: Prentice-Hall, 1964.

17. DuPont, Jean. *Introduction à la musique de jazz.* Vaucluse, France, 1945.

18. Edwards, Paul. *Notions élémentaires sur le jazz.* Liege, Belgium: Club de belgique, 1945.

19. Elliott, Paul. *That Crazy American Music.* New York: Bobbs-Merrill, 1938.

    Contains some interesting historical points on jazz.

20. Ellis, Norman. *Instrumentation and Arranging for the Radio and Dance Orchestra.* New York: G. Schirmer, 1937.

21. Enefer, Douglass S. *Jazz in Black and White.* London: Alliance Press, 1945.

22. Erlich, Lillian. *What Jazz Is All About.* New York: Julian Messner, 1960.

23. Feather, Leonard. *The Book of Jazz.* New York: Meridian Books, 1976.

24. ————. *The New Edition of the Encyclopedia of Jazz.* New York: Bonanza, 1960.

25. Finkelstein, Sidney W. *Jazz: A People's Music.* New
    York: Citadel Press, 1948.

26. Fox, Charles; Peter Gammond; and Alun Morgan. *Jazz on
    Record: A Critical Guide.* London: Hutchinson, 1960.

27. Frankenstein, Alfred V. *Syncopating Saxophones.* Chicago:
    R.O. Ballou, 1925.

28. Ganfield, Jane. *Books and Periodical Articles on Jazz
    in America from 1926-1932.* New York: Columbia Univer-
    sity Press, 1933.

29. Gee, John, ed. *That's a Plenty.* Hemel Hempstead,
    Hertfordshire, England: Society for Jazz Appreciation
    in the Younger Generation, 1945.

30. Gilbert, Douglas. *Lost Chords: The Diverting Story of
    American Popular Songs.* Garden City, New York:
    Doubleday, 1942.

31. Gleason, Ralph J. *Nouvelle histoire du jazz.* Brussels:
    L'Ecran du monde, 1948.

32. Goffin, Robert. *Jam Session.* New York: G.P. Putnam's,
    1958.

33. ————. *Jazz: From the Congo to the Metropolitan.*
    Garden City, New York: Doubleday, 1944.

    A study of the evolution of jazz from the Congo to
    the present, by a Belgian who has been an admirer of
    jazz.

34. ————. *La Nouvelle-Orléans, capital du jazz.* New
    York: Editions de la maison française, 1946.

35. Gold, Robert S. *A Jazz Lexicon.* New York: Knopf, 1964.

36. Goldberg, Isaac. *Tin Pan Alley.* New York: John Day,
    1930.

37. ————. *Jazz Music: What It Is and How to Understand It.*
    Girard, Kansas: Haldeman-Julius, 1927.

38. ————. *George Gershwin: A Study in American Music.*
    New York: Simon & Schuster, 1931.

39. Granz, Norman. *The Jazz Scene*. New York: Knopf, 1947.

40. Graham, Alberta Powell. *Strike Up the Band*. New York:
     Nelson, 1949.

41. Grossman, William L., and Jack W. Farrell. *The Heart
     of Jazz*. New York: New York University Press, 1955.

42. Guinle, Jorge. *Jazz Panorama*. Rio de Janeiro: Livraria
     Agir Editora, 1953.

43. Hirsch, Arthur Z., Jr. *Black and Tan Fantasy*. The
     Sociology of Jazz Music. 1946. (Manuscript copy in
     Schomburg Collection, New York Public Library).

44. Hobson, Wilder. *American Jazz Music*. New York: W.W.
     Norton, 1939.

45. Hodeir, André. *Toward Jazz*. New York: Grove, 1962.

46. ————. *Le jazz, cet inconnu*. Paris: Collection
     harmoniques, 1945.

47. ————, trans. David Noakes. *Jazz: Its Evolution and
     Essence*. New York: Grove, 1956.

48. ————. *Introduction à la musique de jazz*. Paris:
     Librairie larousse, 1948.

49. Hughes, Langston. *The First Book of Jazz*. New York:
     F. Watts, 1955.

50. Jones, Max, ed. *Jazz Photo Album*. London: British
     Yearbooks, 1947.

51. Jones, R.P. *Jazz*. New York: Roy Publishers, 1963.

52. Kaufmann, Helen L. *From Jehovah to Jazz: Music in
     America from Psalmody to the Present*. New York: Dodd,
     Mead, 1937.

53. Lange, Arthur. *Arranging for the Modern Dance Orchestra*.
     New York: Robbins Music, 1927.

54. Lapham, Claude. *Scoring for the Modern Dance Band*.
     New York: Pittman, 1947.

55. Larkin, Philip. *All What Jazz: A Record Diary, 1961-
     1968*. New York: St. Martin's, 1970.
        Articles originally published in the *Daily Telegraph*.

56. Lee, Edward. *Jazz: An Introduction*. London: Kahn and
    Areull, 1972.

57. Leonard, Neil. *Jazz and the White Americans*. Chicago:
    University of Chicago Press, 1962.

58. Longstreet, Stephen. *The Real Jazz, Old and New*.
    Baton Rouge: Louisiana State University Press, 1956.

59. Lucas, John. *Basic Jazz on Long Play*. Northfield,
    Minnesota: Carleton Jazz Club, 1954.

60. McCarthy, Albert. *The Trumpet in Jazz*. London:
    Citizen Press, 1945.

61. ————, et al. *Jazz on Record: The First Fifty Years,
    1917-1967*. New York: Oak, 1968.

62. McRae, Barry. *Jazz Cataclysm*. Cranbury, New Jersey:
    A.S. Barnes, 1967.

63. Mehegan, John. *Jazz Improvisation*. New York: Watson-
    Guptill, 1962.

64. Merriam, Alan P. *Bibliography of Jazz*. Philadelphia:
    American Folklore Society, 1954.

65. Miller, William. *Jazz Impressions*. Melbourne: William
    H. Miller, 1945.

66. Nelson, Stanley Rupert. *All About Jazz*. London: Heath,
    Cranton, 1934.

67. Newton, Francis. *The Jazz Scene*. New York: Monthly
    Review, 1960.

68. Niemoeller, Adolph F. *The Story of Jazz*. Girard, Kansas:
    Haldeman-Julius, 1946.

69. Noble, Peter. *The Illustrated Yearbook of Jazz--1946*.
    Egham, Surrey, England: Citizen Press, 1946.

70. ————. *Transatlantic Jazz: A Short History of American
    Jazz*. London: Citizen Press, 1945.

71. ————. *So This Is Jazz*. Boston: Little, Brown, 1926.

72. Panassie, Hugues. *Le jazz hot*. Paris: Corre, 1934.

73. ———. *Jazz Panorama*. Paris: Deux rives, 1950.

74. ———. *The Real Jazz*. New York: Smith and Durrell,
     1942.

75. Reid, Rufus. *The Evolving Bassist: An Aid in Developing
     a Total Musical Concept for the Double Bass and the
     Four-and-Six String Electric Basses*. Chicago: Myriad,
     1974.

76. Reisner, Robert George, comp. *The Literature of Jazz:
     A Selective Bibliography*. New York: New York Public
     Library, 1959.

77. Rosenthal, Geo. S., ed. *Jazzways: A Yearbook of Hot
     Music*. Cincinnati: Jazzways, 1946.

78. Russo, William. *Jazz Composition and Orchestration*.
     Chicago: University of Chicago Press, 1968.

79. Sargeant, Winthrop. *Jazz: Hot and Hybrid*. New York:
     Dutton, 1946.

80. Schmidt, Joos. *Siegfried Koexistenz oder Integration?
     Die Ausstrahlung des Jazz auf Konzertmusik, Kirchen-
     musik, Oper, Musical, Popular Music und Beat* [Coexis-
     tence or Integration? The Influence of Jazz on Concert
     Music, Church Music, Opera, the Musical, Popular
     Music, and Rock]. Anrath-Willich: M. Bildung, 1971.

81. Shapiro, N., ed. *Hear Me Talkin' to Ya: The Story of
     Jazz by the Men Who Made It*. New York: Rinehart, 1955.

82. Smith, Charles E. *The Jazz Record Book*. New York:
     Smith and Durrell, 1942.

83. Spaeth, Sigmund. *A History of Popular Music in America*.
     New York: Random House, 1948.

84. Stearns, Marshall. *The Story of Jazz*. New York: Oxford
     University Press, 1956.

     A comprehensive study of jazz, chronologically arranged,
     with an extensive bibliography, discography, and syllabus
     of lectures.

85. Tanner, Paul Ora Warren, and Maurice Gerow. *A Study of
     Jazz*. Dubuque, Iowa: Brown, 1964.

86. Toledano, Ralph de. *Frontiers of Jazz.* 2nd ed. New York: Frederick Ungar, 1962.

87. Ulanov, Barry. *A History of Jazz in America.* New York: Viking, 1952.

88. ————. *Handbook of Jazz.* New York: Viking, 1960.

89. ————, and George Simon, eds. *Jazz 1955: The Metronome Yearbook.* New York: Metronome, 1955.

90. Weirick, Paul. *Dance Arranging.* New York: Witmark Educational Publications, 1934.

91. Williams, Martin T. *The Jazz Tradition.* New York: Oxford University Press, 1970.

92. ————, ed. *The Art of Jazz.* New York: Oxford University Press, 1959.

93. ————, ed. *Jazz Panorama.* New York: Macmillan, Crowell-Collier, 1962.

ARTICLES

94. "A Concert to End All Concerts." *Metronome*, Apr. 1948, pp. 13-14.

95. "A Decade of Jazz." *Record Changer*, Aug.-Sept. 1952, p. 67.

96. "A Dialogue on Classical Music and Jazz." *Musical Canada* 7, no. 11 (Nov. 1931): 2, 10.

97. "A French Philosophy of the Musical and Literary Jazz." *New York Times*, 7 Nov. 1926, p. 7.

98. "A Medico on Jazz." *Musical Courier*, 11 Aug. 1927, p. 22.

99. "A New American Idiom." *Musical Leader*, 13 Mar. 1930, p. 6.

100. "A Piano Concerto in the Vernacular to Have Its Day with Damrosch." *New York Times*, 22 Nov. 1925, p. 1.

101. "A Virtuous Revolt Against Jazz." *New York Times*,
     2 Feb. 1926, p. 6.

102. "Accursed Jazz--An English View." *Literary Digest* 61,
     no. 1 (2 Oct. 1926): 28-29.

103. Albam, M. "The Jazz Arranger-Composer: A Thumbnail
     Sketch." *Jazz* 2, no. 3 (Mar. 1963): 7.

104. Aldrich, Richard. "Drawing a Line for Jazz." *New York
     Times*, 10 Dec. 1922, pp. 1-3.

105. "American Dancer Jazzing the 'Marseillaise' Angers
     Friendly Audience in Paris Music Hall." *New York
     Times*, 31 Jan. 1926, p. 4.

106. Anderson, W.R. "Jazz and Real Music." *Musical Times*,
     Oct. 1932, pp. 926-27.

107. "An Attack on Critical Jabberwocky." *Record Changer*,
     Mar. 1949, pp. 13-14.

108. "An Experiment in Music." *Musical Courier*, 21 Feb.
     1924, p. 39.

109. Antheil, George. "American Folk Music." *Forum* 1,
     no. 12 (Dec. 1928): 957-58.

110. ———. "Jazz Is Music." *Forum* 80, no. 7 (July 1928):
     64-67.

111. "Art Mooney Back to Playing Music." *Down Beat*, 16 June
     1950, p. 12.

112. Ashland, Gunnar. "Interpretations in Jazz." *Etude* 65,
     no. 3 (Mar. 1947): 134, 172.

113. Austin, Cecil. "Jazz." *Music and Letters* 6, no. 3
     (1925): 256-68.

     Contains useful historical information. Several
     examples are included.

114. Bagar, Robert. "The Long-Haired Cats." *Musical
     Journal* 14, no. 1 (Jan. 1956): 7, 37.

115. Baker, David N. "The String Player in Jazz." *Down
     Beat*, 5 Mar. 1970, pp. 37-38.

116. "Ban Against Jazz Sought in Ireland." *New York Times*,
      7 Jan. 1936, p. 4.

117. Barnard, Eunice Fuller. "Jazz Is Linked to the Factory
      Wheel." *New York Times*, 30 Dec. 1928, pp. 4-5.

118. Bauer, Marion. "L'Influence du 'jazz band.'" *Revue
      musicale* 5, no. 4 (Apr. 1924): 31-36.

119. Baudue, Ray. "All Jazz Comes from the Blues." *Down
      Beat*, 1 June 1940, p. 19.

120. Beeler, Bruce. "A New Light on Jazz." *Etude* 55,
      no. 6 (June 1937): 406.

121. Belaiev, Victor. "Stravinsky, Weill and Jazz."
      Christian Science Monitor, 18 May 1929, p. 6.

122. Berger, Francesco. "A Jazz Band Concert." *Monthly
      Musical Record* 49, no. 8 (Aug. 1919): 174-75.

123. Berger, Monroe. "Jazz: Resistance to the Diffusion of
      a Culture-Pattern." *Journal of Negro History* 32,
      no. 10 (Oct. 1947): 461-94.

124. Bergman, Dorothy. "Jazz--the Expression of the Age."
      Musician 35, no. 9 (Sept. 1930): 12.

125. Berendt, Joachim Ernest. "Free Jazz, der Neue Jazz der
      60er Jahre" ["Free Jazz, the New Jazz of the 1960's"].
      Melos 34, no. 10 (1967): 343-52.

126. "Berlin Opera Mingles Auto Horn, Films, Jazz." *New
      York Times*, March 3, 1927, p. 2.

127. "Berlin Says Jazz Is Dying." *New York Times*, 15 Apr.
      1926, p. 2.

128. Bernstein, Leonard. "Jazz Forum: Has Jazz Influenced
      the Symphony? Yes." *Esquire*, Feb. 1947, pp. 47,
      152-53.

129. Biddle, Mar. "Jazz in the School Music Program."
      School Musician, Apr. 1942, pp. 10-11.

130. "Blight of Jazz and the Spirituals." *Literary Digest*
      105, no. 2 (12 Apr. 1930): 20.

131.   Blesh, Rudi. "This Is Jazz." *Arts and Architecture*
       66, no. 3 (Mar. 1944): 20-21, 42-43.

132.   Bloom, Clifford. "The Development of Jazz." *Better
       Homes and Gardens*, Apr. 1926, pp. 91, 110.

133.   "Blow It Down." *Time*, 8 Apr. 1946, pp. 45-46.

134.   "Blow! Joshua! Blow! The American People Do Not Enjoy
       Having Their Beloved Melodies and Spirituals Carica-
       tured." *Etude* 59, no. 4 (Apr. 1941): 221, 288.

135.   Bolgen, Kaare A. "An Analysis of the Jazz Idiom."
       Music Teacher's Review 11, no. 5 (Sept.-Oct. 1941):
       3-9.

136.   Borneman, Ernest. "Creole Echoes." *Jazz Review* 2,
       no. 8 (Sept. 1959): 13-16; no. 10 (Nov. 1959): 25-28.

       The author re-examines the origins of jazz and the
       relation of jazz to the musical traditions of Europe
       and Africa. In addition, he introduces new material
       on the influence of the Arabic musical tradition on the
       "Spanish tinge" in jazz and on the importance of the
       "Spanish tinge" in New Orleans jazz.

137.   ———. "The Jazz Cult--Intimate Memories of an
       Acolyte." *Harper's*, Mar. 1947, pp. 241-73.

138.   "Both Jazz Music and Jazz Dancing Barred from All Louis-
       ville Episcopal Churches." *New York Times*, Sept. 19,
       1921, pp. 4-5.

139.   "Both Schools of Critics Wrong." *Down Beat*, 30 July
       1947; 13 Aug. 1947, p. 16.

140.   "Broadcasters Favor 'Swinging' of Bach." *New York Times*,
       28 Oct. 1938, p. 6.

141.   "Brooklyn Academy Opens Its Door to Jazz; Paul Whiteman
       Concert Debuts There." *New York Times*, 8 Jan. 1934,
       p. 3.

142.   Brown, Carlton. "Crisis in Jazz." *Tomorrow* 6, no. 3
       (Mar. 1947): 21-24.

143.   Broyard, Anatole. "Keep Cool, May: The Negro Rejection
       of Jazz." *Commentary* 2, no. 4 (Apr. 1951): 359-62.

144. Brubeck, Dave. "Jazz (Evolvement as an Art Form)."
     Down Beat, 27 Jan. 1950, pp. 12, 15.

145. Bruyr, José. "Un entretien avec ... Darius Milhaud."
     Guide du concert 16, no. 10 (18 Oct. 1929): 55-58.

146. Buchanan, Charles L. "Gershwin and Musical Snobbery."
     Outlook 145, no. 2 (2 Feb. 1927): 146-48.

147. Bukofzer, Manfred. "Soziologie des Jazz." *Melos* 8,
     no. 4 (Aug.-Sept. 1929): 378-91.

148. Cain, Noble. "Choral Fads and Jitterbug Fancies."
     1939. Reprint. *Music Educator's Journal* 26, no. 1
     (Sept. 1939): 26-27.

149. Campbell, E. Simms. "Jam in the Nineties." *Esquire*,
     Dec. 1938, pp. 102-3, 200, 202, 207.

150. "Can Good, Pleasant Band Like Gene Williams' Make a
     Living in These Times?" *Down Beat*, 11 Aug. 1950, p. 2.

151. Canfield, Mary Cass. "Great American Art." *Grotesques
     and Other Reflections*. New York: Harper, 1927, pp. 36-47.

152. Carpenter, John Alden. "Jazz Is Assuming Prominence as
     an American Music Idiom." *Musical Digest* 11, no. 11
     (23 Nov. 1926): 3.

153. Casella, Alfredo. "Alfredo Casella Discusses Jazz."
     Musical Courier, 4 Jan. 1930, p. 7.

154. Cesana, Otto, and Marion Holloway. "Jazz Is American,
     You Snob--and Vastly Overrated." *Musical Digest* 30,
     no. 2 (1948): 12-14.

155. "Changer's Editor Also Blasts Wolff." *Down Beat*,
     15 July 1949, p. 12.

156. Chase, Gilbert. "The Growth of Jazz." *America's Music
     from the Pilgrims to the Present*. New York: McGraw-
     Hill, 1955, pp. 465-89.

     A terse summary of the historical development of jazz.

157. Chatelain, Amy. "Une forme d'art moderne." *Nouvelle
     Revue Suisse* 20, no. 10 (1927): 966-72.

158.   Chop, Max.   "Jazz als Lehrfach." *Signals* 85, no. 1
       (11 Jan. 1928): 43-44.

159.   Chotzinoff, Samuel.   "Jazz: A Brief History." *Vanity
       Fair* 20, no. 6 (June 1923): 10-12.

160.   Clark, Robert.   "Music Education vs. Radio and Dance-
       Hall Rhythm." *Music Educator's Journal* 23, no. 9
       (May 1937): 33-34.

161.   Clarke, E.   "Where Does American Musical Composition
       Stand?" *Etude* 53, no. 12 (Dec. 1935): 704.

162.   "Classical vs. Jazzical Music." *Literary Digest* 65,
       no. 11 (12 June 1920): 40-41.

163.   "Classic in 'Jazz-Tempo.'" *Sheet Music News*, Jan.
       1924, p. 27.

164.   "Classical Jazz and American Music." Alain D. Locke.
       The Negro and His Music. Washington, D.C.: Associates
       in Negro Folk Education, 1936, pp. 106-17.

       Excellent article; good philosophical discussion.

165.   "Composers Protest Jazzing the Classics." *New York
       Times*, 12 Nov. 1922, p. 2.

166.   Comfort, Iris T.   "Sauce for the Classicists." *Etude*
       64, no. 2 (Feb. 1946): 80-113.

167.   "Concerning 'Modern American Music.'" *New York Times*,
       23 Nov. 1924, p. 1.

168.   "Conductors Biased, Says Henry Hadley--Finds an Evil
       Lure in Jazz." *New York Times*, 1 Nov. 1932, p. 5.

169.   Cons, C.L.   "Jargon of Jazz." *American Mercury* 38,
       no. 5 (May 1936): n.p.

170.   "Coolness." *Flair* 1, no. 5 (May 1950): 28-29.

171.   Copland, Aaron.   "Jazz Structure and Influence."
       Modern Music 4, no. 1 (Jan.-Feb. 1927): 9-14.

172.   "Credits Beethoven with Evolving Jazz." *New York Times*,
       17 Sept. 1932, p. 1.

173. Cunliffe, Ronald. "How to Treat Jazz-Mania." *Music Teacher* 8, no. 10 (Oct. 1929): 567-68; (Nov. 1929): 645.

174. Daley, Pete. "Barrelhouse Frank Melrose." *Jazz Record* 32, no. 8 (May 1945): 8-9, 16-17.

175. Damon, S. Foster. "American Influence on Modern French Music." *Dial* 65, no. 8 (15 Aug. 1918): 93-95.

176. "Damrosch Assails Jazz." *New York Times*, 17 Apr. 1928, p. 2.

177. "Dance Music, Harmony Included in Curriculum." *Down Beat*, 2 July 1947, p. 6.

178. David, Hans. "Abschied vom Jazz." *Melos* 9, no. 10 (Oct. 1930): 413-17.

179. Deal, Harry. "Drums on the Mississippi." *Jazz Record* 48, no. 9 (Sept. 1946): 7-9.

180. Decker, Duane. "The Decline of Jazz." *Musician* 27, no. 5 (May 1922): 1.

181. ———. "It's Jazz for Arts' Sake." *Collier's*, 11 Aug. 1951, pp. 28-29.

182. "Delving into the Genealogy of Jazz." *Current Opinion* 67, no. 2 (Aug. 1919): 97-99.

183. Dickerson, Reed. "Hot Music, Rediscovering Jazz." *Harper's*, Apr. 1936, pp. 567-74.

184. Dodge, Roger. "The Hot Solo." *Atlantic Monthly*, July 1944, p. 120.

185. ———. "Harpsichords and Jazz Trumpets." *Hound and Horn* 7, no. 7 (July 1934): 587-608.

186. "Does Jazz Cause Crime?" *Musical Observer*, Aug. 1924, p. 24.

187. Downes, Olin. "More Discussion of Jazz." *New York Times*, 3 Oct. 1926, p. 8.

188. ———. "A Study of Jazz." *New York Times*, 21 May 1939, p. 5.

189. "Downbeat Article Forces a Restatement of Policy."
      Record Changer, Aug. 1949, pp. 5, 17.

190. "Drawing a Line for Jazz." *Metronome*, Jan. 1923, p. 29.

191. Drutmann, Irving. "Anthropology Plus Jazz." *Negro
      Digest* 2, no. 12 (Dec. 1943): 47-48.

192. Dykema, Peter W. "Kind Words for Jazz, But." *Literary
      Digest* 75, no. 20 (18 Nov. 1922): 33-34.

193. "Eddie Condon's Le Jazz Intellectual: Inspired Ad-
      Libbing by Old Master." *Newsweek*, 24 Jan. 1944, p. 62.

194. Eldridge, Thomas R. "Jazzing Classical Music." *New
      York Times*, 7 March 1932, p. 7.

195. "El jazz, influencia y expression." *Ars magazine* 2,
      no. 10 (Oct. 1941): 31.

196. Engel, Carl. "Jazz: A Musical Discussion." *Atlantic
      Monthly*, Aug. 1922, pp. 182-89.

197. "Factory Tests Show Swing Causes Many Girl Employees to
      Spoil Their Work." *New York Times*, 8 Sept. 1938, p. 5.

198. Fairchild, Leslie. "Horse-Sense and Horse-Play in
      Music." *Outlook* 139, no. 1 (14 Jan. 1925): 59-60.

199. Faulkner, Anne Shaw. "Does Jazz Put the Sin in Syncopa-
      tion?" *Ladies Home Journal*, Aug. 1921, pp. 16, 34.

200. Feather, Leonard. "Tempo di Jazz." *Musician* 46, no. 2
      (June-Oct. 1941): 113, 129, 144, 162.

201. ———, and Don Henahan. "Spotlight Review." *Down
      Beat*, 8 Dec. 1960, pp. 36-37.

202. Fellow, Myles. "Keep Jazz Within Its Limits." *Etude*
      62, no. 8 (Aug. 1944): 437, 482.

203. ———. "Speaking of Jazz." *New Republic*, 2 Aug. 1939,
      pp. 363-64.

204. Finck, Henry T. "Jazz—Lowbrow and Highbrow." *Etude*
      42, no. 8 (Aug. 1924): 527-28.

205. "Finds Jazz the Rage with Caucasian Folk." *New York Times*, 29 June 1932, p. 4.

206. Fitzgerald, F. Scott. "Echoes of the Jazz Age." *Scribner's*, Nov. 1931, pp. 459-65.

207. "Founds Jazz Academy." *New York Times*, 28 June 1931, p. 4.

208. Franco, Johan. "Against All 'Arrangements.'" *New York Times*, 13 Nov. 1938, p. 3.

209. Frank, Waldo. "Jazz and Folk Art." *New Republic*, 1 Dec. 1926, pp. 42-43. Reprint. Waldo Frank. *In the American Jungle*. New York: Farrar and Rinehart, 1937, pp. 119-23.

210. Frankenstein, Alfred V. "Jazz Arrives at the Opera." *Review of Reviews* 79, no. 8 (Mar. 1929): 138, 140.

211. Freese, Myron V. "What Jazz Has Done to the Fretted Instruments." *Cadenza* 31, no. 2 (Feb. 1924): 3-7.

212. "French Find Our Jazz Too Soul-Disturbing." *New York Times*, 3 Feb. 1929, p. 8.

213. Garbett, Arthur S. "Why You Like Jazz." *Sunset Magazine*, Mar. 1924, pp. 21-23, 62, 64.

214. Gardner, Carl E. "Ragging and Jazzing." *Metronome*, 1 Oct. 1919, p. 35.

215. Gershwin, George. "The Composer in the Machine Age." *Revolt in the Arts*. Edited by Oliver M. Sayler. New York: Brentano's, 1930, pp. 264-69.

216. ————. "Does Jazz Belong to Art?" *Singing* 1, no. 7 (July 1926): 13-14.

217. Gilbert, Henry F. "Concerning the Jazz Question." *Etude* 53, no. 2 (Feb. 1935): 74.

218. Giles, R.Y. "Jazz Comes of Age." *Scholastic* 27, no. 4 (19 Oct. 1935): 7-8.

219. Gleason, Ralph J. "A Short Analysis of Hot Jazz." *Hobbies*, May 1941, pp. 34-36.

220.   ———. "Perspectives." *Down Beat*, 18 Apr. 1957, pp.
       58-59.

221.   Goldberg, Isaac. "Aaron Copland and His Jazz." *American
       Mercury* 12, no. 9 (Sept. 1927): 63-65.

222.   ———. "Jazz." *Forum* 87, no. 4 (Apr. 1932): 232-36.

223.   Goodbrod, R. Marti. "Conquering the Jazz Craze of Young
       Pianists." *Etude* 52, no. 2 (Feb. 1934): 82.

224.   ———. "Criticising the Critics." *Jazz Session* 7,
       no. 3 (May-June 1945): 18, 30.

225.   Grainger, Percy. "What Effect Is Jazz Likely to Have
       upon the Music of the Future?" *Etude* 2, no. 9 (Sept.
       1924): 593-94.

226.   Greuenberg, Louis. "Der Jazz als Ausgangspunkt."
       Musikblatter des Anbruch 7, no. 4 (Apr. 1925): 196-99.
       Reprint. "Jazz as the Starting Point." *Metronome* 42,
       no. 1 (1 Jan. 1926): 15, 56.

227.   Haggin, B.H. "Gershwin and Our Music." *Nation*, 5 Oct.
       1932, pp. 308-9.

228.   ———. "The Pedant Looks at Jazz." *Nation*, 9 Dec.
       1925, pp. 685-88.

       Contains comments on form and analysis of jazz.

229.   Hamilton, Clarence G. "Jazz and Its Effects." *Etude*
       42, no. 8 (Aug. 1924): 531.

230.   Hammond, John. "History of Jazz at Last on Record:
       A Basic Repertoire of Jazz Records." *New York Times*,
       2 Nov. 1952, pp. 33-34.

231.   Hapke, Walter. "Im Spiegel des Jazz." *Zeitschrift für
       Musik* 48, no. 10 (Oct. 1931): 88-89.

232.   Harap, Louis. "The Case for Hot Jazz." *Musical
       Quarterly* 27, no. 1 (Jan. 1941): 47-61.

       A defense of jazz; also gives Blacks credit for its
       origin and lists outstanding Black contributors to jazz.

233.   Harris, H. Meunier. "A Jazz Bibliography." *Jazzfinder
       '49*. Edited by Orin Blackstone. New Orleans: Orin
       Blackstone, 1949, pp. 129-42.

234. "Has Jazz Hurt Concert-Giving?... Managers say 'No.'" *Musical America*, 14 Nov. 1925, p. 31.

235. Hemming, R. "Hot, Cool, and All That Jazz." *Senior Scholastic*, 6 May 1965, pp. 20-21.

236. Henderson, W.J. "Why Not Mix Jazz and Classics?" *Literary Digest* 91, no. 5 (30 Oct. 1926): 29.

237. Henry, Leigh. "Jazz in Relation to Chamber Music." *Cobbett's Cyclopedic Survey of Chamber Music.* Vol. 2. Edited by Walter Wilson Cobbett. London: Oxford University Press, 1930, pp. 31-34.

238. Hentoff, Nat. "Jazz and Jim Crow." *Commonweal* 73, no. 14 (24 Mar. 1961): 656-58.

239. ————. "Jazz and Race." *Commonweal* 81, no. 1 (8 Jan. 1965): 482-84.

240. ————. "New Faces of Jazz." *Reporter* 25, no. 8 (17 Aug. 1961): 50-52.

241. ————. "Strange Case of Missing Musicians." *Reporter* 20, no. 5 (28 May 1959): 25-27.

242. "Herman Heard Thrills Packed Carnegie Hall." *Down Beat*, 8 Apr. 1946, pp. 1, 15.

243. Hermant, George. "La côte du hot." *Jazz Hot* 4 (Oct.-Nov. 1938): 7.

244. Hershey, Brunet. "Jazz Latitude." *New York Times Magazine*, 25 June 1922, pp. 8-9.

245. Hill, Edward Burlingame. "Copland's Jazz Concerto in Boston." *Modern Music* 4, no. 3 (May-June 1927): 35-37.

246. Hobson, Wilder. "On with the Jazz." *Saturday Review*, 31 May 1952, pp. 44-45.

247. Hodeir, André. "Jazz: Its Evolution and Essence." *Saturday Review*, 17 Mar. 1956, p. 37.

248. Hoffman, Daniel G. "The Folk Art of Jazz." *Antioch Review* 5, no. 3 (Mar. 1945): n.p.

249. ————. "From Blues to Jazz: Recent Bibliographies and
     Discographies." *Midwest Folklore* 5, no. 2 (Summer
     1955): 107-14.

250. Houghton, John Alan. "Darius Milhaud: A Missionary of
     the 'Six.'" *Musical America*, 13 Jan. 1923, pp. 3, 42.

251. Ichaso, Francisco. "Terapeutica de jazz." *Musicalia* 1,
     no. 5 (Sept.-Oct. 1928): 65-96.

252. "Impressions of America." *Jazz Hot* 5, no. 2-3 (Feb.-
     Mar. 1939): 7-13.

253. "Ina Ray Ork Looks Good on TV: Plays Well, Too." *Down
     Beat*, 1 Dec. 1950, p. 13.

254. "Is Jazz the Pilot of Disaster?" *Etude* 43, no. 1 (Jan.
     1925): 5-6.

255. "Is the Popularity of Jazz Music Waning?" *Radio Broad-
     cast*, Dec. 1925, pp. 177-78.

256. "In Praise of Jazz." *Irish Monthly* 62 (1934): 133-43.

257. Irwin, Virginia. "Is Jazz the Pilot of Disaster?"
     Etude 43, no. 1 (Jan. 1925): 5-6.

258. Jackson, Preston. "Jazz Comes to Stay." *Current Opinion*
     77, no. 9 (Sept. 1924): 337-38.

259. ————. "Jazz." *Living Age* 306, no. 9 (31 July 1920):
     280-83.

260. ————. "Jazz Played Art." *Literary Digest* 71, no. 2
     (14 Jan. 1922): 71.

261. ————. "Jazz Origin Again Discovered." *Music Trade
     Review*, 14 June 1919, pp. 32-33.

262. ————. "The Jazz Fiddler." *Etude* 41, no. 6 (June
     1923): 420-21.

263. ————. "The Jazz Hoot." *New Yorker*, 1 Apr. 1950, pp.
     21-22.

264. Jarecki, Tadeusz. "Jazzing Up the Symphony Orchestra."
     Chesterian 8, no. 4 (July-Aug. 1927): 262-68.

265. "Jazz All Over Europe." *New York Times,* 30 Apr. 1929,
      p. 1.

266. "Jazz and American Music." *Twentieth Century Music.*
      Edited by Marion Bauer. New York: G.P. Putnam's,
      1933, pp. 270-77.

267. "Jazz and Classical Music." *Jazz Hot* 5, no. 1 (Jan.
      1939): 5.

268. "Jazzando." *Musical Courier,* 24 Aug. 1922, p. 20.

269. "Jazz and Ragtime Are the Preludes to a Great American
      Music." *Current Opinion* 69, no. 8 (Aug. 1920): 199-
      201.

270. "Jazz and the Disposition." *New York Times,* 13 June
      1927, p. 5.

271. "Jazz as a Diversion and the Subsidence of Hopes That
      It Might Mean a New Musical Force." *New York Evening
      Post,* 21 Dec. 1929.

272. "Jazz as Folk-Music." *Musical America,* 19 Dec. 1925,
      p. 19.

273. "Jazz Analyzed." *Commonwealth* 30, no. 4 (28 Apr. 1939):
      220-23.

274. "Jazz Bitterly Opposed in Germany." *New York Times,*
      11 Mar. 1928, p. 4.

275. "Jazz Coming On." *Musical Courier,* 7 Jan. 1926, p. 30.

276. "Jazz Concerts." *Ebony,* Sept. 1946, pp. 29-34.

277. "Jazz Conservatory for Prague." *New York Times,* 22 Nov.
      1931, p. 5.

278. "Jazz." *Harvard Graduate's Magazine,* Mar. 1926, pp.
      362-65.

279. "Jazz in the Concert Hall." *Musical Opinion* 99, no. 2
      (Feb. 1926): 485-86.

280. "Jazz Is Dead But Tang and Color Will Survive in America's
      Future Classicism Says Grofe, Founder of the 'New
      School.'" *Musical Courier,* 14 May 1932, pp. 9, 16.

281. "Jazz Is Not Music." *Forum* 80, no. 8 (Aug. 1928): 267-71.

282. "Jazzmania." *North American Review* 225, no. 5 (May 1928): 539-44.

283. "Jazz Music and Its Relation to African Music." *Musical Courier*, 1 June 1922, p. 7.

284. "Jazz Music Banned in France." *Musical Leader*, 19 June 1924, p. 586.

285. "Jazz on the Verge." *Time*, 7 Dec. 1936, pp. 62-63.

286. "Jazz Opera or Ballet?" *Modern Music* 3, no. 1 (Jan.-Feb. 1926): 10-16.

287. "Jazz or 'Modern Popular Music' to Be Heard and Discussed at Composers' League Lecture." *Musical Courier*, 7 Feb. 1924, p. 6.

288. "Jazz." *Outlook* 136, no. 5 (5 Mar. 1924): 381-82.

289. "Jazz Reduces Output of Tenors from Naples." *New York Times*, 22 May 1927, p. 2.

290. "Jazz Returns to Europe." *Metronome*, Feb. 1947, pp. 25, 43-45.

291. "Jazz, Says Darius Milhaud, Is the Most Significant Thing in Music Today." *Musical Observer* 22, no. 5: 23.

292. "Jazz." *Scottish Musical Magazine* 11, no. 17 (July 1930): 156.

293. "Jazz Symphony." *Time*, 20 Dec. 1937, pp. 44-45.

294. "Jazz, the Black Peril, and the Bigger Cheeses." *Musical Opinion* 50, no. 5 (4 May 1927): 794-95.

295. "Jazz the Classics." *New York Times*, 7 Dec. 1927, p. 6.

296. "John Hammond ... A Critic and a Crew Haircut." *Music and Rhythm* 2, no. 10 (Oct. 1941): 26.

297. Jones, Isham. "American Dance Music Is Not Jazz." *Etude* 45, no. 8 (Aug. 1924): 526.

298. Jones, S. Turner. "Appreciation through Jazz." *Educational Music Magazine*, Jan.-Feb. 1941, p. 53.

299. Katz, Bernard, and Lola Pergament. "Why They Go for Jazz." *Parents Magazine*, Jan. 1949, pp. 30-31, 96-97.

300. Keepnews, Orrin. "Jazz and America." *Record Changer*, Aug.-Sept. 1952, pp. 31-34.

301. Kiefner, Walter. "Singbewegung und Jass." *Singgemeinde* 8, nos. 8-9 (Aug.-Sept. 1932): 162-69.

302. "King Jazz and the Jazz Kings." *Literary Digest* 88, no. 5 (30 Jan. 1926): 37-42.

     Discusses Vincent Lopez, Paul Whiteman, Roger W. Kahn, and Irving Berlin.

303. Kingsley, Walter. "The Appeal of Primitive Jazz." *Literary Digest* 55, no. 12 (25 Aug. 1917): 28-29.

304. Knowlton, Don. "Anatomy of Jazz." *Harper's* 152, no. 6 (Apr. 1926): 578-85.

305. Kolesch, Mitzi. "Jazz in High Places." *Independent* 116, no. 4 (10 Apr. 1926): 424.

306. Kolodin, I. "Jazz History in Word and Pictures." *Saturday Review*, 14 Jan. 1956, p. 32.

307. Krupa, Gene. "Jazz Forum: Has Jazz Influenced the Symphony? No." *Esquire*, Feb. 1947, pp. 46, 118.

308. Lachenbruch, Jerome. "Jazz and the Motion Picture." *Metronome*, Apr. 1922, p. 94.

309. "Lady Jazz in the Vestibule." *New Republic*, 23 Dec. 1925, pp. 138-39.

     Commentary on the jazz of Gershwin and Damrosch.

310. L'Astruci, Carlo L. "The Professional Dance Musician." *Journal of Musicology* 3, no. 2 (1941): 168-72.

311. Laubenstein, Paul F. "Jazz, Debit and Credit." *Musical Quarterly* 15, no. 3 (Oct. 1929): 606-24.

312. "Leave 'Jazz' Alone." *Musical Courier*, 26 Oct. 1922, p. 21.

313. "Liturgy and Headlines; Jazz Masses." *America* 116, no.
      2 (21 Jan. 1967): 79.

314. Loar, Lloyd. "Is 'Jazz' Constructive or Destructive?"
      Melody 8, no. 6 (June 1924): 3-4.

315. "Looking at Japanese Jazz." *Metronome*, June 1936, pp.
      14, 27.

316. Lloyd, Llewelyn C. "Jazz and the Modern Spirit."
      Monthly Musical Record 56, no. 11 (Nov. 1926): 327-28.

317. Mathews, Haydn M. "Jazz--Its Origin, Effect, Future."
      Flutist 5, no. 2 (Feb. 1924): 32-34.

318. Merriam, Alan P. "A Short Bibliography of Jazz."
      Notes 5, no. 2 (Mar. 1953): 202-10.

319. ————. "Jazz--the Word." *Ethnomusicology* 12, no. 3
      (Sept. 1968): 373-96.

320. ————. "The Dilemma of the Jazz Student Today."
      Record Changer, Nov. 1949, pp. 8, 27.

321. "Meyer Davis Thinks Jazz Symbolic of America." *Metronome*,
      Sept. 1923, pp. 72, 171.

322. Milhaud, Darius. "Development of the Jazz Band and
      North American Negro Music." *Metronome*, 15 Dec. 1925,
      pp. 15-16.

323. ————. "The Jazz Band and Negro Music." *Living Age*
      323 (18 Oct. 1924): 169-73.

324. ————. "L'évolution du jazz-band et de la musique des
      Nègres d'Amérique du nord." *Etudes*. Paris: Aveline,
      1927.

325. Miller, Charles. "Jazz, Pure and Simple." *New Republic*,
      14 Apr. 1947, p. 42.

326. Modlin, Jules. "Notes Towards a Definition of Jazz."
      Needle 1, no. 6 (June 1944): 20-21.

327. Montani, Nicola A. "Says Operatic and 'Jazz' Influence
      Contaminate Our Sacred Music." *Musical America*,
      21 Aug. 1920, p. 24.

328. Moor, Paul. "In Search of a Native Muse." *Theatre Arts* 33, no. 6 (June 1949): 40-41.

329. Mooser, R.A.Y. "Le jazz et la musique." *Dissonances* 16, nos. 3-4 (1943): 41-46.

330. Motherwell, Hiram. "Hitching Jazz to a Star." *Musical America*, 10 Mar. 1929, pp. 13, 55.

331. Mougin, Stephane. "La musique de jazz." *Nouvelle Revue* 113 (1931): 288-96.

332. "Music Clubs Against Jazzing of Classics." *New York Times*, 6 Dec. 1927, p. 2.

333. "Musician Driven to Suicide by Jazz: Wouldn't Play It, Couldn't Get Employment." *New York Times*, 7 April 1922, p. 2.

334. "N.E. Conservatory Starts Jazz Course." *Metronome*, Aug. 1942, p. 7.

335. "Negro Jazz." *Dancing Times*, Oct. 1929, pp. 32-35.

336. Nevin, Gordon B. "Jazz--Whither Bound?" *Etude* 47, no. 4 (Sept. 1929): 655-99.

337. Newell, George. "George Gershwin and Jazz." *Outlook* 148 (29 Feb. 1928): 342-43, 351.

338. Newman, Ernest. "Debunking Jazz." *Literary Digest* 92, no. 13 (26 Mar. 1927): 26-27.

339. ————. "Summing Up Music's Case Against Jazz." *New York Times Magazine*, 6 Mar. 1927, pp. 3, 22.

340. "Never Has Popular Music Been as Classical as Jazz." *Metronome*, 1 July 1926, p. 10.

341. Niles, Abbe. "The Ewe Lamb of Widow Jazz." *New Republic*, Dec. 1929, pp. 164-66.

342. "N.Y.U. Will Teach Jazz." *New York Times*, 15 July 1937, p. 2.

343. "On with the 'Charleston.'" *Literary Digest* 86, no. 12 (19 Sept. 1925): 40, 42.

344.   "Origin of Term JAZZ." *Jazz Session* 8, nos. 7-8 (July-
       Aug. 1945): 4-5.

345.   "Origin of the Word Jazz Traced to West Africa by
       Princeton Men Preparing New Dictionary." *New York
       Times*, 15 Oct. 1934, p. 6.

346.   Osgood, Henry Osborne. "Jazz." *AS* 1, no. 10 (1926):
       513-18.

       Discussion of the origin of the word "jazz."

347.   ————. "The Anatomy of Jazz." *American Mercury* 7,
       no. 28 (Apr. 1926): n.p.

348.   "Our Music Casts Much Influence." *Down Beat* 17, no. 18
       (22 Sept. 1950): 10.

349.   Parker, D.C. "Its Vulgarity Lies over the Land."
       Musical News, 1 Dec. 1928, p. 312.

350.   Patterson, Frank. "Jazz--The National Anthem?" *Musical
       Courier* 84, no. 18 (1922): 18; no. 19 (1922): 6.

351.   ————. "An Afternoon of Jazz." *Musical Courier*,
       14 Feb. 1924, p. 38.

352.   "Peace in the Ranks." *Record Changer*, Mar. 1949, pp.
       11-12.

353.   Peyster, Herbert F. "Jazz Knocks in Vain at the Opera's
       Door." *Musician* 35, no. 3 (Mar. 1929): 12, 30.

354.   "Philadelphia Hears First Complete Jazz Symphony."
       Musical Courier, 11 June 1925, pp. 5, 25.

355.   Pimsleur, Solomon. "Jazzing the Classics." *New York
       Times*, 6 Nov. 1932, p. 6.

356.   "Primitive Savage Animalism, Preacher's Analysis of
       Jazz." *New York Times*, 3 Mar. 1922, p. 7.

357.   Reynolds, Robert R. "The Aframerican Viewpoint." *Jazz
       Session* 7, no. 3 (May-June 1945): 19.

358.   Riesenfeld, Paul. "Der Amerikanismus in der heutigen
       Musik." *Rheinische Musik und Theater-Zeitung* 29
       (16 June 1928): 303-5.

359. Rogers, B. "Capacity House Fervently Applauds as Jazz Invades Realm of Serious Music." *Musical America*, 23 Feb. 1924, p. 32.

360. Rogers, M. Robert. "Jazz Influence on French Music." *Musical Quarterly* 21, no. 1 (Jan. 1935): 53-68.

361. Rostland, Claude. "Modern Jazz with Dance." *Musical America*, June 1960, p. 12.

362. Saenger, Gustav. "The Ambitions of Jazz in Artistic Form." *Musical Observer*, Jan. 1926, p. 5.

363. Sargent, Norman and Tom. "Negro-American Music, or the Origin of Jazz." *Musical Times*, June-Aug.-Sept. 1931, n.p.

364. "Says Jazz Originated in Old French Music." *New York Times*, 25 Mar. 1928, p. 7.

365. "Says Most Jazz Critics Are Not Qualified." *Down Beat*, 15 Feb. 1941, pp. 8, 16.

366. "Says Jazz Threatens Christian Civilization." *New York Times*, 16 Dec. 1934, p. 7.

367. Schenke, Jean-Gustave. "Reflexions sur le rhythme du plain-chant et du jazz-band." *Musical Courier* 26, no. 13 (1 Nov. 1924): 516-17.

368. Schoen, Ernst. "Jazz und Kunstmusik." *Melos* 6, no. 12 (Dec. 1927): 512-19.

369. Schuller, Gunther. "The Future of Form and Jazz." *Saturday Review*, 12 Jan. 1957, pp. 62-63, 67-68.

370. ———. "Is Jazz Coming of Age?" *Musical America*, Feb. 1959, pp. 8-9.

371. "Seven Jazz Books." *Saturday Review*, 11 Feb. 1967, p. 61.

372. Skinrood, C.O. "Eva Gauthier Silences Hissing of Jazz Songs in Milwaukee Recital." *Musical America*, 23 Feb. 1924, p. 13.

373. Slotkins, J.S. "Jazz and Its Forerunners as an Example of Acculturation." *American Sociological Review* 8 (1943): 570-75.

374. Smith, Charles E. "Folk Music, the Roots of Jazz."
      Saturday Review, 29 July 1950, n.p.

375. Smith, S. Stephenson. "The Gayer Arts." *The Craft of
      the Critic*. New York: Thomas Y. Crowell, 1931, pp.
      279-96.

376. "Some English Observations upon a First Hearing of a
      Jazz Band Concert." *Metronome*, Oct. 1922, pp. 84-85.

377. "Some Further Opinions on 'Jazz' by Prominent Writers."
      Metronome, Aug. 1922, pp. 27-28.

378. "Some Notes on Use and History: Cornet and Trumpet."
      Record Changer, Oct. 1950, p. 9.

379. "Soprano Sax Comeback." *Down Beat*, 1 Apr. 1940, p. 2.

380. "Sousa Expects Jazz to Wane: Denies It Is Truly American."
      New York Times, 26 Apr. 1928, n.p.

381. Stearns, Marshall. "Almost Fair Enough." *H.R.S. Society
      Ray* 3, no. 1 (Jan. 1939): 6-7.

382. "Stearns Completes Plans for a U.S. Jazz Institute."
      Down Beat, 17 June 1949, p. 11.

383. Strauss, D. "French Critics and American Jazz."
      American Quarterly 17, no. 3 (Fall 1965): 582-87.

384. "Stravinsky as a Symptom." *American Mercury* 4, no. 4
      (Apr. 1925): 465-68.

385. Tallmadge, William H. "What Is Jazz?" *Music Educators
      Journal* 42, nos. 1-2 (Sept.-Oct. 1955): 31-33.

386. Taylor, Nicholas G.B. "The Language of the Jitterbug."
      Better English 2, no. 5 (1938): 51.

387. ————. "American Jazz Is Not African." *New York
      Times*, 19 Sept. 1926, p. 8.

388. ————. "Jazz Music and Its Relation to African Music."
      Musical Courier 84, no. 22 (1922): 7.

389. "The Blight of Jazz and the Spiritual." *Literary Digest*
      55, no. 15 (12 Apr. 1950): 10.

390. "The Decline of Jazz." *Musician* 27, no. 5 (May 1922): 1.

391. "The Doctor Looks at Jazz." *Literary Digest* 46, no. 10
      (3 Sept. 1927): n.p.

      Contains a doctor's (neuropath's) view of why people
      like jazz.

392. "The Function of the Critic in Jazz." *Metronome*, Aug.
      1949, pp. 16-17.

393. "The Influence of 'Jazz.'" *Monthly Musical Record* 57,
      no. 8 (1 Aug. 1927): 233.

394. "The Jazz Band and Negro Music." *Living Age* 323, no. 10
      (18 Oct. 1924): 169-73.

395. "The Jazz Beat: Note on Small Bands." *Saturday Review*,
      27 Sept. 1947, p. 47.

396. "The Jazz Beat: Sic Transit Something or Other."
      Saturday Review, 28 Aug. 1948, p. 55.

397. "The National Music Fallacy: Is American Music to Rest
      on a Foundation of Ragtime and Jazz?" *Arts and
      Decoration* 20, no. 2 (Feb. 1924): 26, 62.

398. "The Need for Racial Unity in Jazz: A Panel Discussion."
      Down Beat, 11 Apr. 1963, pp. 16-21.

399. "The Relation of Jazz to American Music." *American
      Composers on American Music*. Edited by Henry Cowell.
      Stanford: Stanford University Press, 1933, pp. 186-87.
      Reprint. Elie Siegmeister, ed. *The Music Lover's
      Handbook*. New York: William Morrow, 1943, pp. 728-29.

400. "The Riotous Return of Mr. Antheil." *Literary Digest*
      43, no. 5 (30 Apr. 1927): 26-27.

      Comments on Antheil's jazz concerts and interpreta-
      tion.

401. "The Jazz Invasion." *Behold America*. Edited by Samuel
      Daniel Schmalhausen. New York: Farrar and Rinehart,
      1931, pp. 499-513.

402. "The Quarries for Jazz." *Literary Digest* 89, no. 9
      (29 May 1926): 27.

      Paul Whiteman's views on jazz.

403. Thompson, Oscar. "Jazz, as Art Music, Piles Failure on
      Failure." *Musical America* 43, no. 3 (13 Feb. 1926):
      3, 23.

404. Thompson, R.F. "Jazz Roots in Nigeria." *Saturday Review*,
      11 Apr. 1964, pp. 52-53.

405. "The Cult of Jazz." *Vanity Fair* 24, no. 6 (June 1925):
      54, 118.

406. Van Gogh, Rupert. "The Evolution of Jazz." *West African
      Review* 6, no. 3 (Mar. 1935): 15-17.

      Discusses Black elements in jazz.

407. "Variationettes." *Musical Courier*, 4 May 1922, p. 21.

408. "Vienna Is Alarmed by Inroads of Jazz." *New York Times*,
      15 Apr. 1928, p. 4.

409. "Waltz-Kings and Jazz-Kings." *New Statesman*, 17 Apr.
      1926, pp. 13-14. Reprint. W.J. Turner. *Musical
      Meanderings*. London: Methuen, 1928, pp. 59-64.

410. "Warns White Races They Must Drop Jazz." *New York
      Times*, 20 Sept. 1927, p. 3.

411. Webster, James D. "The Bango Gave Us Jazz--Believe It
      or Not!" *Metronome*, Aug. 1940, p. 40.

412. "What Europeans Write About Jazz." *Down Beat*, 13 Aug.
      1947, pp. 10-11.

413. "When We Have Jazz Opera." *Musical Canada* 6, no. 10
      (Oct. 1925): 13-14.

414. "When European Composes Jazz." *Literary Digest* 46,
      no. 11 (17 Mar. 1928): 25-26.

      Has some excellent comments on jazz by Maurice Ravel.

415. "Where Is Jazz Leading America?" *Etude* 42, no. 8
      (Aug. 1924): 517-18.

416. "Where the *Etude* Stands on Jazz." *Etude* 42, no. 8
      (Aug. 1924): 515.

417. "Where Jazz Was Born." *Pageant*, Feb. 1945, pp. 93-95.

418. "Where Jazz Is Taking Us Musically." *Current Opinion*
      77 (Dec. 1924): 746-47.

419. "White Jazzmen Today Are Superior to Negroes." *Music
      and Rhythm* 2, no. 8 (Aug. 1941): 24-25.

420. "Who Invented Jazz?" *Collier's*, 3 Jan. 1925, p. 38.

421. "Why Not Mix Jazz and Classics?" *Literary Digest* 91,
      no. 5 (30 Oct. 1926): 29.

422. "Will South American Music Kill Jazz?" *Music and Rhythm*
      2, no. 4 (Apr. 1942): 9-10, 48-49.

423. Williams, B. "Sounds of Jazz, Big Bands Again Pour Out
      from Nashville Scene." *Billboard*, 1 Apr. 1967, p. 4.

424. Williams, Martin T. "Jazz at the Movies." *Saturday
      Review*, 15 July 1967, p. 49.

425. ————. "The Bystander." *Down Beat*, 20 June 1963,
      p. 43.

426. ————. "Jazz Composition--What Is It?" *Down Beat*,
      15 Feb. 1962, pp. 20-23.

427. Wilson, Edmund. "The Jazz Problem." *New Republic*,
      13 Jan. 1926, pp. 217-19.

428. Wolff, D. Leon. "Are Critics Jazz's Worst Enemy?"
      Down Beat, 9 Apr. 1947, pp. 15-16.

THESES AND DISSERTATIONS

429. Anderson, Edgar W., Jr. "An Investigation of Jazz
      Instruction in Texas Secondary Schools." Master's
      thesis, Houston State Teacher's College, 1959.

430. Apetz, Harry B. "The Place of the Dance Band in the
      High School Educational Program." Master's thesis,
      Texas Christian University, 1949.

431. Bauman, Dick. "A Dissection of the History and Musical
      Product of Stan Kenton"; "Jazz Education in the
      Public School Music Program"; "The Third Stream."

Master's thesis, Northwest Missouri State University, 1970.

432. Becker, Howard Saul. "The Professional Dance Musician in Chicago." Master's thesis, University of Chicago, 1949.

433. Berritt, Hugh G. "Developing a High School Stage Band." Master's thesis, Manhattan School of Music, 1958.

434. Bonsanti, Neal J. "A Survey of Stage Band Curricula in the High Schools of Florida." Master's thesis, University of Miami, 1968.

435. Briscuso, Joseph James. "A Study of Ability in Spontaneous and Prepared Jazz Improvisation Among Students Who Possess Different Levels of Musical Aptitude." Ph.D. dissertation, University of Iowa, 1972.

436. Burton, Roger V. "The Personality of the Contracted Studio Musician: An Investigation Using the Guilford-Zimmerman Temperament Survey." Master's thesis, University of Southern California, 1955.

437. Chuckanzeff, John L. "Popular Dance Music in High School Instrumental Teaching." Master's thesis, Eastman School of Music, 1938.

438. Coker, Jerry. "The Presentation of an Introduction to the Theory of Jazz Improvisation." Master's thesis, Sam Houston State Teacher's College, 1960.

439. Damron, Bert Lee, Jr. "The Development and Evaluation of a Self-Instructional Sequence in Jazz Improvisation." Ph.D. dissertation, Florida State University, 1973.

440. DeShore, Thomas Jake. "Dance Bands and Public School Music." Master's thesis, Florida State University, 1973.

441. Duke, John R. "Teaching Musical Improvisation: A Study of 18th and 19th Century Methods." Ph.D. dissertation, George Peabody College, 1972.

442. Faulkner, Robert Roy. "Studio Musicians: Their Work and Career Contingencies in the Hollywood Film Industry." Ph.D. dissertation, University of California, 1968.

443. Gold, Robert S. "A Jazz Lexicon." Ph.D. dissertation, New York University, 1962.

444. Good, Melvin Lee. "A Study of the Effectiveness of Public School Music in the Opinions of Selected Dance Band Musicians." Master's thesis, Northwestern University, 1954.

445. Hansen, Chadwick Clarke. "The Ages of Jazz: A Study of Jazz in Its Cultural Context." Ph.D. dissertation, University of Minnesota, 1956.

446. Hilligoss, C. Adair. "Materials and Methods for High School Stage/Dance Bands." Master's thesis, Washington State University, 1961.

447. Hortse, Ralph John. "The Development of a Functional Knowledge of Theory through Simplified Dance Orchestra Arranging." Master's thesis, Montana State University, 1970.

448. Hoyt, Charles. "Jazz and Its Origin." Bachelor's thesis, Wesleyan University, 1953.

449. Johnson, James Winfred. "The Status and Administration of Student Dance Bands in Colleges and Universities in the United States." Master's thesis, North Texas State Teacher's College, 1947.

450. Keathley, Kenneth E. "A Proposed Guitar Method for High School Dance Bands." Master's thesis, Sam Houston State Teacher's College, 1955.

451. Konowitz, Bertram Lawrence. "Jazz Improvisation at the Piano--A Textbook for Teachers." Ph.D. dissertation, Columbia University, 1969.

452. Lambrecht, Clarence Julius. "A Survey of Texas High School Dance Bands." Master's thesis, University of Texas, 1961.

453. Marinac, William. "Course Outline for Teachers' Use in Lecture of Jazz Appreciation 1912." Master's thesis, Vandercook College of Music, 1971.

454. McCauley, John Willys. "Jazz Improvisation for the B-Flat Soprano Trumpet: An Introductory Text for

Teaching Basic Theoretical and Performance Principles."
Ph.D. dissertation, Louisiana State University and
Mechanical College, 1973.

455.   McDaniel, William Theodore, Jr.   "Differences in Music
       Achievement, Musical Experiences, and Background
       Between Jazz-improvising Musicians and Non-improvising
       Musicians at the Freshman and Sophomore College Levels."
       Ph.D. dissertation, University of Iowa, 1974.

456.   Merriam, Alan P.   "Instruments and Instrumental Usages
       in the History of Jazz."   Master's thesis, Northwestern
       University, 1948.

457.   Midyett, Gene H.   "The Place of the Dance Band in the
       High School Program."   Master's thesis, University of
       Southern California, 1949.

458.   Minkler, Chester.   "Applying Dance Band Arranging
       Techniques in Scoring Music for the High School
       Concert Band."   Master's thesis, Boston University,
       1950.

459.   Morton, Jean.   "Some Physiological Effects of Jazz and
       Classical Music."   Master's thesis, University of
       Pittsburgh, 1935.

460.   Nanry, Charles Anthony.   "The Occupational Subculture
       of the Jazz Musician: Myth and Reality."   Ph.D.
       dissertation, Rutgers, The State University of New
       Jersey, 1970.

461.   Parmen, Milton C.   "The Place of the Dance Band in the
       School Music Program."   Master's thesis, Ohio State
       University, 1942.

462.   Patterson, Willis Perry.   "A Critical Study of the Jazz-
       Vaudeville Drama (1923-1934) in the United States."
       Ph.D. dissertation, University of Denver, 1965.

463.   Rulli, Joe R.   "The Stage Band as a Teaching Tool for
       the Performance of Contemporary Band Literature."
       Master's thesis, University of Wyoming, 1971.

464.   Salvatore, Joseph A.   "Jazz Improvisation: Principles
       and Practices Relating to Harmonic and Scalic Resources."
       Ph.D. dissertation, Florida State University, 1970.

465. ————. "A Guide for Ad-Lib Playing on the Trumpet."
     Master's thesis, Pennsylvania State University, 1962.

466. Sample, Alexander Claude, Jr. "A Plan for Stimulating
     Interest and Motivation in High School Instrumental
     Music through the Utilization of the Dance Orchestra."
     Master's thesis, Texas Southern University, 1955.

467. Smith, Hugh L. "Literary Manifestation of a Romanticism
     in American Jazz." Ph.D. dissertation, University of
     New Mexico, 1955.

468. Stanley, John W. "An Analysis and Comparison of Four
     Texts on Arranging and Composing for Jazz Orchestra."
     Master's thesis, Sam Houston Teacher's College, 1964.

469. Stuart, Mary Louise. "Unit Organization of the Topic
     Jazz in the Senior High School." Master's thesis,
     Boston University, 1953.

470. Stebbins, Robert Alan. "The Jazz Community: The
     Sociology of Musical Sub-culture." Ph.D. dissertation,
     University of Minnesota, 1954.

471. Tanner, Paul O.W. "A Technical Analysis of the Develop-
     ment of Jazz." Master's thesis, University of Cali-
     fornia, Los Angeles, 1962.

472. Tuozzolo, James Michael. "Trumpet Techniques in Selec-
     ted Works of Four Contemporary American Composers:
     Gunther Schuller, Mayer Kupferman, William Sydeman,
     and William Fabrizio." Ph.D. dissertation, University
     of Miami, 1972.

473. Von Haupt, Lois. "Jazz: An Historical and Analytical
     Study." Master's thesis, New York University, 1945.

474. Weitz, Lowell Eugene. "The Stage Band as a Part of the
     High School Music Program." Ph.D. dissertation,
     University of Missouri at Kansas City, 1964.

475. Went, Barry. "Statewide Survey on the Present Status
     of Jazz Bands in Michigan." Master's thesis,
     Michigan State University.

476. Wickiser, Duane A. "A Progressive Method on How to
     Improvise." Master's thesis, Millikin University,
     1965.

477. Wucher, Jay R.   "Jazz Bands and Concert Band Performance
      Skills of Selected Undergraduate Instrumental Music
      Education Majors at the University of Southern Missis-
      sippi." Master's thesis, University of Southern
      Mississippi, 1972.

478. Wylie, F.E., Jr.   "An Investigation of Some Aspects of
      Creativity in Jazz Musicians." Ph.D. dissertation,
      Wayne State University, 1962.

B. PRE-SWING

This category contains selected information on
performers, composers, and arrangers as well
as on jazz styles that were prominent before
the swing era.

BOOKS

479. Allen, Walter C., and Brian A.L. Rust. *King Joe Oliver*.
      London: Sedgwick & Jackson, 1954.

480. Armstrong, Louis. *Satchmo: My Life in New Orleans*.
      New York: Prentice-Hall, 1954.

481. Asbury, Herbert. *The French Quarter*. New York:
      Ballantine, 1973.

482. Bechet, Sidney. *Treat It Gentle*. New York: Hill &
      Wang, 1960.

      Among those who helped record and edit the tapes on
      which this book is based are Joan Reid, Desmond Flowers,
      and John Ciardi.

483. Blesh, Rudy. *Shining Trumpets: A History of Jazz*.
      New York: Knopf, 1946.

      A concise history of jazz from the early days to
      modern times (mid- to late forties). Contains musical
      examples and a discography.

484. Borenstein, Larry. *Preservation Hall Portraits*. Baton
      Rouge: Louisiana State University Press, 1960.

485. Brunn, H.O. *The Story of the Original Dixieland Jazz
      Band*. Baton Rouge: Louisiana State University Press,
      1960.

      An extensive, detailed study of the Original Dixieland

Jazz Band. A somewhat biased view of the origin of
early jazz.

486.   Buerkle, Jack V., and Danny Barker. *Bourbon Street
          Black: The New Orleans Black Jazzman*. New York:
          Oxford University Press, 1973.

487.   Charters, Samuel B. *Jazz: A History of the New York
          Scene*. Garden City, New York: Doubleday, 1962.

       A very detailed look at how blues and jazz began in
New York. About two-thirds of the book deals with jazz
before 1917. Also contains a good section on Scott
Joplin and ragtime music, and a good bibliography with
a very detailed discography.

488.   Chilton, John. *Who's Who of Jazz: Storyville to Swing
          Street*. Philadelphia: Chilton, 1972.

489.   Condon, Eddie. *We Called It Music: A Generation of
          Jazz*. New York: Henry Holt, 1947. Reprint. Westport,
          Connecticut: Greenwood, 1974.

       A story of the growth of jazz with a detailed appen-
dix, compiled by John Swingle, listing the Chicago bands
and Eddie Condon recordings.

490.   Davis, J.P., ed. *The American Negro Reference Book*.
          Englewood Cliffs, New Jersey: Prentice-Hall, 1966.

       Chapters 20, 21, and 24 contain some information
concerning early jazz.

491.   Dodds, W., and L. Gorci. *The Baby Dobbs Story*. Los
          Angeles: Contemporary Press, 1959.

492.   Eaton, Jeanette. *Trumpeter's Tale: The Story of Young
          Louis Armstrong*. New York: William Morrow, 1955.

493.   Feather, Leonard. *New Edition of the Encyclopedia of
          Jazz*. New York: Horizon Press, 1960.

       Includes discussion of Louis Armstrong.

494.   ———. *The New Encyclopedia of Jazz in the Sixties*.
          New York: Horizon Press, 1965.

       Includes discussion of Louis Armstrong.

495. Gillis, Frank J., and John W. Miner. *Oh, Didn't He Ramble: The Life Story of Lee Collins as Told to Mary Collins.* Urbana: University of Illinois Press, 1974.

496. Goffin, Robert. *Horn of Plenty: The Story of Louis Armstrong.* Translated from French by James F. Bezov. New York: Allen, Towne and Heath, 1947.

497. ————. *La Nouvelle-Orléans, capitale du jazz.* New York: Editions de la maison française, 1946.

498. Hadlock, Richard, ed. *Jazz Masters of the Twenties.* 1966. Reprint. New York: Macmillan, 1974.

    Chapters on Louis Armstrong, Earl Hines, Bix Beiderbecke, Fats Waller, James P. Johnson, Don Redman, Bessie Smith, Fletcher Henderson, Jack Teagarden, and Eddie Lang.

499. *International Who's Who, 1965-1966.* London: Europa, 1966.

    Includes information on Louis Armstrong.

500. James, Burnett. *Bix Beiderbecke.* Cranbury, New Jersey: A.S. Barnes, 1961.

501. *Jazz Records: 1897-1942 Revised Edition.* London: Storyville Publications, 1970.

502. *Jelly Roll Morton's New Orleans Memories.* New York: Consolidated Records, n.d.

503. Jepsen, Jorgen Grunnet. *Discography of Jelly Roll Morton.* Vols. 1 and 2. Stanhope, New Jersey: Walter C. Allen, n.d.

504. Johnson, George. *The Five Pennies: The Biography of Jazz Band Leader Red Nichols.* New York: Dell, 1959.

505. Jones, Cliff. *New Orleans and Chicago Jazz.* London: Discographical Society, 1944.

506. ————, ed. *J.G. Higginbottom.* London: Discographical Society, 1944.

507. Jones, Maz, and John Chilton. *Louis: The Louis Armstrong Story, 1900-1971.* Boston: Little, Brown; London: Studio Vista, 1971.

508. King, Grace E. *New Orleans: The Place and the People*.
      1895. Reprint. Westport, Connecticut: Negro Univer-
      sities Press, 1967.

509. Kmen, Henry A. *The Roots of Jazz: The Negro and Music
      in New Orleans, 1791-1900*. Urbana: University of
      Illinois Press, 1977.

510. ————. *Music in New Orleans: The Formative Years,
      1791-1841*. Baton Rouge: Louisiana State University
      Press, 1966.

      Relates the social history of White New Orleans
      music. Also contains some information on the pre-
      history of the early jazz era.

511. Lambert, G.E. *Johnny Dodds*. London: Cassell, 1961.

512. Longstreet, Stephen. *Sportin House: A History of the
      New Orleans Sinners, and the Birth of Jazz*. Los
      Angeles: Sherbourne Press, 1965.

513. Martinez, Raymond. *Portraits of New Orleans Jazz: Its
      People and Places*. New Orleans: Hope Publications,
      1971.

514. McCarthy, Albert; Alun Morgan; Paul Oliver; and Max
      Harrison. *Jazz on Record: A Critical Review of the
      First 50 Years: 1917-1967*. London: Hanover Books,
      1968.

515. McCarthy, Albert J. *Louis Armstrong*. Cranbury, New
      Jersey: A.S. Barnes, 1961.

516. Mendel, R.W.S. *The Appeal of Jazz*. London: P. Allan,
      1927.

      An interesting historical source on early jazz;
      describes the roots and origin of jazz.

517. Miller, William. *Three Brass (O'Brien, Kaminsky, Sher-
      lock)*. Melbourne: William H. Miller, 1945.

518. Mouly, R. *Sidney Bechet, notre ami*. Paris: La table
      ronde, 1959.

519. Panassie, Hugues. *Louis Armstrong*. 1971. Reprint.
      New York: Scribner's, 1974.

520. Schuller, Gunther. *Early Jazz: Its Roots and Musical Development.* New York: Oxford University Press, 1968.

An excellent and extensive study of early jazz and its origin. The book covers rhythm, form, harmony, melody, timbre, and improvisation of jazz. Also contains information on some early jazz performers.

521. Shapiro, Nat, and Nat Hentoff, eds. *The Jazz Makers.* New York: Rinehart, 1957.

Treats Jelly Roll Morton, Baby Dodds, Louis Armstrong, Jack Teagarden, Bix Beiderbecke, and Pee Wee Russell.

522. Smith, Jay, and Len Guttridge. *Jack Teagarden.* London: Cassell, 1960.

523. Stambler, Irwin, ed. *Encyclopedia of Popular Music.* New York: St. Martin's, 1965.

Contains information on Louis Armstrong.

524. Tallant, Robert. *Voodoo in New Orleans.* New York: Macmillan, 1966.

525. Williams, Martin T. *Jazz Masters of New Orleans.* New York: Macmillan, 1967.

526. ————. *Jelly Roll Morton.* Cranbury, New Jersey: A.S. Barnes, 1962.

ARTICLES

527. "The Air Is Filled with Music." *Time*, 14 Mar. 1949, p. 44.

528. "Albert Nicholas: Artist in Exile." *Jazz Monthly*, Sept. 1961.

529. "American Bandsmen in London." *Musical Opinion* 46, no. 5 (May 1923): 733-34.

530. "An Interview with Sidney Bechet." *Record Changer*, June 1969, pp. 9-10.

531. Ansermet, Ernest. "Sidney Bechet in 1919." *The Art of Jazz*. Edited by Martin T. Williams. New York: Oxford University Press, 1959, pp. 3-7.

532. "The Appeal of the Primitive Jazz." *Literary Digest* 55, no. 8 (25 Aug. 1917): 28-29.

      Some interesting comments on the origin and appeal of jazz.

533. "Are the White Chicagoans of the '20's Overrated? No." *Music and Rhythm* 11, no. 10 (Oct. 1941): 45, 56.

534. "Armstrong's Nostalgia Envelops Bop City." *Billboard*, 3 Sept. 1949, p. 14.

535. "Armstrong to Make Another Europe Trip." *Down Beat*, 3 Nov. 1950, p. 3.

536. Armstrong, Lil. "About Early Chicago Days." *Down Beat*, 1 June 1951, p. 12.

537. ———. "Lil Tells of First Time She Met Louis." *Down Beat*, 14 July 1950, p. 18.

538. Armstrong, Louis. "Joe Oliver Is Still King." *Record Changer*, July 1950, n.p.

539. ———. "Louis in Jazz and Swing." *Metronome*, June 1945, pp. 26-27.

540. ———. "Jazz on a High Note." *Esquire*, Dec. 1951, pp. 85-86, 209-12.

541. ———. "Berigan Can't Do No Wrong." *Down Beat*, 1 Sept. 1941, p. 7.

542. ———. "Scanning the History of Jazz." *Jazz Review* 3, no. 6 (July 1960): 6-10.

543. ———. "Louis on the Spot." *Record Changer*, July-August 1950, pp. 23-24, 44.

544. Armstrong, Lucille. "Louis' Favorite Dish." *Record Changer*, July-Aug. 1950, p. 18.

545. "Art Hodes Band Achieves a 'Rarely-Heard Unity.'" *Down Beat*, 15 Dec. 1950, p. 11.

546. Asbury, Herbert. "Congo Square." *The French Quarter.* New York: Knopf, 1936.

547. Avakian, George M. "How I Found the Unissued Armstrongs." *Jazz Information* 2, no. 12 (6 Dec. 1940): 17, 24.

548. ————. "Paul Mares, New Orleans Rhythm Kings." *Record Changer*, Nov. 1949, p. 10.

549. "Back to Chicago." *Time*, 21 July 1941, p. 40.

550. Bankhead, Tallulah. "Louis the End--and Beginning--Tallulah." *Down Beat*, 14 July 1950, pp. 1, 19.

551. Barker, Danny. "Jelly Roll Morton in New York." *Jazz Review* 2, no. 4 (May 1959): 12-15.

552. ————. "A Memory of King Bolden." *Evergreen Review*, no. 37 (Sept. 1965).

553. Barrelhouse, Dan. "Has Louis Armstrong Passed His Peak as a Jazz Leader?" *Down Beat*, July 1939, p. 24.

554. Beall, George. "The New Orleans Rhythm Kings." *Frontiers of Jazz.* 2nd ed. Edited by Ralph de Toledano. New York: Frederick Ungar, 1962, pp. 82-91.

555. ————. "Forgotten Giants." *Jazz Information* 2, no. 12 (20 Dec. 1940): 12-20.

556. Bechet, Sidney, et al. "In Praise of Satchmo." *Record Changer*, July-Aug. 1950, pp. 12-13.

556a. Benford, Robert J. "Louis Armstrong: Bibliography." *Record Changer*, July-Aug. 1950, pp. 33-35.

557. Biemiller, Carl L. "Armstrong and His Hot-Noters Point a Trend." *Holiday*, Oct. 1948, pp. 13-14.

558. "Bix Beiderbecke." *Down Beat*, 1 Aug. 1940, p. 10.

559. "Bix and Carmichael." *Jazz Finder* 1 (Mar. 1948): 18.

560. "Bix at Lake Forest." *Esquire*, Mar. 1944, pp. 59, 144-45.

561. "Bobby Hackett Is a Great Cornet Player." *Music and Rhythm* 11, no. 1 (Jan. 1942): 27.

562.   Bontemps, Arna, and Jack Conroy. "An American Original
       (Jelly Roll Morton)." *Jam Session*. Edited by Ralph
       J. Gleason. New York: G.P. Putnam's, 1958.

563.   "Bop Will Kill Business Unless It Kills Itself First--
       Louis Armstrong." *Down Beat*, 7 Apr. 1948, pp. 2-3.

564.   Borneman, Ernest. "The Roots of Jazz." *Jazz*. Edited
       by Nat Hentoff and Albert McCarthy. New York: Rine-
       hart, 1959, pp. 1-21.

565.   Breck, Poak. "This Ain't Bunk; Bunk Taught Louis."
       Down Beat, June 1939, p. 4.

566.   Broun, Heywood Hale. "Satchmo 40, Looks Good for
       Another 20 Years." *PM*, 11 May 1941.

567.   Bruell, Anton. "Jazz Dazzler! Louis Armstrong." *Vanity
       Fair* 45, no. 11 (Nov. 1935): 39.

568.   "Bud Freeman." *Down Beat*, 1 June 1941, p. 10.

569.   "Buddy Bolden." *Hot Club Magazine*, Feb. 1967, pp. 3-4.

570.   Bushkin, Joe. "Old Satchmo, the Gourmet." *Down Beat*,
       14 July 1950, p. 12.

571.   "Bunk's an Amazing Story." *Down Beat*, 26 Aug. 1949,
       pp. 6-7.

572.   "Bunk Didn't Teach Me." *Record Changer*, July-Aug. 1950,
       p. 30.

573.   "Bunk Discography." *Down Beat*, 26 Aug. 1949, p. 6.

574.   "Bunk Johnson Rides Again." *Time*, 24 May 1943, pp.
       63-64.

575.   "Bunk Johnson." *Ebony*, Mar. 1946, pp. 33-37.

576.   "Bunk Johnson: An Appreciation." *Jazz Journal* 11, no. 9
       (Sept. 1969): 2-3.

577.   "Bury Jelly Roll Morton on Coast." *Down Beat*, 1 Aug.
       1941, p. 13.

578.   "Care of the Lip." *Record Changer*, July-Aug. 1950,
       p. 30.

579. Carew, Roy. "Let Jelly Roll Speak for Himself." *Record Changer*, Dec. 1952, n.p.

580. Carey, Mutt. "New Orleans Trumpet Players." *Jazz Music* 3, no. 4 (1946): 10-12.

581. Charters, Samuel B. "Willie Geary 'Bunk' Johnson." *Jazz* 18 (1958): n.p.

582. "Chicago, Chicago, That Toddlin Town: How King and Ol' Satch Dug It in the Twenties." *Esquire's 1947 Jazz Book*. Chicago: Esquire, 1946, pp. 40-43.

583. "Chicago jazz, au temps des gangsters--." *Hot Club Magazine*, June 1946, pp. 6-7, 9.

584. "Chicago Style?--It's a Phony Myth!" *Music and Rhythm* 1, no. 3 (Mar. 1941): 35-40.

585. "Chicago Style All Bunk Bud Freeman Asserts, Ain't No Such Animal." *Down Beat*, 1 Dec. 1942, p. 4.

586. Chilton, Charles. "Jackson and the Oliver Band." *Jazz Music* 6 (1947): 59.

587. Chotzinoff, Samuel. "Jazz: A Brief History." *Vanity Fair* 22, no. 6 (June 1923): 69.

588. "Church Jazz Wedding Utilizes Saxophone." *New York Times*, 14 Nov. 1926, n.p.

589. Clark, Dave. "Educated Cat Stole My Mute Idea--Joe Oliver." *Down Beat*, 1 Mar. 1960, p. 8.

590. Collins, Mary, and John W. Miner. "From Lee Collins' Story." *Evergreen Review*, no. 37 (Mar. 1965): n.p.

591. Cons, Carl. "Bunny Berigan Teams Up with Bix." *Music and Rhythm* 2, no. 7 (June 1942): 50.

592. Cotler, Gordon. "Preservation Hall." *Holiday*, May 1970, pp. 54-55.

593. Covarrubias. "Impossible Interview: Fritz Kreisler vs. Louis Armstrong." *Vanity Fair* 45, no. 2 (Feb. 1936): 33.

594. Delaunay, Charles. "Louis Armstrong." *Hot Discography*.
     New York: Commodore Records, 1963, pp. 35-52.

595. Deutsch, Hermann. "Louis Armstrong." *Esquire*, Oct.
     1935, pp. 70, 138.

596. ————. "Louis Armstrong: A Trumpet Call for the Little
     Black Waif Grown Up Playing Hot Notes for White Folks."
     Esquire, Oct. 1935, pp. 70, 138.

597. "Discography of Jimmie Noone." *Jazz Information* 2
     (8 Nov. 1940): 15-22.

598. "Dodds and Bolden Were Smiling." *Down Beat*, 1 Dec.
     1948, p. 7.

599. Dodge, Roger Pryor. "Louis Armstrong." *Jazz*, no. 12
     (Dec. 1943): 5.

600. ————. "New Jazz." *Dancing Times*, Oct. 1929, pp. 32-
     35.

601. "Discography: Leon Bismark (Bix) Beiderbecke." *Recordi-
     ana* 1, nos. 6-7 (June-July 1944): 3-4.

602. "Dixieland Bandwagon." *Time*, 24 Apr. 1950, p. 104.

603. "Dixie 1950." *Metronome*, May 1950, pp. 24, 28.

604. "Dixieland Jazz in Brussels." *Hot Club Magazine*,
     Feb. 1946, pp. 6-7.

605. "Dixie Jubilee Once More Proves Box Office Bonanza."
     Down Beat, 17 Nov. 1950, pp. 1, 13.

606. "Dixieland Shrine." *Newsweek*, 16 Oct. 1944, pp. 105-6.

607. "Don Ewell Goes Back to New Orleans Rags." *Down Beat*,
     4 Nov. 1946, p. 12.

608. Drob, Harold. "Bunk Johnson--An Appreciation, Part I."
     Record Changer, Nov. 1952, n.p.

609. Dugan, James. "Old Man Jiver." *Collier's*, 9 Feb. 1946,
     pp. 27, 51-52.

610. Ebel, Bud. "Old Wolverines Couldn't Read So I Pulled
     Out." *Down Beat*, 15 June 1942, p. 5.

611. Edwards, Eddie. "Once Upon a Time." *Jazz Record* 55, no. 5 (1 May 1947): 5-6.

612. "Emmet Hardy." *Down Beat*, 15 Aug. 1940, p. 6.

613. Erskin, Gilbert M. "Last of the New Orleans Rhythm Kings." *Down Beat*, 10 May 1962, n.p.

614. Estes, Stephen A. "The 'New' Jazz." *Music Lover's Magazine*, Sept. 1922, p. 7.

615. Europe, James Reese. "A Negro Explains Jazz." *Literary Digest* 61, no. 4 (1919): 28-29.

    Contains excellent comment on the origin of the term "jazz," as well as Europe's remarks on his experiences in Paris, how he organized his band, etc.

616. "Europe--With Kicks." *Holiday*, June 1950, pp. 8-12, 14-16.

617. Ewen, David. "Louis Armstrong." *Men of Popular Music*. New York: Ziff Davis, 1944, pp. 51-62.

618. "Fans Who Misinterpreted Now Are Forgetting Bunk." *Down Beat*, 15 Dec. 1948, p. 6.

619. Farber, Manny. "New Orleans Survival." *New Republic*, 21 Feb. 1944, pp. 242-43.

620. ———. "Old Man with an Hour." *New Republic*, Jan. 1946, p. 448.

    An analysis of six Bunk Johnson recordings.

621. Feather, Leonard. "Satchmo Remembered." *Down Beat*, 9 July 1970, p. 21.

622. ———. "Lombardo Grooves Louis!" *Metronome*, Sept. 1949, p. 18.

623. ———. "Ferdinand Joseph Morton--A Biography." *Jazz Music* 2, nos. 2-3 (Feb.-Mar. 1944): 86-101.

624. "Frank Trumbauer." *Down Beat*, 1 Nov. 1940, p. 10.

625. "Figs Might Do Well to Take a Hint from Bop--Make New Dixie Sounds." *Down Beat*, 6 May 1949, p. 2.

626. Foster, Pops. "Forty-Eight Years on the String Bass."
Jazz Record 53, no. 9 (Mar. 1947): 18, 32.

627. Freedman, Marvin. "Satchmo Terrific Solo Style Met and
Filled Dixieland Ensemble." *Down Beat*, June 1939, p.4.

628. "From Louis' Photo Album." *Record Changer*, July-Aug.
1950, pp. 28-29.

629. Gabler, Milt. "Hot Renaissance of Dixieland Jazz."
New York Times Magazine, 24 Sept. 1950, pp. 26-27.

630. Gagliane, Nick. "King Louis' Triumph Tempered." *Down
Beat*, 8 Apr. 1949, p. 18.

631. Garroway, Dave. "Everyone Owes Debt to Louis, Says
Garroway." *Down Beat*, 14 July 1950, pp. 1, 19.

632. Gayer, Dixon. "Chicago, Chicago--." *Metronome*, Oct.
1943, pp. 37-38.

633. ———, and George Hoefer. "Chicago Jazz History."
Esquire, Feb. 1946, pp. 51-55.

634. ———. "'Get in B Flat' Led Joe Oliver to the Throne."
Down Beat, 15 Sept. 1941, p. 16.

635. Gleason, Ralph J. "Bunk Johnson and His New Orleans
Band." *RCA Victor Album H J 7*.

636. Goffin, Robert. "Where Jazz Was Born." *Pageant*, Feb.
1945, pp. 93-96.

637. ———. "Louis Armstrong." *Jazz from the Congo to the
Metropolitan*. Garden City, New York: Doubleday, 1944,
pp. 114-29.

638. Goines, Leonard. "Jazz Piano of the 20's." *Allegro* 71,
no. 4 (Apr. 1972): 12.

639. Graver, Bill. "Dixieland Clarinet." *Record Changer*,
Aug. 1948, pp. 11-12.

640. Green, Benny. "His Name ... a Household Word?" *Jazz
Review* 2, no. 2 (Feb. 1959): 18-19.

About Louis Armstrong.

641. Greene, Robert S. "Bix: He Was an Emotion More Than Anything Else." *Record Changer*, May 1949, pp. 8, 20.

642. Gualtne, Tom. "Pee Wee's Last Days." *Down Beat*, 12 June 1969, pp. 20, 42.

643. Greenbaum, Lucy. "Saga of 'Satchmo.'" *New York Times*, 4 May 1947, n.p.

644. Deleted.

645. Grossman, W.L. "From Jelly Roll to Brubeck: Is This Progress?" *Crisis* 63, no. 15 (8 Aug. 1955): 414-15.

646. Guilliams, A.E. "Detrimental Effects of Jazz on Our Younger Generation." *Metronome*, Feb. 1923, p. 59.

647. Gushee, Larry. "King Oliver." *Jazz Panorama*. Edited by Martin Williams. New York: Crowell-Collier, 1962, pp. 20-26.

648. Hadlock, Richard. "The State of Dixieland." *Jazz Review* 2, no. 9 (Oct. 1959): 6-16.

    A musical analysis, including examples, of 13 recent releases, some being reissues. The article includes examples that compare the interpretations of "originals" with different performers, e.g., Pee Wee Russell and Charles Parker on "Embraceable You."

649. ————. "Sidney Bechet: How to Live Music." *San Francisco Examiner*, 17 Jan. 1965.

650. Haggin, B.H. "Music." *Nation*, 3 July 1939, pp. 653-54.

    Contains Wilder Hobson's view of jazz.

651. Haig, Kenneth. "Bury the Dead." *Jazz Information* 2, no. 8 (9 Aug. 1940): 17-18.

652. Hansen, C. "Social Influences on Jazz Style Chicago, 1920-30." *American Quarterly* 12, no. 1 (Winter 1960): 493-507.

653. Harrison, Max. "Review of the Sidney Bechet-Mezz Mezzrow 1945-1947 Recordings." *Jazz Monthly* 12, no. 2 (Feb. 1966): n.p.

654. Hayakawa, S.I. "35th and State: Reflections on the
      History of Jazz." *Poetry*, 17 March 1945, n.p.

655. Haynes, Don C. "Bunk's 2nd Try Proves His Horn the
      Real Thing." *Down Beat*, 7 Oct. 1946, p. 19.

656. "Happy Birthday, Louis, from ..." *Down Beat*, 14 July
      1950, pp. 2-3.

657. "Hear That Ragtime Band." *Jazz Record* 18, no. 3 (March
      1966): 6-7.

658. "Henderson 'Had to Get Louis' for Roseland Ork." *Down
      Beat*, 14 July 1950, pp. 4-5.

659. Hennessey, Mike. "Albert Nicholas! From New Orleans to
      Paris." *Down Beat*, 12 June 1969, pp. 16-17.

660. Deleted.

661. Hennessey, Thomas Joseph. "The Black Chicago Establish-
      ment 1919-1930." *Journal of Jazz Studies* 2, no. 1
      (Dec. 1974): 15-46.

662. Hentoff, Nat. "Garvin Bushell and New York Jazz in the
      1920's." *Jazz Review* 2, no. 1 (Jan. 1959): 11-14;
      no. 2 (Feb. 1959): 9-11; no. 3 (Apr. 1959): 16-17, 40.

      An in-depth discussion of the life and music of
      Garvin Bushell. Also contains some information on
      important jazz musicians of the 1920's.

663. Heyward, Du Bose. "Jasbo Brown." *American Mercury* 6,
      no. 9 (Sept. 1925): 7-9.

664. Hillman, J.C. "Tommy Ladnier." *Jazz Journal* 7, no. 8
      (Aug. 1965): n.p.

665. Hines, Earl. "Earl Hines Picks 'Five Greatest Jazzmen.'"
      Down Beat, 15 July 1941, p. 7.

666. "'Hitch-Hiking' Has Hurt Hot Music." *Down Beat*, 1 June
      1940, p. 5.

667. Hobson, Wilder. "Beiderbecke and Bailey." *Saturday
      Review*, 26 Apr. 1952, pp. 62-63.

668. ————. "Mr. Armstrong's Earlier Works." *Saturday
      Review*, 28 Apr. 1951, pp. 52-53.

669. Hodes, Art. "Bunk Johnson at Stuyvesant Casino." *Down Beat*, 28 Feb. 1963, n.p.

670. ————. "Muggsy." *Down Beat*, 18 May 1967, pp. 23, 46.

671. Hoefer, George. "All of Bix' Okeh Records Listed." *Down Beat*, 1 Nov. 1960, p. 12.

672. ————. "Armstrong Pleases Jazz Lovers in Chicago Bash." *Down Beat*, 3 Dec. 1947, p. 11.

673. ————. "Luis Russell." *Down Beat*, 8 Nov. 1962, pp. 9-11.

674. ————. "Will the Louis Sides on Cylinder Ever Turn Up?" *Down Beat*, 14 July 1950, p. 11.

675. Hourwich, Rebecca. "Where the Jazz Begins." *Collier's*, 23 Jan. 1926, p. 14.

676. "How I Found the Unissued Armstrongs." *Jazz Information* 2, no. 12 (6 Dec. 1940): 17, 24.

677. "How Louis Has Influenced Jazz." *Down Beat*, 5 Nov. 1947, p. 2.

678. Deleted.

679. Hulsizer, Kenneth. "Jelly Roll Morton in Washington." *Jazz Music* 2, nos. 2-3 (Feb.-Mar. 1944): 109-16.

680. "Ils cherchaient une ville ... Notes sur les styles Nouvelle-Orléans et Chicago." *Hot Club Magazine*, Mar. 1946, pp. 6-7.

681. Irving, Carter. "Jazz Brings First Dance of the City." *New York Times*, 14 July 1925, p. 9.

682. "Is Jess Stacy the Greatest White Pianist?" *Music and Rhythm* 2, no. 6 (July 1941): 84-85.

683. "Is the White Cornet Style Dead?" *Music and Rhythm* 2, no. 4 (Apr. 1942): 19-20.

684. "It's 70 for Satch." *Ebony*, Sept. 1970, pp. 80-82.

685. "Jack Teagarden." *Down Beat*, 1 Dec. 1940, p. 10.

686.   Jackson, Bee.   "Hey! Hey! Charleston."   *Collier's*,
          10 Dec. 1927, pp. 12, 34.

687.   Jackson, Preston.   "King Oliver."   *Frontiers of Jazz*.
          Edited by Ralph de Toledano.   New York: Oliver Durrell,
          1947, pp. 75-82.

688.   ――――.   "King Oliver--Daddy of the Trumpet."   *Hot News*,
          May 1935, pp. 5-9; July 1935, pp. 3, 16.

689.   ――――.   "Lillian Armstrong."   *Jazz Hot* 5, nos. 2-3
          (Feb.-Mar. 1939): 13.

690.   James, Harry.   "My Ten Favorite Trumpeters."   *Music and
          Rhythm* 2 (Dec. 1941): 16-17.

691.   "Jay C. Higginbotham."   *Down Beat*, 15 Mar. 1941, p. 10.

692.   "The Jazz Beat: The Best Band in the Land."   *Saturday
          Review*, 24 Apr. 1948, p. 63.

693.   "Jazz Origin Again Discovered."   *Music Trade Review* 68,
          no. 24 (1919): 32-33.

694.   "Jazz Pre-History--and Bunk Johnson."   *Frontiers of
          Jazz*.   Edited by Ralph de Toledano.   New York: Oliver
          Durrell, 1947, pp. 91-103.

695.   "Jelly Roll's Library of Congress Wax Date World's
          Longest Session."   *Down Beat*, 24 Sept. 1947, p. 11.

696.   "Jelly Roll Morton."   *Down Beat*, 15 Apr. 1940, n.p.

697.   "Jelly Roll Morton's Washington Documentary."   *Jazz
          Record*, June 1947, pp. 24-25.

698.   "Jelly Roll Morton on Records."   *Jazz Information* 2
          (Nov. 1941): 25-28.   Reprint. Ralph de Toledano, ed.
          Frontiers of Jazz.   New York: Oliver Durrell, 1947,
          pp. 108-14.

699.   "Jelly Would Flash That G-note, Laugh in Your Face."
          Down Beat, 1 Aug. 1961, p. 4.

700.   Jepsen, Jorgen Grunnet.   "Discographie de Sidney Bechet."
          Les cahiers du jazz, nos. 10-11, n.p.

701.   "Jessy Stacy."   *Down Beat*, 1 Mar. 1941, p. 10.

702. "Jimmy Noone." *Jazz Information* 2, no. 4 (21 Mar. 1941):
      10-12, 30.

703. "Jimmy Noone." *Down Beat*, 15 Feb. 1941, p. 10.

704. "Jimmy Noone." *Jazz Information* 2, no. 10 (4 Oct.
      1940): 6-9.

705. "Joe Oliver Is Still King." *Record Changer*, June-Aug.
      1950, pp. 10-11.

706. "Johnny Dodds Discography." *Jazz* 1, no. 9 (n.d.):
      23-26.

707. "Johnny Dodds." *Jazz Information* 2, no. 2 (23 Aug.
      1940): 6-9, 24.

708. "Johnny Dodds." *Down Beat*, 1 Apr. 1940, p. 10.

709. Johnson, Bunk. "Bunk Johnson's Talking Records."
      Record Changer, June-July 1943, pp. 32-35.

710. ————, and Frederick Ramsey, Jr. "I Am Writing You
      This Letter." *Jazz*, no. 6 (June 1942): 6-8.

711. Johnson, George. "The Wolverines and Bix." *Frontiers
      of Jazz*. Edited by Ralph de Toledano. New York:
      Oliver Durrell, 1947, pp. 123-36.

712. Kahn, H. "Bebop? One Long Search for the Right Note,
      Says Louis Armstrong." *Melody Maker*, 12 Nov. 1949,
      p. 3.

713. Kay, F.W. "Basin Street Stroller: New Orleans and Tony
      Jackson." *Jazz Journal* 4, no. 6 (June 1951): 1-3.

714. Kay, George W. "The Shep Allen Story." *Jazz Journal*
      16, no. 2 (Feb. 1963): n.p.

715. Keepnews, Orin. "Jelly Roll Morton." *The Jazz Makers*.
      Edited by Nat Shapiro and Nat Hentoff. New York:
      Evergreen Books, 1958, pp. 3-18.

716. ————. "Dixieland." *Art of Jazz*. New York: Oxford
      University Press, 1959, pp. 57-59.

717. "Kid Ory Comes Back to Bizz." *Down Beat*, 1 Sept. 1942,
      p. 2.

718. "Kid Ory, Famous Armstrong Trombonist." *Metronome,*
        Sept. 1942, p. 7.

719. King, Bruce. "The Gigantic Baby Dodds." *Jazz Review*
        3, no. 7 (Aug. 1960): 12-16.

720. ————. "A Reassessment of New Orleans Jazz on American
        Music Records, Part 3." *Jazz Monthly* 5, no. 4 (Apr.
        1959): 14-17.

721. "King Louis Elected King of Zulus for Mardi Gras."
        Down Beat, 29 Dec. 1948, p. 11.

722. "King Louis 1st." *Look,* 23 Mar. 1943, pp. 64-66.

723. "King Oliver." *Down Beat,* 15 May 1940, p. 13.

724. "King Oliver." *Frontiers of Jazz.* Edited by Ralph de
        Toledano. New York: Oliver Durrell, 1947, pp. 75-81.

725. "King Oliver Is Dead." *Jazz Hot* 4, nos. 4-5 (Apr.-May
        1938): 9.

726. Kmen, Henry. "The Roots of Jazz and the Dance in Place
        Congo: A Reappraisal." *Anuario interamericano de
        investigacion musical* 8 (1972): 5-16.

727. "La famille Bechet." *Hot Club Magazine* 15, no. 3 (Mar.
        1947): 3-4, 16.

728. Lang, Iain. "Chicago." *Jazz in Perspective: The Back-
        ground of the Blues.* London: Hutchinson, 1943, pp.
        58-62. Reprint. New York: Da Capo, 1976.

729. Lax, John. "Chicago's Black Jazz Musicians in the
        Twenties: Portrait of an Era." *Journal of Jazz
        Studies* 1, no. 2 (June 1974): 107-27.

730. "Leon Rappola." *Down Beat,* 15 Oct. 1940, p. 10.

731. Lim, Harry. "Way Down Yonder." *Metronome,* Oct. 1943,
        pp. 26, 38.

732. "Louis Armstrong." *Current Biography 1944.* New York:
        H.W. Wilson, 1945, pp. 15-17.

733. "Louis Armstrong." *Down Beat,* 15 Dec. 1939, p. 10.

734. "Louis Armstrong Discography." *Down Beat*, 14 June 1950, pp. 14-15.

735. "Louis Armstrong." *Metronome*, Jan. 1947, p. 26.

736. "Louis Armstrong Abroad." *Disques* 1, no. 2 (Feb. 1931): 535.

737. "Louis Armstrong in Mardi Gras Role." *Variety*, 12 Jan. 1949, p. 43.

738. "Louis Armstrong in Scandinavia." *Melody Maker*, 15 Oct. 1949, p. 3.

739. "Louis, Babe Ruth Go Hand in Hand." *Down Beat*, 14 July 1950, p. 10.

740. "Louis Center of New Commotion." *Down Beat*, 2 July 1947, p. 3.

741. "Louis: King of the Zulus." *Melody Maker*, 26 Mar. 1949, p. 3.

742. "Louis Always Has Golden Song to Offer: Hobson." *Down Beat*, 14 July 1950, pp. 1, 19.

743. "Louis the First." *Time*, 21 Feb. 1949, pp. 52-58.

744. "Louis Today." *Record Changer*, July-Aug. 1950, p. 27.

745. "Louis Writes Life Story." *Down Beat*, 5 May 1950, p. 1.

746. "Louis Bash Doesn't Blow Up Storm; Weather Does." *Down Beat*, 24 Feb. 1950, p. 18.

747. "Louis Armstrong Plays with Concert Group in Carnegie Hall 'Pops.'" *New York Herald Tribune*, May 1948.

748. "Louis Armstrong." *Présence africaine* 4 (1948): 687-89.

749. "Louis and the Waif's Home." *Record Changer*, July-Aug. 1950, pp. 8, 43.

750. "Louis Armstrong in the Past and Today." *Jazz Information* 2 (21 Feb. 1941): 11-13.

751. "Lucas Hails Dixie Uprising." *Down Beat*, 3 Nov. 1950, p. 5.

752. Lucas, John. "Dawn of Dixieland--Famous Orks, Sidemen."
      Down Beat, 20 May 1946, pp. 12, 15; "Jazz Grows Up to
      BG and Woody," 17 June 1946, pp. 7, 23.

753. Lover, William C. "Louis Armstrong Discography." *Jazz*
      1, no. 12 (Dec. 1943): 18-21.

754. Ludwig, William. "Jazz, the Present-Day Live Issue in
      the Development of American Music." *Metronome*, May
      1922, pp. 78-79.

755. Mangurian, David. "George Lewis: A Portrait of the New
      Orleans Clarinetist." *Down Beat*, 29 Aug. 1963, n.p.

756. Marshall, Kaiser. "When Armstrong Came to New York."
      Jazz Record, no. 4 (Apr. 1963): 4-5.

757. "Mary Lou Williams." *Down Beat*, 15. Dec. 1940, p. 12.

758. McCarthy, Albert J. "The Story of Tommy Ladnier."
      Record Changer, July 1946, pp. 9-11.

759. ————. "Louis Armstrong: Discography." *Record
      Changer*, June-Aug. 1950, pp. 37-42.

760. ————. "Jelly-Roll Morton Discography." *Jazz Music*
      11, nos. 2-3 (Feb.-Mar. 1944): 102-6.

761. "Memphis 5 Gives Dixie a Needed Shot in the Arm." *Down
      Beat*, 1 June 1949, p. 18.

762. Mercer, G. "The First Fifty Years of Jazz." *Second
      Line* 18, nos. 5-6 (May-June 1967): 49; nos. 7-8
      (July-Aug. 1967): 73.

763. Merriam, Alan, and Robert J. Benford. "Louis Armstrong:
      Bibliography." *Record Changer*, June-Aug. 1950,
      pp. 33-35.

764. Meryman, Richard. "An Interview with Louis Armstrong."
      Life, 15 Apr. 1966, n.p.

765. Miller, Charles. "New Orleans in New York." *New
      Republic*, 25 Nov. 1946, p. 694.

766. Miller, Paul Edward. "Are the White Chicagoans of the
      20's Overrated? Yes." *Music and Rhythm* 2, no. 10
      (Oct. 1941): 45, 57.

767. Mitchell, Charles H. "Louis Armstrong." *Disques* 1, no. 11 (Nov. 1930): 387.

768. Moerman, Ernst. "Louis Armstrong." *Negro*. London: Wishart, 1934, p. 205.

769. Moon, Bucklin. "Louis Armstrong and Fletcher Henderson--Paramount 14003 Prince of Wails." *Record Changer*, Apr. 1949, p. 17.

770. Moore, A.L.H. "Paul Whiteman, the Reformer of Music." *British Musician* 5, no. 6 (June 1929): 165-67.

771. Moore, Fred. "King Oliver's Last Tour." *Jazz Record* 31 (Apr. 1945): 10-12.

772. Morgenstern, Dan. "Louis Armstrong: 1900-1971." *Down Beat*, 16 Sept. 1971, pp. 12-14.

    Brief history of Louis Armstrong including tributes and comments.

773. Morton, Jelly Roll. "From Jelly Roll Morton Remembers." *Black Joy*. Chicago: Cowles, 1971, pp. 89-100.

774. ————. "A Fragment of an Autobiography." *Record Changer*, Mar. 1944, pp. 15-16.

775. ————. "A New Orleans Funeral" and "A Discourse on Jazz." *Jam Session*. Edited by Ralph J. Gleason. New York: G.P. Putnam's, 1958, pp. 12-31.

776. ————. "I Created Jazz in 1902." *Down Beat*, Aug. 1938, p. 3.

777. "Muggsy Spanier." *Down Beat*, 1 Dec. 1940, p. 10.

778. "Muggsy Spanier." *Metronome*, Nov. 1941, pp. 14, 67.

779. "Mugsy and Men Blow a Questionable Storm." *Down Beat*, 11 Feb. 1948, p. 6.

780. Murphy, Turk, and Lester Koenig. "New Orleans Has a Future." *Record Changer*, Nov. 1949, pp. 12-13, 28-29.

781. Murray, Ken. "Louis, Bix Had Most Influence on Der Bingle." *Down Beat*, 14 July 1950, p. 16.

782.   "My Best on Wax." *Down Beat*, 7 Apr. 1950, p. 11.

783.   "New Orleans Comes to New York." *Esquire*, Mar. 1946,
        pp. 93-94, 114.

784.   "N'Orlans Disclaims Honor as Jazz Parent." *Metronome*,
        Nov. 1936, p. 27.

785.   "New Orleans." *Hot Club Magazine*, May 1946, p. 7.

786.   "New Orleans Jazz Revival Sparks Formation of Crack
        Crew." *Down Beat*, 3 Nov. 1950, p. 11.

787.   "New Orleans' Musicians of Long Ago." *Louisiana His-
        torical Quarterly* 31, no. 1 (Jan. 1948): 130-39.

788.   "New Orleans Memories." *Record Changer*, Oct. 1948,
        pp. 6-7.

789.   "New Orleans Recollections." *Record Changer*, Nov. 1943,
        n.p.

790.   "The New Orleans Rhythm Kings." *Frontiers of Jazz*.
        Edited by Ralph de Toledano. New York: Oliver
        Durrell, 1947, pp. 82-90.

791.   "New Orleans Today." *Jazzways*. Edited by George S.
        Rosenthal. Cincinnati: Jazzways, 1946, pp. 59-87.

792.   Niles, Abbe. "Ballads, Songs and Snatches on 'Sweet
        Jazz.'" *Bookman* 67, no. 4 (June 1968): 422-24.

793.   "1949 Dixieland Jubilee." *Record Changer*, Dec. 1949,
        pp. 6-7.

794.   "Noone's Energy vs BG's Finesse." *Down Beat*, 1 Oct.
        1942, p. 8.

795.   Nordell, Rod. "Danceable--Happy Dixieland Jazz."
        Christian Science Monitor Magazine, 13 May 1950,
        p. 16.

        Information on the state of jazz in 1950.

796.   "Oh, Mr. Jelly." *Jazz Record* 17, no. 2 (Feb. 1944):
        8-10.

797.   "Okay, So Bix Didn't Copy from Louis." *Down Beat*,
        1 May 1942, p. 18.

798. "Old Bunk Opens in New York." *New Republic*, 22 Oct. 1945, pp. 528-29.

799. "Ol' Satch and Horn in Best Jazz Concert of Town Hall Series." *New York Daily News*, 19 May 1947, pp. 7-8.

800. "On the River Boats." *Record Changer*, July-Aug. 1950, pp. 9, 43, 44.

801. "Orleans Jazz a Real Who's Who." *Down Beat*, 15 Dec. 1945, p. 12; 1 Jan. 1946, p. 15; 14 Jan. 1946, p. 14. Pt. II entitled "Orleans Jazz Greats Concluded."

802. Ory, Kid. "Louis Was Just a Little Kid in Knee Pants; Ory." *Down Beat*, 14 July 1950, p. 8.

803. "Ory Rhythm." *Record Changer*, Jan. 1949, pp. 13, 21.

804. Ostransky, Leroy. "New Orleans Style." *The Anatomy of Jazz*. Seattle: University of Washington Press, 1960. Reprint. Westport, Connecticut: Greenwood, 1973.

805. Otto, Albert S. "Dixieland Jubilee." *Record Changer*, Jan. 1949, pp. 6-7.

806. Panassie, Hughes. "Jelly Roll Morton on Records." *Frontiers of Jazz*. Edited by Ralph de Toledano. New York: Frederick Ungar, 1962, pp. 108-15.

807. "Paul Mares: New Orleans Rhythm King." *Record Changer*, Nov. 1949, pp. 17, 31.

808. Perry, William. "New Orleans Style." *Record Changer*, Mar. 1950, pp. 9, 18.

809. Pierce, N. "Early Jazz." *Time*, 3 May 1968, p. 64.

810. "The Phenomenal Resurgence of the Spasm Band." *Record Changer*, Dec. 1950, pp. 8, 17.

811. "Preservation Hall: New Orleans." *Ebony*, May 1965, pp. 64-66.

812. "The Professional Viewpoint." *Record Changer*, June-Aug. 1950, pp. 31, 46, 47.

813. Race, S. "Louis Armstrong Description of Bop." *Jazz Journal* 3, no. 1 (Jan. 1950): 6.

814. Ramsey, Frederic, Jr. "Satchmo." *Jazzways*. Edited by
     George S. Rosenthal. Cincinnati: Jazzways, 1946, pp.
     110-11.

815. ———. "King Oliver." *Jazzmen*. Edited by Frederic
     Ramsey, Jr., and Charles Edward Smith. New York:
     Harcourt, Brace, 1939, pp. 59-95; "King Oliver in
     Savannah." *Saturday Review*, 17 Mar. 1956, pp. 30-31,
     40-41.

     The *Saturday Review* article is on King Oliver's last
     days in Savannah, Georgia.

816. "Rare Morton Piano Roll Discovered in Junk Shop." *Down
     Beat*, 17 Nov. 1950, p. 7.

817. "Re-Recording Etched of Picou 'High Society' Ride."
     Down Beat, 22 Sept. 1950, pp. 6, 7.

818. "Record Companies Go All Out for Dixieland." *Down Beat*,
     7 Apr. 1950, p. 1.

819. "Red Nicholas." *Down Beat*, Sept. 1939, p. 30.

820. "Red Norvo." *Down Beat*, 15 June 1940, p. 10.

821. "Red Norvo Trio 'Astounding, Impeccable.'" *Down Beat*,
     17 Nov. 1950, p. 4.

822. Reda, J. "De Jelly-Roll Morton, a Mon." *Jazz Magazine*,
     Nov. 1963, pp. 20-23.

823. "Reluctant Millionaire." *Ebony*, Nov. 1964, pp. 136-38,
     140-42.

     On Louis Armstrong.

824. "Reverend Satchelmouth." *Time*, 29 Apr. 1946, pp. 47-48.

     On Louis Armstrong.

825. Reynolds, Robert R. "The Afro-American Viewpoint."
     Jazz Session 7, nos. 5-6 (May-June 1945): 19.

826. "The Rhythm Section--Sidney Bechet: No Peers, Few
     Equals." *Esquire*, July 1945, pp. 76-77.

827. Deleted.

828. Rohlf, Wayne H. "Emmet Hardy Never Taught Bix, Says Pal." *Down Beat*, 15 Jan. 1942, p. 6.

829. "Roses for Satchmo." *Down Beat*, 9 July 1970, pp. 15-19.

    A tribute to Louis Armstrong from about 90 musicians.

830. Russell, William. "Jelly Roll Morton and the Frog-i-more Rag." *The Art of Jazz*. Edited by Martin T. Williams. New York: Oxford University Press, 1959, pp. 33-43.

831. ————. "Louis Armstrong." *Jazzmen*. Edited by Frederic Ramsey, Jr., and Charles Edward Smith. New York: Harcourt, Brace, 1939, pp. 119-42.

832. ————. "New Orleans Music." *Jazzmen*. Edited by Frederic Ramsey, Jr., and Charles Edward Smith. New York: Harcourt, Brace, 1939, pp. 7-39.

833. ————. "Play That Thing, Mr. Johnny Dodds." *Jazz Information* 2, no. 8 (23 Aug. 1940): 10-11.

834. Rust, B., comp. "Jazz Records, A-Z, 1897-1931." *Matrix* 46, no. 4 (Apr. 1963): 9.

835. Sanction, Tommy. "Portrait of a New Orleans Jazz Man." *Down Beat*, 9 Feb. 1967, pp. 20-22.

    Life and music of Kid "Punch" Miller. Also mentions several other early jazz musicians.

836. Sanjek, Russell. "Bunny Berigan: He Is Either Very Good or Very Lousy." *Music and Rhythm* 1, no. 11 (Nov. 1940): 37-39.

837. Sargant, Norman, and Tom Sargant. "Negro-American Music on the Origin of Jazz." *Musical Times*, July 1931, pp. 653-55; Aug. 1931, pp. 751-52; Sept. 1931, pp. 847-48.

838. "Satchmo--An Appreciation of Louis Armstrong." *Flair*, Nov. 1950, pp. 36-37, 107.

839. "Satchmo Comes Back." *Time*, 1 Sept. 1947, p. 32.

840. "Satchmo's Downbeat Scrapbook." *Down Beat*, 9 July 1970, pp. 20, 30.

    Contains excellent highlights from Louis Armstrong's musical career.

841. "Satchmo Europe Trip Successful: Plan Second Tour."
     Billboard, 22 Oct. 1949, p. 13.

842. "Satchmo's Genius Still Alive." *Down Beat*, 4 July 1947,
     p. 3.

843. "Satchmo Goes Back Home." *Ebony*, July 1956, n.p.

844. "'Satchelmouth' Symbol of Best Negro Music." *Down Beat*,
     March 1938, p. 4.

845. Sexton, Susie. "Paul Whiteman Made Jazz Contagious."
     American Magazine, July 1924, pp. 74-75.

846. Shain, Cy. "New Orleans Trumpeters." *Jazz Record* 54,
     no. 11 (Nov. 1946): 16.

847. Shelton, Jerry. "Echo of Louie Chorus Heard in Grand
     Canyon." *Down Beat*, May 1936, n.p.

848. Siders, Harvey. "Los Angeles Love-In for Louis." *Down
     Beat*, 20 Aug. 1970, pp. 21, 33.

849. "Sidney Bechet." *Down Beat*, 15 July 1940, p. 10.

850. Simon, George T. "Armstrong, Commercialism and Music."
     Metronome, Oct. 1949, p. 38.

851. ———. "Dixie 1950." *Metronome*, May 1950, pp. 24, 28.

852. ———. "Mugsy Spanier." *Metronome*, Oct. 1941, pp. 14,
     47.

853. "60-Year-Old 'Bunk' Johnson, Louis' Tutor, Sits in the
     Band." *Down Beat*, 15 Aug. 1941, p. 11.

854. Slate, Lane. "It Smacks of Showmanship--With Reference
     to Sidney Catlett." *Jazz Session* 5, nos. 1-2 (Jan.-
     Feb. 1945): 14-15.

855. Slotkin, J.S. "Jazz and Its Forerunners as an Example
     of Acculturation." *American Sociological Review* 8,
     no. 10 (Oct. 1943): 570-75.

856. Smith, Charles E. "Folk Music, the Roots of Jazz."
     Saturday Review, 29 July 1950, pp. 35-36.

857. ———. "New Orleans Style." *Modern Music* 18, no. 4
     (1941): 235-41.

858. ———. "The Austin High School Gang." *Jazzmen*. Edited by Frederic Ramsey, Jr., and Charles Edward Smith. New York: Harcourt, Brace, 1939, pp. 161-82.

859. ———. "Time Out of Hand." *Record Changer*, Jan. 1950, p. 11.

860. ———. "White New Orleans." *Jazzmen*. Edited by Frederic Ramsey, Jr., and Charles Edward Smith. New York: Harcourt, Brace, 1939, pp. 39-59.

861. "Some Thoughts on the Jazz Revival." *Record Changer*, Nov. 1948, pp. 14, 23.

862. Souchon, Edmond. "King Oliver: A Very Personal Memoir." *Jazz Review* 3, no. 4 (May 1960): 8-12.

The author recalls the influence of Joe "King" Oliver on him from his early childhood (age 4), around 1901.

863. "Souchon Contributes to New Orleans Jazz Lore." *Down Beat*, 7 Apr. 1950, p. 11.

864. "Stale Bread's Sadness Gave Jazz to the World." *Literary Digest* 61, no. 4 (26 Apr. 1919): 47-48.

865. "State Dept. Says 'Thanks, Louis.'" *Down Beat*, 14 July 1950, p. 1.

866. Stearns, William. "Dunn Thought We Could Carve Armstrong; Used to Jump Up and Take All of Louie's Solos." *Down Beat*, Apr. 1937, p. 8.

867. Steinhard, Erich. "Whitemans Jazzorchester im Paris." *Auftakt* 6 (1926): 221-22.

868. Steiner, John. "Chicago." *Jazz*. Edited by Nat Hentoff and Albert McCarthy. New York: Rinehart, 1959, pp. 137-71.

869. ———. "Story of Emmet Hardy Told by New Orleans Musicians." *Down Beat*, 15 May 1940, pp. 8-9.

870. "Storyville." *True*, Nov. 1947, pp. 32-33, 100, 105.

871. "Sullivan Piano Shines at N.Y. Dixieland Bash." *Down Beat*, 21 Apr. 1950, p. 18.

872. Surpin, Alan. "Bud Freeman: Tenor with Tenure." *Down Beat*, 24 June 1971, p. 15.

873. "Sweet Corn at Glen Island." *Time*, 2 June 1947, pp. 69-70.

874. "Sweet PaPa Jelly Roll." *Record Changer*, Feb. 1948, pp. 6-7.

875. "Symphonic Jazz." *Flutist* 6, no. 2 (Feb. 1925): 25-27.

876. "A Symposium on Louis Armstrong: The Man Who Revolutionized Jazz." *Saturday Review*, 4 July 1970, n.p.

      Contains a cover story and three articles that discuss Louis Armstrong's life, artistic development, and influence on jazz. Authors are Stanley Dance, Bud Freeman, Milt Gabler, and Jack Bradley.

877. "The Tailgate Jazz Band." *Record Changer*, Feb. 1950, pp. 7, 16.

878. Taubman, H. "A Half-Century with Satchmo." *Negro Digest* 8, no. 6 (June 1950): 23-28.

879. Teagarden, Jack. "The Ten Greatest Trombone Players." *Music and Rhythm* 2, no. 6 (June 1942): 14.

880. "Teagarden Plans to Quit Armstrong." *Down Beat*, 26 Aug. 1969, n.p.

881. "There Is a Chicago Style!--Mares." *Down Beat*, 15 Feb. 1943, p. 4.

882. Thompson, Bob. "Jazz! Chicago! Muggsy!" *Record Changer*, Oct. 1948, pp. 11, 19.

883. Thompson, Kay C. "An Interview with Sidney Bechet." *Record Changer*, July 1949, n.p.

884. Tiegel, E. "Dixieland Comes Out Swinging and Ringing at Monterey Fest." *Billboard*, 25 May 1968, p. 8.

885. Tracy, Jack. "Alvin Adds to Dixie Revival." *Down Beat*, 2 June 1950, p. 2.

886. Traill, Sinclair. "Armstrong Completes His Half-Century of European Concerts." *Melody Maker*, 12 Nov. 1949, p. 2.

887. "Trumpeter Freddie Keppard Walked Out on Al Capone!"
     Music and Rhythm 11, no. 6 (June 1941): 13-17.

888. "Trumpeter's Jubilee." *New York Times*, 26 Oct. 1941,
     pp. 5-6.

889. Ulanov, Barry. "Another Month, Another Boom." *Metro-
     nome*, June 1950, p. 34.

890. ————. "History of Jazz." *Metronome*, July 1950, pp.
     18-20; Aug. 1950, pp. 14-15, 20.

891. "Ulceratedly Yours, Louis Armstrong." *Down Beat*,
     14 July 1950, pp. 1, 19.

892. "Way Down Yonder." *Time*, 31 Jan. 1949, p. 39.

893. Weirick, Paul. "Where the Word 'Jazz' Started." *Music
     Trade Review* 68, no. 18 (1919): 50.

894. Wettling, George. "A Tribute to Baby Dodds." *Down
     Beat*, 29 Mar. 1962, p. 21.

895. ————. "Wettling Calls Chicago Jazz New Orleans."
     Metronome, May 1941, pp. 22-23, 30.

896. "What Are They Doin' to Satchmo?" *Down Beat*, 24 Sept.
     1947, p. 7.

897. "What Is New Orleans Style?" *Record Changer*, Mar. 1948,
     p. 16.

898. "A Whiteman Concert." *New York Times*, 22 Apr. 1924,
     p. 4.

899. Whiteman, Paul. "New Concepts in Present Day Music."
     Etude 57, no. 4 (Apr. 1939): 227.

900. ————. "This Thing Called Jazz." *Rotarian* 54, no. 6
     (June 1939): 346.

901. "Willie Bunk Johnson, Last of the Olympians." *Record
     Changer*, Sept. 1949, p. 12.

902. Williams, Martin. "For Louis Armstrong at 70." *Down
     Beat*, 9 July 1970, pp. 22-23.

     The impact of Louis Armstrong on jazz.

903. Williams, Martin, ed. "Jazz Panorama." *Jazz Review* (1962), 105-16.

    Includes discussion of Louis Armstrong.

904. Wilson, John S. "Armstrong Explains Stand Against Bop." *Down Beat*, 30 Dec. 1949, p. 3.

905. ————. "Real New Orleans Sound." *High Fidelity*, Sept. 1963, pp. 59-61.

906. Wolff, D. Leon. "Bop Nowhere, Armstrong Just a Myth." *Down Beat*, 17 June 1949, pp. 1, 19.

907. "Wolverine Days." *Swing Music* 14, no. 3 (Autumn 1936): 30-32.

THESES AND DISSERTATIONS

907a. Hennessey, Thomas Joseph. "From Jazz to Swing: Black Jazz Musicians and Their Music, 1917-1935." Ph.D. dissertation, Northwestern University, 1973.

907b. Hoyt, Charles A. "Jazz and Its Origin." Bachelor's thesis, Wesleyan University, 1953.

C. SWING

This category contains information on a select
number of composers, arrangers, directors, and
performers who were significant contributors
to the big bands of the thirties and forties,
e.g., Count Basie, Duke Ellington, Don Redman,
and Benny Goodman. A select number of entries
on other jazz musicians of the same period are
also included.

BOOKS

908. Aasland, Benny H. *The "Wax Works" of Duke Ellington.*
Stockholm: B.H. Aasland, 1954.

909. Allen, Walter C. *Hendersonia: The Music of Fletcher
Henderson and His Musicians: A Biography-Discography.*
Highland Park, New Jersey: Author, 1973.

910. Antrim, Doren Kemp, ed. *Paul Whiteman, Jimmy Dorsey,
Rudy Vallee, Freddie Rich: Giving Their Secrets of
Dance Band Success.* New York: Famous Stars, 1936.

911. Armstrong, Louis. *Swing That Music.* New York: Longmans,
Green, 1936.

Contains an introduction by Rudy Vallee and a section
edited by Horace Gerlach with special examples of swing
music contributed by Benny Goodman, Tommy Dorsey, Joe
Venuti, and others. Includes a piano score by the
author and Horace Gerlach, accompanied by improvisation
supplied by ten musicians for their particular instruments.

912. Arnaud, Noel. *Duke Ellington.* Paris: Messager boeteus,
1950.

913. Berend, David. *Swing Style for the Piano.* New York:
Amsco Music, 1937.

914. Calloway, Cab. *Cab Calloway's Catalogue*. New York:
      Mills Artists, 1938.

915. Carey, Dave, and Albert McCarthy. *The Directory of
      Recorded Jazz and Swing Music*. Vols. 1-3. Fording-
      bridge and Hampshire: Delphic Press, 1949.

916. Charters, S., and L. Kunstadt. *Jazz: A History of the
      New York Scene*. Garden City, New York: Doubleday,
      1962.

917. Cons, Carl, and George Von Physter. *Destiny: A Study
      of Swing Musicians*. Chicago: Down Beat Publishing,
      1938.

918. Dance, Stanley. *The World of Duke Ellington*. New York:
      Scribner's, 1970.

919. ————. *The World of Swing*. New York: Scribner's,
      1974.

      Contains information on many swing musicians, in-
      cluding Freddie Green, Count Basie, Willie Smith, Sy
      Oliver, Benny Carter, Coleman Hawkins, Roy Eldridge,
      Jonah Jones, Lionel Hampton, Stuff Smith, Chick Webb,
      Mildred Bailey, Billie Holiday, and many more.

920. Davis, John R.T. *The Music of Thomas "Fats" Waller*.
      London: J.F. Publications, 1950.

921. Ellington, Edward Kennedy. *Music Is My Mistress*.
      Garden City, New York: Doubleday, 1973.

922. Erlich, Lillian. *What Jazz Is All About*. New York:
      Julian Messner, 1962.

      The history of jazz is examined throughout. The
      author, however, focuses primarily on the careers of
      Fletcher Henderson, Benny Goodman, Count Basie, and
      Billie Holiday.

923. Fernett, Gene. *Swing Out: Great Negro Dance Bands*.
      Midland, Michigan: Pendell, 1970.

      A descriptive book with many pictures of the great
      Black band leaders and their bands. Much biographical
      information on many of the big names of the big-band
      era.

924. Fox, Charles. *Fats Waller*. New York: A.S. Barnes, 1961.

925. Gammond, Peter. *Duke Ellington: His Life and Music*. London: Phoenix House, 1958.

926. Goffin, Robert. *Jazz from Congo to Swing*. Translated by Ray Sonin. London: Musicians Press, 1946.

927. Goodman, Benny, and Irving Kolodin. *The Kingdom of Swing*. Harrisburg, Pennsylvania: Stackpole, 1939.

   The life and musical career of Benny Goodman.

928. Graham, Alberta P. *Strike Up the Band!: Bandleaders of Today*. New York: Nelson, 1949.

929. Graves, Charles, ed. *100 Facts on Swing Music*. London: Naldrett Press, 1948.

930. Hibbs, Leonard, comp. *21 Years of Swing Music on Brunswick Records*. London: Leonard Hibbs, 1924.

931. Holiday, Billie, and William Dufty. *Lady Day Sings the Blues*. New York: Doubleday, 1956.

932. Horricks, Raymond. *Count Basie and His Orchestra*. London: Victor Gollancz, 1957.

   History of the Count Basie band and biographies of individual musicians.

933. Howard, John Tasker. *Our Contemporary Composers*. New York: Thomas Y. Crowell, 1941.

   Includes information on Duke Ellington.

934. Hughes, Langston. *The First Book of Jazz*. New York: Franklin Watts, 1954.

   Contains some information on swing.

935. Jackson, Edgar. *Swing Music*. Middlesex, England: Gramophone, 1948.

936. ————, and Leonard Hibbs. *Encyclopedia of Swing*. London: Decca Records, 1941.

937. Johnson, Frank, and Ron Wilk. *Jam: An Annual of Swing Music*. Sydney and New South Wales: Tempo Publishing, 1938.

938. Jones, LeRoi. *Blues People*. New York: William Morrow,
      1967.

      Contains some information on Black swing musicians.

939. Keepnews, Orrin, and Bill Grauer, Jr. *A Pictorial
      History of Jazz: People and Places from New Orleans
      to Modern Jazz*. New York: Crown, 1966.

940. Kinnell, Bill, ed. *Jazz Orchestras*. England: Chilwell,
      1943.

941. Kirkeby, W. *The Story of Fats Waller*. New York: Dodd,
      Mead, 1966.

942. Lambert, George E. *Duke Ellington*. New York: A.S.
      Barnes, 1961.

      Primarily a biographical sketch of Duke Ellington with
      special emphasis on his music. Also contains a selected
      discography.

943. McCarthy, Albert. *Big Band Jazz*. New York: G.P. Put-
      nam's, 1974.

      Has outstanding information on the historical develop-
      ment of big bands. Also contains excellent photos.

944. ————. *Coleman Hawkins*. London: Cassell, 1963.

945. Miller, Glenn. *Glenn Miller's Method for Orchestral
      Arranging*. New York: Mutual Music Society, 1943.

946. Miller, Paul Eduard. *Down Beat's Yearbook of Swing*.
      1939. Reprinted as *Miller's Yearbook of Popular
      Music*. Chicago: Down Beat Publishing, 1943.

947. Montgomery, Elizabeth Rider. *Duke Ellington: King of
      Jazz*. Champaign, Illinois: Garrard, 1972.

948. Myrus, Donald. *I Like Jazz*. New York: Macmillan, 1964.

      The author presents a detailed account of the origin
      of swing. Some biographical information on selected
      musicians is included.

949. Panassie, Hughes. *Hot Jazz Hot: The Guide to Swing
      Music*. New York: Witmark, 1936. Reprint. Westport,
      Connecticut: Negro Universities Press, 1974.

950. ————. *La musique de jazz et le swing.* Paris: Correa, 1945.

951. Russell, Ross. *Jazz Style in Kansas City and the South-west.* Berkeley and Los Angeles: University of California Press, 1971.

An excellent source that illustrates that the same kind of musical renaissance that occurred in New Orleans was about to take place in Kansas City and the Southwest. Some of the musicians discussed are Count Basie, Charles Parker, and Lester Young.

952. Simon, George T. *The Big Bands.* Rev. ed. New York: Macmillan, 1971.

A guide to swing era orchestras.

953. Smith, Willie ("The Lion"), and George Hoefer. *Music on My Mind: The Memoirs of an American Pianist.* Garden City, New York: Doubleday, 1964.

954. Specht, Paul L. *How They Became Name Bands: The Modern Technique of a Danceband Maestro.* New York: Fine Arts Publications, 1941.

955. Stambler, Irwin, ed. *The Encyclopedia of Popular Music.* New York: St. Martin's, 1965.

Contains information on Duke Ellington and Fats Waller.

956. Stewart, Rex. *Jazz Masters of the Thirties.* New York: Macmillan, 1972.

Contains information on Duke Ellington, Coleman Hawkins, Fletcher Henderson, Ben Webster, John Kirby, and others.

957. *Swing: The Guide to Modern Music.* Detroit: Cats Meow Publishing, 1938.

958. Toledano, Ralph de, ed. *Frontiers of Jazz.* 2nd ed. New York: Frederick Ungar, 1947.

Primarily a collection of articles on jazz, some taken from the *National Review, Fortune,* and *Down Beat,* as far back as the early thirties. Some very good biographical information on Duke Ellington, Billie Holiday, Jelly Roll Morton, Benny Goodman, Bessie Smith, Louis Armstrong, and others who have contributed to jazz.

959. Trazegmes, Jean de. *Duke Ellington*. Brussels: Hot
      club de Belgique, 1946.

960. Treadwell, Bill. *Big Book of Swing*. New York:
      Cambridge House, 1946.

961. Ulanov, Barry. *A History of Jazz in America*. New York:
      Viking, 1955. Reprint. New York: Da Capo Press, 1972.

      Focuses on Benny Goodman and his contributions to
      swing.

962. ————. *Duke Ellington*. New York: Creative Age Press,
      1946.

963. Williams, Martin T. *The Art of Jazz*. New York: Oxford
      University Press, 1959.

      A collection of essays on jazz. Contains biographical
      information on Bessie Smith, Billie Holiday, Duke
      Ellington, Bix Beiderbecke, and others.

                              ARTICLES

964. "Act of the Year: Art Tatum." *Metronome*, Jan. 1944,
      p. 23.

965. Albertson, Chris. "Jimmy Rushing: A Sturdy Branch of the
      Learning Tree." *Down Beat*, 13 Nov. 1969, pp. 17, 38.

966. "Andy Kirk's Story." *Jazz Review* 2, no. 4 (Feb. 1959):
      11.

967. Armitage, Jack. "Billie Holiday." *Jazz Hot* 4, nos. 6-
      7 (June-July 1938): 9.

968. Balliett, Whitney. "Our Local Correspondents: A Day
      with the Duke." *New Yorker*, 27 June 1970, pp. 52-55.

969. "Band of the Year: Lionel Hampton." *Metronome*, Jan.
      1944, p. 21.

970. "Bands That Stay on Top: And Why." *Metronome*, Oct. 1935,
      pp. 19, 57.

971. "Bands That Stay on Top: Analyzing the Stylists."
      Metronome, Nov. 1935, pp. 19, 51.

972. Barnett, Charlie. "My Band Does Not Imitate Duke's."
      Down Beat, 15 June 1941, pp. 2, 19.

973. "Barney Bigard Is Leaving Duke." *Down Beat*, 15 July
      1942, p. 2.

974. "Basie Discography." *Down Beat*, 17 Nov. 1950, p. 14.

975. "Basie Best of What's Left?" *Down Beat*, 13 Jan. 1950,
      p. 21.

976. Basie, Count. "Critics in the Doghouse." *Down Beat*,
      July 1939, p. 18.

977. "Basie Led the Greatest Rhythm Machine in Jazz." *Down
      Beat*, 24 Mar. 1950, p. 11.

978. Basie, W. "Jazz in the Year 2000." *Sepia*, May 1958,
      pp. 28-33.

979. "Ben Pollack." *Down Beat*, 1 May 1941, p. 10.

980. Beneke, Tex. "Swing Was Never King." *Metronome*, Feb.
      1947, pp. 20-21, 37.

981. ————. "Benny's Band Bust Up; Shaw Grabs." *Metronome*,
      Aug. 1940, p. 9.

982. "Benny Carter." *Down Beat*, 15 Sept. 1940, p. 10.

983. "Benny Goodman." *Metronome*, Feb. 1947, p. 22.

984. "Benny Goodman." *Down Beat*, 1 Feb. 1940, p. 10.

985. "Benny Goodman, Glenn Miller Voted Champs!" *Down Beat*,
      1 Jan. 1942, pp. 1, 21-22.

986. "Benny Goodman: Jazz Immortal." *Look*, 12 June 1945,
      pp. 34, 36, 38, 40-41.

987. "Benny Goodman Makes a Comeback." *Life*, 20 Aug. 1945,
      p. 117.

988. "Benny's New Band Is Too Much Like Benny's Old Band."
      Down Beat, 15 Mar. 1941, p. 6.

989. "Benny Goodman: 1949." *International Musician* 48, no.
      10 (Oct. 1949): 15-16.

990. "Benny Goodman on Redman." *Metronome*, Oct. 1943, p. 26.

991. "Benny Rides Again." *New Republic*, 6 Oct. 1947, p. 37.

992. "B.G. Swing King and Favorite." *Metronome*, Aug. 1940,
      pp. 7, 15.

993. Berigan, Bunny. "This Thing Called Swing." *Metronome*,
      Sept. 1937, pp. 65, 89.

994. "Big Jay McNeely." *Ebony*, May 1963, pp. 60-64, 66.

995. "Billie Holiday Concert Makes Jazz History." *Down Beat*,
      11 Mar. 1946, p. 1.

996. "Billie Holiday's Tragic Life." *Ebony*, July 1956, pp.
      20-22.

997. "Billie Holiday." *Jazz* 1, no. 7 (July 1945): 3-4.

998. "Billie Holiday." *Look*, 3 Sept. 1946, p. 59.

999. Blesh, Rudi. "Billie Holiday." *Eight Lives in Jazz
      Combo: U.S.A.* Philadelphia: Chilton, 1971, pp. 217-
      30.

1000. "Bunny Berigan Dies After Long Illness." *Down Beat*,
      15 June 1942, p. 1.

1001. Campbell, E. Simms. "Swing, Mr. Charlie." *Esquire*,
      Feb. 1936, pp. 100-103, 183.

1002. Carter, Elliot. "Once Again Swing: Also 'American
      Music.'" *Modern Music* 16, nos. 1-2 (Jan.-Feb. 1939):
      99-100.

1003. "Charlie Christian." *Metronome*, Aug. 1947, p. 27.

1004. "Charlie Christian Dies in New York." *Down Beat*,
      15 Mar. 1942, pp. 1, 20.

1005. Chasdel, J. "Swing from Paris." *Hot Club Magazine*,
      Jan. 1946, pp. 10-11.

1006. "Chick Webb." *Down Beat*, 1 Jan. 1941, p. 10.

1007. Clar, Mimi. "The Style of Duke Ellington." *Jazz Review* 2, no. 3 (Apr. 1959): 6-11.

A musical analysis including examples of Ellington's style. An excellent article.

1008. Clinton, Larry. "Swing Grows Up: A Prophecy for Days to Come." *Good Housekeeping*, Oct. 1938, pp. 13, 92.

1009. "Coleman Hawkins." *Down Beat*, 15 Feb. 1940, p. 18.

1010. "Coleman Hawkins." *Hot Club Magazine*, Aug. 1946, pp. 6-7.

1011. "Coleman Hawkins." *Look*, 9 Mar. 1943, p. 62.

1012. "Coleman Hawkins." *Ritmo y melodia* 5, nos. 5-6 (May-June 1948): n.p.

1013. "College Gives Ellington Honorary Doctor's Degree." *Down Beat*, 14 Jan. 1965, p. 9.

On the occasion of Milton College's (Wisconsin) presenting Duke an honorary doctor of humanities degree. A campaign was begun as well to bring his accomplishments in music to the attention of the Pulitzer Prize Committee.

1014. "Concerts Rex Stewart." *Hot Club Magazine*, Apr. 1948, pp. 7-8.

1015. Connell, Tom. "B.G.: The King of Swing Abdicates." *Metronome*, Aug. 1946, p. 41.

1016. "Cootie Williams." *Look*, 15 May 1945, p. 78.

1017. "Cootie Williams." *Metronome*, June 1941, p. 28.

1018. "Count Basie." *Down Beat*, 15 June 1941, p. 10.

1019. "Count Basie." *Look*, 21 Mar. 1944, p. 78.

1020. "Count Basie Picks the 12 Best Pianists." *Music and Rhythm* 2, no. 1 (Jan. 1942): 19, 45.

1021. "Critic Rapped: Crowds Pleased." *Down Beat*, 25 Feb. 1948, p. 16.

1022. Cumps, Marcel. "Rex Stewart à Bruxelles." *Hot Club Magazine*, Apr. 1948, p. 9.

1023. Dance, Helen. "The Immutable Cootie Williams." *Down Beat*, 4 May 1967, pp. 20-22, 35-36.

1024. Dance, Stanley. "A Matter of Inspiration and Interpretation." *Down Beat*, 23 Feb. 1967, pp. 18-19.

      The life and musical career of Billy Strayhorn.

1025. ————. "Count Basie: An American Institution." *Down Beat*, 18 Apr. 1968, pp. 18-20.

1026. ————. "Ecumenical Ellington: Concert in San Francisco's Grace Cathedral." *Saturday Review*, 16 Oct. 1965, pp. 70-71.

1027. ————. "Ed Wilcox: Lunceford Ace." *Down Beat*, 3 Oct. 1968, pp. 20-22.

1028. ————. "Ellington Marches On." *Down Beat*, 21 Mar. 1968, pp. 18, 44-45.

1029. ————. "Otra, Otra: Ellington Conquers Latin America." *Down Beat*, 12 Dec. 1968, pp. 16, 42.

1030. Davies, Ron. "Lettre ouverte aux modernistes." *Hot Club Magazine*, May 1946, pp. 8-9.

1031. Dickerson, Reed. "Hot Music: Rediscovering Jazz." *Harper's*, Apr. 1936, pp. 567-574.

1032. ————. "Digging for Swing." *New Republic*, 6 Oct. 1947, p. 41.

1033. "Don Redman." *Down Beat*, 15 Nov. 1940, p. 10.

1034. "Don Redman, Composer-Arranger." *Jazz Review* 2, no. 10 (Nov. 1959): 6-13.

1035. "Don Redman Dies of Heart Attack." *Down Beat*, 14 Jan. 1965, p. 8.

1036. "Don't Stop Swinging the Classics--Scott." *Music and Rhythm* 2, no. 1 (Jan. 1942): 17, 45.

1037. Dugan, James. "The Duke." *Time*, 19 May 1947, pp. 47-48.

1038. "The Duke of Jazz." *Time*, 1 Feb. 1943, pp. 54-55.

1039. "Duke, Benny, Artie Top 1941 Discs." *Metronome*, Jan. 1942, pp. 18-27.

1040. "Duke Draws Sell-Out Crowd Who Sit on Hands." *Down Beat*, 11 Feb. 1946, pp. 1, 12-13.

1041. "Duke Ellington." *Current Biography 1941*. New York: H.W. Wilson, 1942, pp. 260-62.

1042. "Duke Ellington." *Down Beat*, 15 Jan. 1940, p. 10.

1043. "Duke Ellington." *Look*, 22 June 1947, pp. 64, 66-67, 69.

1044. "Duke Ellington." *Metronome*, Apr. 1947, p. 18.

1045. "Duke Fuses Classical and Jazz!" *Down Beat*, 15 Feb. 1943, pp. 12-13.

1046. "Duke Invades Carnegie Hall." *New York Times*, 17 Jan. 1943, pp. 20-30.

1047. "Duke, James Lead Bands of 1942." *Metronome*, Jan. 1942, pp. 10-11, 39.

1048. "Duke Marks His Band's 20 Fabulous with Ellington Week and Carnegie Concert." *Newsweek*, 1 Feb. 1943, p. 50.

1049. "Duke Sweeps '48 Band Poll." *Down Beat*, 29 Dec. 1948, pp. 1, 12-13.

1050. "Earl Hines." *Down Beat*, 1 July 1940, p. 23.

1051. Ebert, Alan. "Duke: Loving You Madly." *Essence*, Sept. 1974, pp. 51, 84.

    Contains a series of quotations on the music and man (Ellington) by several show business and music personalities, e.g., Lena Horne, Perry Como, and Erroll Garner.

1052. Edwards, Calvin. "The Duke Is Gone." *Sepia*, July 1974, pp. 79-82.

1053. Ehrlich, Evelyn. "Carnegie Concert Has Below Par Ellington." *Down Beat*, 28 Jan. 1946, p. 3.

1054. Ellington, Duke. "Jazz as I Have Seen It." *Swing*, June 1940, pp. 11, 22.

1055. "Ellington's Annual Chicago Concert 'A Gala Evening.'"
       Down Beat, 10 Mar. 1950, p. 7.

1056. "Ellington Cops Both Crowns." *Down Beat*, 1 Jan. 1947,
       pp. 1, 20.

1057. "Ellington Fails to Top Himself." *Down Beat*, 16 Dec.
       1946, p. 2.

1058. "Ellington Pleases Concert Crowd." *Down Beat*, 14 Jan.
       1948, p. 3.

1059. "Ellington Wins Swing Poll." *Down Beat*, 1 Jan. 1943,
       pp. 1, 13-14.

1060. Emge, Charles. "Jimmy Blanton Takes a Last Ride."
       Down Beat, 15 Aug. 1942, p. 12.

1061. "Erskine Hawkins." *Current Biography 1941.* New York:
       H.W. Wilson, 1942, pp. 269-71.

1062. "Erskine Hawkins." *Jazz* 1, no. 4 (Mar. 1945): 7.

1063. "Fats Waller." *Down Beat*, 15 Jan. 1941, p. 10.

1064. "Fats Waller Demonstrates Swing, Even Defines It."
       Metronome, Feb. 1936, pp. 19, 33.

1065. "Fats Waller in Carnegie Hall." *New York World Tele-
       gram*, 15 Jan. 1942.

1066. "Fats Waller: Portrait." *Jazz* 1, no. 3 (Mar. 1945):
       14.

1067. Feather, Leonard. "Harold Jones: The Beat Behind
       Basie." *Down Beat*, 15 Apr. 1971, pp. 18, 38.

1068. ————. "King of the Big Band Road." *Down Beat*,
       17 Apr. 1969, p. 18.

       Reasons for Duke Ellington's continued supremacy.

1069. "Fletcher Henderson." *Down Beat*, 15 Nov. 1939, p. 23.

1070. Frederick, Lewis. "Why Glenn Miller's Music Gets the
       Girls." *Liberty*, 26 Oct. 1940, pp. 45-46.

1071. "Full Discography of Ben Pollack and Band." *Down Beat*,
       14 Jan. 1946, p. 19.

1072. Garceau, Phil. "The Price of Swing." *Jazz Parody.*
Edited by Charles Harvey. London: Spearman, 1948,
pp. 69-76.

1073. Gelly, D. "The Count Basie Octet." *Jazz Monthly* 9,
no. 7 (July 1963): 9-11.

1074. "Gene Krupa." *Down Beat*, 1 Nov. 1939, p. 20.

1075. Gitler, Ira. "Ever-Ready Teddy Edwards." *Down Beat*,
27 July 1967, pp. 21-22.

1076. Gleason, Ralph J. "Basie Will Always Have a Swinging
Band." *Down Beat*, 17 Nov. 1950, pp. 1-2.

1077. ————. "Fatha' Hines: Daddy of Em All." *Negro Digest*
9, no. 11 (Nov. 1950): 22-26.

1078. ————. "Glenn Miller Precise." *Metronome*, Jan. 1962,
pp. 10, 25.

1079. "Glenn Miller Commissioned a Captain." *Metronome*,
Oct. 1942, pp. 5, 9.

1080. "Glenn Miller." *Current Biography 1942.* New York:
H.W. Wilson, 1943, pp. 597-99.

1081. Goodman, Benny. "Jam Session." *Pictorial Review* 39,
no. 5 (May 1938): 15.

1082. ————. "When Swing Meets the Classics." *Scribner's*,
Mar. 1941, pp. 90-92.

1083. Gordon, Frank. "Billie Holiday." *Ebony*, Jan. 1965,
pp. 28-33.

   Discusses and compares the style of Billie Holiday
with that of other blues-jazz singers.

1084. Gould, Jack. "News of the Night-Clubs: The Decline of
Swing." *New York Times*, 7 Aug. 1938, p. 4.

1085. Gray, Glen. "Casa Loma Made Swing Commercial." *Down
Beat*, 15 May 1940, pp. 3, 14.

1086. Guillod, Eric. "Lester Young." *Hot Club Magazine*,
Mar. 1947, pp. 10-11.

1087. Hadlock, Dick. "The Ultimate Ellington Tribute." *Down
       Beat*, 27 Nov. 1969, pp. 12, 30.

1088. Hall, Henry. "British Bands Cannot Feel Swing."
       Metronome, Oct. 1935, pp. 17, 33.

1089. Hammond, John. "The Advent of Charlie Christian."
       Down Beat, 25 Aug. 1966, pp. 22-23.

1090. "Hamp's Pianist Reared by Band." *Down Beat*, 1 Oct.
       1943, pp. 14, 17.

1091. Hansen, Millard. "Coleman Hawkins Discusses Tenor
       Sax." *Music and Rhythm* 2, no. 12 (June 1941): 80-81.

1092. Harris, Pat. "'Jazz Dead,' Says Teddy Powell, Trying
       Comeback." *Down Beat*, 16 June 1950, p. 7.

1093. Harvey, Holman. "It's Swing." *Delineator* 129, no. 11
       (Nov. 1936): 10-11.

1094. Hawkins, Coleman. "He Has Great Pride as He Follows
       the Miller Style But ... He's Not Following Glenn
       at All." *Metronome*, May 1948, pp. 15-16.

1095. ————. "Twelve Greatest Tenor Men." *Music and Rhythm*
       2, no. 8 (Aug. 1941): 10-12.

1096. Heckman, Don. "Henderson 'Had to Get Louis' for Rose-
       land Ork." *Down Beat*, 14 July 1950, pp. 4-5.

1097. ————. "Pres and Hawk, Saxophone Fountainheads."
       Down Beat, 3 Jan. 1963, n.p.

1098. Henderson, Fletcher. "He Made the Band Swing."
       Record Changer, July-Aug. 1950, pp. 15-16.

1099. Hentoff, Nat. "One More Time: The Travels of Count
       Basie." *Jazz Review* 4, no. 1 (Jan. 1961): 4-8.

       A discussion of the Basie band of 1960, with some
       historical and musical information on Count Basie.

1100. Herman, Woody. "Herman Attacks Mathematics in 'Pro-
       gressivism.'" *Down Beat*, 5 May 1948, pp. 1, 3.

1101. Herschberg, J. "Kansas City: The Jazz Scene." *ALA
       Bulletin* 62, no. 5 (May 1968): 517-18.

1102. Hobson, Wilder. "Bix Beiderbecke and the Swing Tradition." *Musical Record* 1, no. 10 (Oct. 1933): 168-71.

1103. Hodeir, Andre. "Du coté de chez Basie." *Jazz Review*
1, no. 2 (Dec. 1958): 6-9. [In English]

1104. Hoefer, George. "Coleman Hawkins' Pioneer Days."
Down Beat, 5 Oct. 1967, pp. 20-22.

1105. Holiday, Billie. "I'm Cured for Good." *Ebony*, July
1949, pp. 26-32.

1106. "Horace Henderson's College Band Started Him to the
Top." *Down Beat*, 1 Sept. 1940, p. 16.

1107. Howard, Buddy. "Ellington Celebrates 20th Year in
Music." *Down Beat*, 1 Apr. 1942, p. 4.

1108. Howard, John Tasker. "Swing and Its Performers."
Our Contemporary Composers. New York: Thomas Y.
Crowell, 1941, pp. 290-95.

1109. "How to Do the Bop Hop: Benny Goodman Band Introduces
New Dance Steps on Its Tour." *Ebony*, July 1949,
pp. 23-25.

1109a. "'I'm Not Slipping'--Duke Ellington." *Down Beat*, 17
June 1946, pp. 4, 14.

1110. "Introducing Duke Ellington." *Fortune*, Aug. 1935,
pp. 47-49, 90, 92, 94-95.

1111. Ioakimidis. "Ellington's Drummers." *Jazz Journal* 16,
no. 1 (Jan. 1963): 4-5.

1112. "Ivie Joined the Duke for Four Weeks, Stays with Band
for 12 Years." *Down Beat*, 15 July 1942, p. 31.

1113. "'The Jazz Beat--Ellington the Nonpareil." *Saturday
Review*, 29 Nov. 1947, p. 62.

1114. "Jazz Is Where You Find It." *Esquire*, Feb. 1944,
pp. 35, 129-30.

1115. "Jazz Off the Record, Lester Young." *Down Beat*, 4 May
1955, n.p.

1116. "Jay McShann Relates His Musical Career." *Jazz Monthly*
4, no. 3 (Mar. 1958): 3.

1117. "Jimmy Dorsey." *Down Beat*, 1 Sept. 1940, p. 10.

1118.   "Jimmy Dorsey 'On the Way Back.'" *Down Beat*, 24 Mar.
        1950, pp. 3, 7.

1119.   "The Jukes Take Over Swing." *American Mercury* 51, no.
        10 (Oct. 1940): 172-77.

1120.   Kallen, Horace Meyer. "Swing as Surrealist Music."
        Art and Freedom. New York: Duell, Sloan and Pearce,
        1942, pp. 831-34.

1121.   "Kansas City Brass--The Story of Ed Lewis." *Jazz
        Review* 2, no. 4 (May 1959): 16-19.

1122.   Karberg, Paul F. "Joe Sanders and His Nighthawks."
        Swing Music 14, nos. 5-6 (May-June 1936): 57-58.

1123.   "Keep That Bass Moving, Says Willie (the Lion) Smith."
        Down Beat, 1 Feb. 1942, pp. 16-17.

1124.   Kellogg, J.F. "Benny Morton's Trombone Tops." *Music
        and Rhythm* 1, no. 4 (Apr. 1941): 78-79.

1125.   "The Killer-Diller." *Saturday Evening Post*, 7 May
        1938, pp. 22-23.

1126.   "The Kingdom of Swing." *The Music Lover's Handbook*.
        Edited by Elie Siegmeister. New York: William
        Morrow, 1943, pp. 718-28.

1127.   Kirby, John. "My Favorite Bass Players." *Music and
        Rhythm* 2, no. 5 (May 1942): 10, 44.

1128.   Kolodin, Irving. "What About Swing." *Parents Magazine*,
        Aug. 1939, pp. 18-19.

1129.   Koonce, Dave. "Late Jimmy Blanton Bassdom's Greatest."
        Metronome, Aug. 1946, pp. 48-49.

1130.   "Lady Day Returns." *Record Changer*, June 1948, pp.
        8-9.

1131.   Lawrence, Robert. "Fats Waller Presents Carnegie Hall
        Recital." *New York Herald Tribune*, 15 Jan. 1942.

1132.   "Lester Young." *Jazz Monthly* 6, no. 10 (Oct. 1960): n.p.

1133.   "Let Freedom Swing." *New York Times*, 6 Nov. 1938,
        p. 3.

1134. Levin, A.F. "Life Goes to a Party to Listen to Benny
       Goodman and His Swing Band." *Life*, 1 Nov. 1937,
       pp. 120-22, 124.

1135. ————. "Swing Glories in Its Humble Origin." *Musician*
       44, no. 4 (Apr. 1939): 66.

1136. ————. "Swing Marches On." *Musician* 44, no. 12 (Dec.
       1939): 219.

1137. Levin, Michael. "Coleman Hawkins: One of Great Forces
       in Jazz." *Down Beat*, 20 Oct. 1950, pp. 2, 3.

1138. "Lion Tracked to His Lair--Or Willie Smith's Story."
       Down Beat, 1 Jan. 1947, p. 14.

1139. "Lionel Hampton." *Jazz* 1, no. 2 (Feb. 1946): 3, 5.

1140. "Lionel Hampton." *Look*, 29 June 1943, p. 66.

1141. "Lionel Hampton's Million-Dollar Band Business."
       Ebony, Aug. 1949, pp. 20-24.

1142. "Lionel Hampton on Vibes et al." *Metronome*, Oct. 1943,
       pp. 32, 68.

1143. Locke, Bob. "Jean Goldkette Band Was the Greatest--
       Morgan." *Down Beat*, 15 Mar. 1942, p. 8.

1144. Lodwick, John. "Machine Jazz." *Swing Music* 14, no. 3
       (Autumn 1936): 26.

1145. "Looking at the World's Ace Swing Clarinetists."
       Metronome, Sept. 1936, pp. 39, 45.

1146. Martinez, Andrade Roberto. "La musica de 'Jazz' y
       'Swing.'" *Ha revista nacional des S.E.U.*, Apr.
       1945, pp. 35-36.

1147. McDonough, Johnny. "Reminiscing in Tempo." *Down Beat*,
       17 Apr. 1969, pp. 16-17.

1148. ————. "Inside Ellington." *Down Beat*, 25 July 1968,
       pp. 20-21, 40.

       Mercer Ellington discusses Duke and the band.

1149. McKaie, Andy. "Billie Holiday: An Appreciation."
       Crawdaddy, July 1972, pp. 46-47.

1150. McKinley, Ray. "'Ooh, What You Said, Tex!'" *Metro-nome*, Mar. 1947, pp. 19, 39-41.

1151. McNamara, Helen. "Pack My Bags and Make My Getaway:
       The Odyssey of Jimmy Rushing." *Down Beat*, 3 Apr.
       1965, pp. 22-25.

1152. Mehegan, John. "The Case for Swinging." *Down Beat*,
       20 Aug. 1959, pp. 43-44.

1153. Mezzrow, Milton. "Lionel Hampton." *Jazz Hot* 5, nos.
       3-4 (Feb.-Mar. 1939): 11.

1154. Milhaud, D. "Jazz Band and Negro Music." *Living Age*
       323 (18 Oct. 1944): 169-73.

       Contains some biographical information on Count Basie,
       Fletcher Henderson, and Duke Ellington, and outlines
       the jazz bands and their acceptance by vaudeville
       audiences. Somewhat limited information is given on
       each composer.

1155. "Money Invested in Swing Music Will Keep It Alive,
       Says Miller." *Down Beat*, 15 Apr. 1940, p. 6.

1156. Morgenstern, Dan. "Keep It Swinging." *Down Beat*,
       20 Mar. 1969, pp. 22-23.

       Cozy Cole's musical career, musicians, background,
       and styles.

1157. ————. "Lester Leaps In." *Down Beat*, 3 Apr. 1969,
       pp. 19-20.

       Lester Young honored for 30 years in jazz. His
       personality and style are described.

1158. ————. "Swinging at the White House." *Down Beat*,
       12 June 1969, p. 14.

       On Duke Ellington at the White House in honor of his
       70th birthday.

1159. Mosher, J. "Moten and Lee Are Patron Saints of Kansas
       City Jazz." *Down Beat*, 1 Jan. 1941, pp. 8, 18.

1160. ————. "Swing Band Is Born." *Collier's*, 20 May 1939,
       pp. 17, 32, 34.

1161. "The Music Goes 'Round and Around.'" *New Republic*, 29 Jan. 1936, pp. 334-35.

1162. "Musical Blasphemies: Thomas (Fats) Waller." *Music and Rhythm* 1, no. 4 (Apr. 1941): 31.

1162a. "My Story, by Andy Kirk as Told to Frank Driggs." *Jazz Review* 2, no. 2 (Feb. 1959): 12-18.

1163. Nicholson, Roger. "The Swing to Strings." *Music and Rhythm* 2, no. 10 (Oct. 1941): 36, 56.

1164. "No More Swing?" *Scribner's*, Nov. 1936, pp. 70-71.

1165. "No One's Energy vs. BG's Finesse." *Down Beat*, 1 Oct. 1942, p. 8.

1166. Deleted.

1167. Oakley, Helen. "Duke Ellington." *Jazz Hot* 12, no. 11 (Nov. 1936): 5-6.

1168. "One-Nighter Car Jump Kills Great Saxist Chu Barry." *Metronome*, Dec. 1941, p. 8.

1169. Ortiz Oderigo, Nestor R. "El arte de Harry Carney." *Ritmo y melodia* 4, no. 9 (Sept. 1947): 18-20.

1170. Palmer, Tom. "Fatha' Hines Thumbs His Nose at Jazz." *Music and Rhythm* 2, no. 11 (Nov. 1941): 10.

1171. Panassie, Hugues. "Alto Saxophonists." *Jazz Hot* 13, no. 12 (Dec. 1936): 3-6.

1172. Perrin, Michael. "Duke Ellington à la Salle Pleyel." *Présence Africaine*, no. 5 (1948): 861-62.

1173. Petit, Georges. "Duke Ellington et son orchestre." *Europe Nouvelle* 16 (5 Aug. 1933): 740.

1174. Poling, James W. "Music After Midnight." *Esquire*, June 1936, pp. 92, 131-32.

1175. "Pollock's Band Broke Up Slowly." *Metronome*, Nov. 1941, pp. 18-19.

1176. "Pollock Says Firehouse 5 Is Just a Cornball Crew." *Down Beat*, 5 May 1950, p. 12.

1177.   Postif, François. "Lester: Paris 1959." *Jazz Review*
        2, no. 8 (Sept. 1959): 6-10.

        An interview which took place one week before Lester
        "Prez" Young's death.

1178.   "Pres Talks About Himself, Copycats." *Down Beat*,
        4 May 1949, p. 15.

1179.   Reisner, Robert. "The Last Days of Lester Willis
        Young." *Down Beat*, 17 June 1949, pp. 1, 12.

1180.   "Reputation Shredded, Duke Should Disband." *Down Beat*,
        17 June 1949, pp. 1, 12.

1181.   "Rex Wows Parisians." *Down Beat*, 14 Jan. 1948, p. 3.

1182.   Rowland, Sam. "Debunking Swing." *Esquire*, Aug. 1936,
        pp. 79, 111.

1183.   Rubba, Joseph V. "Much Ado About Swinging." *Metronome*,
        Aug. 1936, pp. 9-10.

1184.   Russell, Ross. "The Parent Style and Lester Young."
        The Art of Jazz. Edited by Martin Williams. New
        York: Oxford University Press, 1959, pp. 207-15.

1185.   Rust, Brian. "The Fletcher Henderson Band." *Jazz
        Journal* 2, no. 11 (Nov. 1949): 4-5.

1186.   "The Saga of Tommy Dorsey." *International Musician* 48,
        no. 11 (Nov. 1949): 16.

1187.   Schaap, Walter E. "Fats Waller." *Jazz Hot* 32, nos.
        7-8 (July-Aug. 1939): 11.

1188.   Schillinger, Joseph. "At Long Last--Here It Is--An
        Explanation of Swing." *Metronome*, July 1942, pp. 19,
        23.

1189.   Schuller, Gunther. "Early Duke." *Jazz Review* 2, no.
        11 (Dec. 1959): 6-14; 3, no. 1 (Jan. 1960): 18-23;
        3, no. 2 (Feb. 1960): 18-26.

        The life and early musical style of Duke Ellington.
        Also included are some pertinent historical information
        and numerous musical examples. An excellent series of
        articles.

1190. ———. "The Ellington Style: Its Origins and Early
       Development." *Jazz*. Edited by Nat Hentoff and
       Albert McCarthy. New York: Rinehart, 1959, pp. 231-
       75.

1191. Schulz, Dietrich. "Swing Fever in Germany." *Swing
       Music* 14, no. 3 (Autumn 1936): 23, 94.

1192. Secor, E.A. "Just What Really Is Swing Music?" *Etude*
       58, no. 4 (Apr. 1940): 240.

1193. "Shaw's New Ork Proves 'Can't Turn Clock Back.'" *Down
       Beat*, 21 Apr. 1950, p. 8.

1194. Smith, Charles Edward. "Swing." *New Republic*, 16 Feb.
       1938, pp. 39-41.

1195. Smyth, Ian Monro. "Jimmy Lunceford and His Orchestra."
       Jazz Hot 3, nos. 11-12 (Nov.-Dec. 1937): 3-17.

1196. ———. "Swing Bassistes." *Jazz Hot* 12, no. 11 (Nov.
       1936): 9-10.

1197. "The Spirit of Jazz." *New Republic*, 30 Dec. 1936,
       pp. 269-71.

1198. "Spirituals to Swing." *Modern Music* 21, no. 1 (Jan.
       1946): 224-25.

1199. "Spirituals to Swing." *Time*, 2 Jan. 1939, pp. 23-24.

1200. Stearns, Marshall. "Swing." *The Story of Jazz*. New
       York: Oxford University Press, 1973, pp. 197-217.

       Presents a historical and musical discussion of
       swing.

1201. Stewart, Rex. "Flow Gently, Sweet Rhythm." *Down Beat*,
       15 June 1967, pp. 23-25, 52, 53.

       Life and musical career of John Kirby.

1202. ———. "Harry Carney: Boss Boutano." *Down Beat*,
       2 Nov. 1967, pp. 20-22, 35.

1203. Stone, Richard. "Basie and Bop." *Record Changer*,
       Dec. 1948, p. 10.

1204.   Deleted.

1205.   "The Story of Duke's Boss." *Music and Rhythm* 2, no. 6
        (June 1942): 14.

1206.   Strate, Marvin W. "Swing: What Is It?" *Musical
        America*, 25 May 1936, pp. 6-7.

1207.   Strayhorn, Billy. "Billy Strayhorn on Pianists."
        Metronome, Oct. 1943, pp. 29, 66.

1208.   "Swing." *Jazzways*. Edited by George S. Rosenthal.
        Cincinnati: Jazzways, 1946, pp. 48-51, 104-5.

1209.   "Swing." *New Republic*, 16 Feb. 1938, pp. 39-41.

1210.   "Swing." *New York Times*, 19 Nov. 1939, pp. 14, 19.

1211.   "Swing Again." *Modern Music* 15, no. 2 (Mar.-Apr.
        1938): 160-66.

1212.   "Swing Fiesta by Goodman." *New York Times*, 22 May
        1938, p. 3.

1213.   "Swing Glories in Its Humble Origin." *Musician* 44,
        no. 4 (Apr. 1939): 66, 68.

1214.   "Swing High." *Vogue*, 15 Mar. 1936, pp. 90-91, 112,
        114.

1215.   "Swing in Philadelphia." *Metronome*, July 1946, pp. 16-
        17, 28-29.

1216.   "Swing Marches On." *Musician* 44, no. 12 (Dec. 1939):
        219.

1217.   "Swing Music." *Modern Music* 13, no. 3 (May-June 1936):
        12-17.

1218.   "Swing Music Produces These." *Life*, 21 Feb. 1938, pp.
        4-7.

1219.   "Swing That Music." *The Music Lover's Handbook*. Edited
        by Elie Siegmeister. New York: William Morrow, 1943,
        pp. 711-18.

1220. "Swing Viewed as 'Musical Hitlerism': Professor Sees Fans Ripe for Dictator." *New York Times*, 2 Nov. 1938, p. 3.

1221. "Swing: What Is It?" *New York Times*, 5 Sept. 1937, n.p.

1222. "'Swinging' Bach." *New York Times*, 30 Oct. 1938, n.p.

1223. "Swinging the Blues." *Hot Club Magazine*, Feb. 1946, pp. 3, 5.

1224. Taubman, H. "Swing and Mozart, Too." *New York Times Magazine*, 29 Dec. 1939, p. 74.

1225. "Teddy Wilson." *Down Beat*, 1 Apr. 1941, p. 10.

1226. "Teddy Wilson." *Metronome*, July 1947, p. 20.

1227. "The Ten Greatest Trombone Players." *Music and Rhythm* 2, no. 6 (June 1942): 14.

1228. "Thanks, Mr. Redman, for Modern Style." *Metronome*, June 1941, pp. 20-21, 25, 26.

1229. "Things You Can Discover at an Ellington Concert." *Down Beat*, 29 Dec. 1946, p. 15.

1230. "Thomas Wright (Fats) Waller." *Current Biography 1942*. New York: H.W. Wilson, 1943, pp. 862-64.

1231. Thompson, Virgil. "Swing Music." *Modern Music* 13, no. 3 (May-June 1936): 12-17.

1232. Tilford, William Roberts. "Swing, Swing, Swing." *Etude* 55, no. 12 (Dec. 1937): 777-78, 835.

1233. Toll, Ted. "Ellington Lauded as All Time Greatest." *Down Beat*, 1 Sept. 1940, p. 3.

1234. "Tommy Dorsey." *Down Beat*, 15 May 1941, p. 10.

1235. "TD's One of the Finest Dance Bands in the Country." *Down Beat*, 8 Sept. 1950, p. 3.

1236. "Tricky Sam Nanton, 42, Dies on Tour with Duke." *Down Beat*, 12 Aug. 1946, p. 9.

1237. "Two Decades with the Duke." *Ebony*, Jan. 1946, pp. 11-19.

       Information on Duke Ellington's musical style from "Soda Fountain Rag" to his current (1946) hit, "Black, Brown and Beige."

1238. "Ventura Could Climb Right to Top." *Down Beat*, 19 May 1950, p. 23.

1239. "Walter Page's Story." *Jazz Review* 1, no. 10 (Nov. 1958): 15-18.

1240. "Warns of Effects of 'Swing' on Youth." *New York Times*, 26 Oct. 1938, p. 8.

1241. "A Weary Duke Errs by Not Rehearsing with Ork." *Down Beat*, 28 July 1948, p. 2.

1242. "Webster in Royal Return to Duke." *Down Beat*, 1 Dec. 1948, p. 1.

1243. Weidemann, Erik. "Lester Young on Records." *Jazz Review* 2, no. 8 (Sept. 1959): 11-13.

1244. "What About Swing?" *Parents Magazine*, Aug. 1939, pp. 18-19.

1245. Wheelock, Raymond. "Did Swing Come from the Indians?" *Educational Music Magazine*, Nov. 1943, pp. 20-21, 50.

1246. Whiteman, Paul. "All-American Swing Band." *Collier's*, 10 Sept. 1935, pp. 9-12, 63.

1247. ————. "Why I Hate Glenn Miller's Music." *Music and Rhythm* 2, no. 3 (Mar. 1942): 7, 46, 48.

1248. "William Count Basie." *Current Biography 1942*. New York: H.W. Wilson, 1943, pp. 55-57.

1249. Williams, Cootie. "Why I Quit Duke Ellington After 11 Years." *Music and Rhythm* 1, no. 12 (Dec. 1940): 9, 97.

1250. Williams, Richard. "Basie Swinglish." *House Beautiful*, Feb. 1944, pp. 94-95.

1251. "Willie Smith." *Ebony*, June 1949, pp. 41-43.

1252. "Woody, Basie Work with Small Units, Explain Why."
      Down Beat, 24 Mar. 1950, pp. 5-7.

1253. Yaw, Ralph. "What Is Swing?" *Metronome*, May 1936,
      pp. 22, 35.

1254. "You Gotta' Swing! Says the Count." *Metronome*, May
      1947, pp. 19, 46.

1255. "You'll Never Walk Alone; Not with the Miller Tag."
      Down Beat, 17 June 1949, p. 3.

1256. Zolotow, Maurice. "The Duke of Hot." *Saturday Evening
      Post*, 7 Aug. 1943, pp. 24-25, 57, 59.

D. BOP

This category contains information on select
performers as well as on the development of
Bop. Also included are entries on Bop criticism
and influence.

BOOKS

1257. Allen, Steve. *Bop Fables*. New York: Simon & Schuster,
      1955.

1258. Burley, Dan. *Dan Burley's Original Handbook of Harlem
      Jive*. New York: Author, 1944.

1259. Dorsett, Lyle W. *The Pendergast Machine*. New York:
      Oxford University Press, 1968.

      Background information on Kansas City.

1260. Edlun, Martin, ed. *Jazzhistorier: From Blues till Bop*.
      Stockholm: Folket i Bilds Forlag, 1960.

1261. Edwards, Carlos V. *The Giants of Bebop*. Urbana:
      University of Illinois Press, 1962.

1262. Edwards, Paul, ed. *Esquire's Jazz Book*. New York:
      A.S. Barnes, 1945.

1263. *Esquire's Jazz Book, 1944-1947*. New York: Smith and
      Durrell, 1944-1947.

1264. Evans, George. *Bebop, comment le jouer, comment
      l'écrire*. Brussels, 1948.

1265. Feather, Leonard. *The Encyclopedia of Jazz in the
      Sixties*. New York: Horizon Press, 1967.

1266. ————. *Inside Be-Bop*. New York: J.J. Robbins, 1949.

1267.   ———. *Inside Jazz*. New York, 1949.

History and technical analysis of jazz, together with biographies of jazzmen. Covers the period 1940-1949.

1268.   ———. *The New Edition of the Encyclopedia of Jazz*. New York: Horizon Press, 1960.

1269.   Gitler, Ira. *Jazz Masters of the Forties*. New York: Macmillan, 1966.

Contains information on Charlie Parker, Dizzy Gillespie, Bud Powell, J. Johnson, Oscar Pettiford, Kenny Clarke, Max Roach, Dexter Gordon, Lennie Tristano, Lee Konitz, and Todd Dameron.

1270.   Goffin, R. *Nouvelle histoire du jazz, du congo au bebop*. Brussels: L'écran du monde, 1948.

1271.   Goldberg, J. *Jazz Masters of the Fifties*. Edited by Martin Williams. New York: Macmillan, 1965.

Journalistic in style with no index. Chapters on Gerry Mulligan, Thelonious Monk, Art Blakey, Miles Davis, Sonny Rollins, the Modern Jazz Quartet, Charles Mingus, Paul Desmond, Ray Charles, John Coltrane, Cecil Taylor, and Ornette Coleman. Includes a discography of each musician.

1272.   Green, B. *The Reluctant Art: Five Studies in the Growth of Jazz*. London: MacGibbon & Kee, 1962.

Essays on the work of Benny Goodman, Billie Holiday, Bix Beiderbecke, Lester Young, and Charlie Parker.

1273.   Griffin, Nard. *To Be, or Not to Bop*. New York: Leo B. Workman, 1948.

1274.   Harrison, Max. *Charlie Parker*. London: Cassell, 1960.

1275.   James, Michael. *Dizzy Gillespie*. London: Cassell, 1959.

1276.   Jepsen, Jorgen Grunnet. *A Discography of Thelonious Monk and Bud Powell*. Copenhagen: Karl E. Knudsen, 1969.

1277.   Jones, Cliff. *Jazz in New York*. London: Discographical Society, 1944.

1278. McCarthy, Albert, ed. *Jazzbook: 1947.* London: Nicholson and Watson, 1948.

1279. ————. *PL Jazzbook: 1946 and 1947.* London: Editors Petry, 1948.

1280. Miller, Paul Eduard. *Esquire's Jazz Book: 1944.* New York: A.S. Barnes, 1944.

1281. ————. *Esquire's 1946 Jazz Book.* New York: Smith and Durrell, 1946.

1282. Patane, Giuseppe. *Be-bop ou pas be-bop? Ou, à la découverte du jazz.* Geneva: Editions Sabaudia, 1951.

1283. Russell, Ross. *Bird Lives: The High Life and Hard Times of Charlie (Yardbird) Parker.* New York: Charterhouse, 1973.

1284. Spellman, A.B. *Black Music: Four Lives (in the Bebop Business).* New York: Pantheon Books, 1970.

     A brief biographical description of Cecil Taylor, Ornette Coleman, Jackie McLean, and Herbie Nichols.

1285. Wilson, John S. *Jazz: The Transition Years.* New York: Meredith, 1966.

     A history of jazz from 1940 to 1960; covers Charlie Parker, Dizzy Gillespie, etc.

ARTICLES

1286. Ager, Shana. "Bebop." *Mademoiselle*, Jan. 1948, pp. 88-89, 132-33.

1287. "Armstrong Explains Stand Against Bop." *Down Beat*, 30 Dec. 1949, p. 3.

1288. Avakian, George. "B.G. and Bebop." *Newsweek*, 27 Dec. 1948, pp. 66-67.

1289. Bacon, Paul. "The High Priest of Be-Bop: The Inimitable Mr. Monk." *Record Changer*, Nov. 1949, p. 29.

1290. Balliett, Whitney. "Jazz Records: The Great Gillespie." *New Yorker*, 7 Nov. 1959, pp. 158-64.

1291.   ————. "The Measure of Bird." *Saturday Review*,
         17 Mar. 1956, pp. 33-34.

         Written a year after Parker's death, this article
         spotlights his contributions to jazz, his musical
         style, and his life.

1292.   Banks, Dave. "Be-Bop Called Merely the Beginning of a
         New Creative Music Form." *Down Beat*, 11 Feb. 1948,
         p. 16.

1293.   "Band of the Year: Dizzy Gillespie." *Metronome*, Jan.
         1949, pp. 17-18.

1294.   Basie, Count. "Be-Bop Seems Here to Stay." *Cue*,
         5 June 1948, p. 14.

1295.   "Bebop Fashions: Weird Dizzy Gillespie Mannerisms
         Quickly Picked Up as Accepted Style for Bebop
         Devotees." *Ebony*, Dec. 1948, pp. 31-33.

1296.   "Bebop Is Not Jazz." *Jazz Record* 21, no. 3 (Mar. 1947):
         n.p.

1297.   "Be-Bop??!!--Man, We Called It Kloop-Mop!!" *Metronome*,
         Apr. 1947, pp. 21, 44-45.

1298.   "Bebop: New Jazz School Is Led by Trumpeter Who Is Hot,
         Cool, and Gone." *Life*, 11 Oct. 1948, pp. 139-42.

         On Dizzy Gillespie.

1299.   "Bebop and Old Masters." *New Republic*, 30 June 1947,
         p. 36.

1300.   "Bebop's the Easy Out, Claims Louis." *Metronome*, Mar.
         1948, pp. 14-15.

1301.   Bel, André de, and Marcel Cumps. "Dizzy in Belgium."
         Hot Club Magazine, Mar. 1948, pp. 5-7.

1302.   "The Billy Eckstine Band." *Jazz Journal* 13, no. 11
         (Nov. 1960): n.p.

1303.   "Birdland Applies Imagination to Jazz." *Down Beat*,
         27 Jan. 1950, p. 3.

1304.   "Bird, Backed by Strings, Disappoints at Birdland."
         Down Beat, 25 Aug. 1950, p. 4.

1305. "Bird Speaks." *Jazz Journal* 17, no. 5 (May 1964): n.p.

1306. "'Bird' Wrong: Must Get a Beat: Diz." *Down Beat*, 7 Oct. 1949, pp. 1, 12.

1307. "Bop at End of Road, Says Dizzy." *Down Beat*, 8 Sept. 1950, p. 1.

1308. "Bop Confused Benny." *Metronome*, Oct. 1949, pp. 15, 35.

1309. "Bop's Dixie to Monk." *Metronome*, Apr. 1948, pp. 20, 34-35.

1310. "Bop Horn: A Discography." *Record Changer*, July 1948, pp. 11-13, 28.

1311. "Bop Man Haig Serious and Well-Schooled." *Down Beat*, 3 June 1949, p. 12.

1312. "Bop Nowhere, Armstrong Just a Myth." *Down Beat*, 17 June 1949, pp. 1, 19.

1313. "Bop Rhythm." *Record Changer*, July 1948, pp. 11-13, 28.

1314. "Bop Will Kill Business Unless It Kills Itself First-- Louis Armstrong." *Down Beat*, 7 Apr. 1948, pp. 2-3.

1315. "Bopera on Broadway." *Time*, 20 Dec. 1948, pp. 63-64.

1316. Boyer, Richard C. "Bop." *New Yorker*, 3 July 1948, pp. 28-32, 34-37.

1317. "Brass Instrumentation in Be-Bop." *Record Changer*, Jan. 1949, pp. 9-10, 21.

1318. "Brew Brews Bop on Pres Kick." *Down Beat*, 1 July 1949, p. 7.

1319. Burns, J. "The Lipster (Bop)." *Jazz Journal* 21, no. 7 (July 1968): 3-4.

1320. "Claim French Can't Get Yet with Bop." *Down Beat*, 7 Oct. 1946, pp. 4, 17.

1321. Crawford, Marc. "Requiem for a Tortured Heavyweight." *Down Beat*, 10 Oct. 1966, pp. 12-13.

    Reflections on Bud Powell's life.

1322.   Dameron, Tadd. "The Case for Modern Music." *Record Changer*, Feb. 1948, pp. 5, 16.

1323.   Dexter, Dave, Jr. "The Bird." *The Jazz Story*. Englewood Cliffs, New Jersey: Prentice-Hall, 1964, pp. 145-56.

        Concerned more with the personal, not the musical, life of Charlie Parker. An account of the Bird's troubles with heroin, women, and booze.

1324.   "Dix Sacrifices Spark to Get His 'Bop with Beat.'" *Down Beat*, 13 Jan. 1950, p. 8.

1325.   "Dizzy's Discussion." *Hot Club Magazine*, May 1947, pp. 3-5.

1326.   "Eckstine: A Lush Voice and Musical Imagination Have Made Him a Top Crooner." *Look*, 30 Aug. 1949, p. 92.

1327.   Eldridge, Roy. "Roy Eldridge on Trumpeters." *Metronome*, Oct. 1943, p. 27.

1328.   "Europe Goes Dizzy." *Metronome*, May 1948, pp. 18-19, 35.

1329.   "The Evolution of Bop." *Record Changer*, Mar. 1948, pp. 9-10, 18.

1330.   Farrell, Barry. "The Loneliest Monk." *Time*, 28 Feb. 1964, pp. 84-88.

        Relates the success of one of Monk's European tours, tells his life story, and describes his musical influences Says his is a relatively quiet and reserved life.

1331.   Farres, Enrique. "El jazz, la musica progresista y el publica." *Club de ritmo* 41, no. 9 (Sept. 1949): 5.

1332.   "Fats Navarro Dies in NYC." *Down Beat*, 11 Aug. 1950, p. 1.

1333.   Feather, Leonard. "Diz Strikes Happy Compromise Between Jazz, Commercialism." *Down Beat*, 8 Feb. 1952, p. 2.

1334.   "52nd Re-Bop Street." *Hot Club Magazine*, 1 Oct. 1947, p. 10.

1335.   "Figs Might Do Well to Take a Hint from Bop--Make New
        Dixie Sounds." *Down Beat*, 6 May 1949, p. 2.

1336.   "Folks Find New Word to Mangle." *Down Beat*, 15 Dec.
        1950, p. 10.

1337.   "From Heebie Jeebies to Bebop." *Saturday Review*,
        30 Oct. 1948, p. 51.

1338.   Gazzaway, Don. "Conversation with Buster Smith."
        Jazz Review 1, no. 11 (Dec. 1959): 18-23; 3, no. 1
        (Jan. 1960): 11-15; 3, no. 2 (Feb. 1960): 12-17.

        An in-depth interview concerning Smith's life and
        musical career. Also included are his recollections
        of Charles Parker's performing in his band. The inter-
        view was recorded in August, 1959.

1339.   Gillespie, Dizzy. "The Years with Yard." *Down Beat*,
        25 May 1961, pp. 21-23.

1340.   "Gillespie's Crew Great Again, But May Break Up."
        Down Beat, 16 June 1950, p. 1.

1341.   Gillespie, Dizzy. "Interview by M. Edey, Jr." *Paris
        Review* 9, no. 3 (Fall 1965): 137-46.

1342.   Gitler, Ira. "Bird Still Lives." *Down Beat*, 2 Apr.
        1970, pp. 16-17.

        The life and music of Charles Parker.

1343.   Gleason, Ralph J. "Dizzy Getting a Bad Deal from Music
        Biz: Gleason." *Down Beat*, 17 Nov. 1950, p. 14.

1344.   Gonzalez, Pearl. "Monk Talk." *Down Beat*, 28 Oct.
        1971, pp. 12-13.

        Thelonious Monk's opinions on jazz and things of
        the day.

1345.   Hadlock, Dick. "Earl Hines on Charlie Parker." *Jazz
        Review* 3, no. 9 (Nov. 1960): 12-14.

1346.   Hakim, Radik. "The Charlie Parker Ko Ko Date." *Jazz
        Review* 2, no. 2 (Feb. 1959): 11-12.

1347.   Hallock, Ted. "Bop Jargon Indicative of Intellectual
        Thought." *Down Beat*, 28 July 1948, p. 4.

1348.   Hamblett, Charles. "Music--Sm-o-oth & Boppy: New
        Fashion in Rhythm." *Illustrated Weekly of India*,
        19 Dec. 1948, pp. 38-39.

1349.   Henderson, Harry, and Sam Shaw. "And Now We Go Be-Bop!"
        Collier's, 20 Mar. 1948, pp. 16-17, 88.

1350.   Hobson, Wilder. "Farewell to the Bird." *Saturday
        Review*, 30 Apr. 1955, pp. 54-55.

        Brief comments about Parker's life and musical
        ability, with reviews of recordings of Parker's com-
        positions by other performers.

1351.   Hoefer, George. "Klook--Hot Box." *Down Beat*, 28 Mar.
        1963, pp. 20, 23.

1352.   ————. "Earl Hines in the 1940's." *Down Beat*,
        25 Apr. 1963, n.p.

1353.   "How Deaf Can You Get?" *Time*, 17 May 1948, p. 74.

1354.   "The Jazz Beat: Memo on Bebop." *Saturday Review*,
        30 Aug. 1947, pp. 18-19.

1355.   "Jazz Is Neurotic--Stan." *Down Beat*, 14 Jan. 1948,
        pp. 1, 18-19.

1356.   Jepsen, Jorgen Grunnet. "Jazz Records, 1942-1962."
        Jazz Journal 16, no. 10 (Oct. 1963): 13.

1357.   Kahn, H. "Bebop? One Long Search for the Right Note,
        Says Louis Armstrong." *Melody Maker*, 12 Nov. 1949,
        p. 3.

1358.   Koch, Lawrence. "A Numerical Listing of Charlie
        Parker's Recordings." *Journal of Jazz Studies* 2,
        no. 2 (June 1975): 86-95.

1359.   ————. "Ornithology: A Study of Charlie Parker's
        Music." *Journal of Jazz Studies* 2, no. 1 (Dec.
        1974): 61-88; 2, no. 2 (July 1975): 86-96.

        Excellent harmonic and melodic analysis of Parker's
        music.

1360.   Lapham, Lewis H. "Monk: High Priest of Jazz." *Saturday
        Evening Post*, 11 Apr. 1964, pp. 70-74.

        On Monk's personality, life, and musical style.

1361. Lawrence, Elliot. "Dance Music, Not Bop, Is Our Bread,
       Butter: Elliot." *Down Beat*, 19 May 1950, p. 18.

1362. "Les avis de ... sur le Be-bop." *Hot Club Magazine*,
       May 1947, pp. 8-9.

1363. "Les Beboppers." *Hot Club Magazine*, May 1947, pp. 6-7.

1364. "Magnificent Monk of Music." *Ebony*, May 1959, pp. 120-
       22.

1365. "Man, Tatum Is Jazz--Big Tea." *Down Beat*, 1 July 1942,
       p. 11.

1366. Manskleid, Felix. "Dizzy on Charlie Parker." *Jazz
       Review* 4, no. 1 (Jan. 1961): 11-14.

       Gillespie recalls meeting and performing with Charlie
       Parker.

1367. McDonough, John. "Bird Discovered." *High Fidelity &
       Musical America*, Nov. 1974, pp. 95-96.

       Contains review of six newly-released Parker recordings,
       recorded by him from 1946 to 1947. Also contains informa-
       tion on Parker's performance abilities.

1368. McKean, Gilbert. "The Diz and the Bebop." *Esquire*,
       Oct. 1947, pp. 212-16.

1369. "Metronome's Records of the Year." *Metronome*, Jan.
       1947, pp. 28-29.

1370. Morrison, Allan. "The Man Behind the Horn." *Ebony*,
       June 1964, pp. 143-44, 146, 148-49, 151.

       Discusses the musical contributions of Dizzy Gillespie.

1371. "Nothing But Bop? 'Stupid,' Says Miles." *Down Beat*,
       27 Jan. 1950, pp. 18-19.

1372. "An Opera for the Bird." *Down Beat*, 5 May 1966, n.p.

1373. Owens, Thomas. "Applying the Melograph to 'Parker's
       Mood.'" *Selected Reports in Ethnomusicology* 2, no. 1
       (1974): 167-75.

1374. Pease, Sharon A. "Bop Harmony a Contribution of Jimmy
       Jones." *Down Beat*, 8 Apr. 1949, p. 12.

1375.   "Pianist Monk Getting Long Awaited Break." *Down Beat*,
        11 Feb. 1948, p. 11.

1376.   "Pops Pops Top on Sloppy Bop." *Metronome*, Oct. 1949,
        pp. 18, 25.

1377.   "The Private Life of Billy Eckstine." *Ebony*, Mar.
        1949, pp. 54-59.

1378.   "Professor Explains Bop." *Down Beat*, 25 Feb. 1949,
        p. 3.

1379.   Item deleted.

1380.   Raes, Jack. "Que pensez-vous de Be-bop?" *Hot Club
        Magazine*, May 1947, pp. 11, 13-14.

1381.   Reddick, L.D. "Dizzy Gillespie in Atlanta." *Phylon*
        1, no. 1 (First Quarter 1949): 44-49.

1382.   Reisner, Robert G. "Charlie Parker: A Biography in
        Interviews." *Jazz Review* 3, no. 8 (Sept.-Oct. 1960):
        6-16; 3, no. 9 (Nov. 1960): 8-12; 4, no. 1 (Jan. 1961):
        10-12.

        An excellent series of articles which details the
        life and musical career of Charles Parker. Also in-
        cluded is a list of interviews from musicians and lay-
        men who knew him.

1383.   ————. "Requiescat in Pace: Bud Powell--1924-1966."
        Down Beat, 8 Sept. 1966, p. 13.

1384.   "The Relation of the Blues to Bop." *Record Changer*,
        Nov. 1949, pp. 15-16.

1385.   "The Rhythm Section: Dizzy, 21st Century Gabriel."
        Esquire, Oct. 1945, pp. 90-91.

1386.   "Room for Two Schools of Jazz Thought Today." *Down
        Beat*, 4 Nov. 1946, pp. 10, 13.

1387.   "Roy Eldridge." *Down Beat*, 15 Apr. 1941, p. 10.

1388.   "Roy Eldridge." *Metronome*, May 1947, p. 25.

1389.   Russell, Ross. "Jay McShann, New York--1208 Miles."
        Jazz and Pop 7, no. 9 (Sept. 1968): 18-23.

1390. ————. "Bebop." *The Art of Jazz*. Edited by Martin T. Williams. New York: Oxford University Press, 1959, pp. 187-214.

1391. ————. "Be-bop Instrumentation." *Record Changer*, Nov. 1949, pp. 12-13, 22-23.

1392. ————. "Be-bop: Reed Instrumentation." *Record Changer*, Feb. 1949, pp. 6-7, 20.

1393. ————. "Bop Horn: A Discography." *Record Changer*, Feb. 1949, p. 10.

1394. ————. "Bop Rhythm." *Record Changer*, July 1948, pp. 11-13, 28.

1395. ————. "Brass." *The Art of Jazz*. Edited by Martin T. Williams. New York: Oxford University Press, 1959, pp. 202-07.

1396. ————. "Brass Instrumentation in Be-Bop." *Record Changer*, Jan. 1949, pp. 9-10, 21.

1397. ————. "Fat Girl! The Legacy of Fats Navarro." *Down Beat*, 19 Feb. 1970, pp. 14-16, 33.

Theodore (Fats) Navarro's musical career and style.

1398. ————. "The Legendary Joe Albany." *Jazz Review* 2, no. 3 (Apr. 1959): 18-20.

1399. Schillinger, Mort. "Dizzy Gillespie's Style, Its Meaning Analyzed." *Down Beat*, 11 Feb. 1946, pp. 14-15.

1400. Schuller, Gunther. "Thelonious Monk at Town Hall." *Jazz Review* 2, no. 5 (June 1959): 6-9.

1401. Stearns, Marshall. "Re-bop, Be-bop and Bop." *Harper's*, Apr. 1950, pp. 89-96.

1402. Stine, Jack. "American Jazz, 1949." *Jazz Journal* 2, no. 10 (Oct. 1949): 4-5.

1403. Stone, Richard. "Basie and Bop." *Record Changer*, Dec. 1948, p. 10.

1404. "Stravinsky, Bird, Vibes Gas Roach." *Down Beat*, 3 June 1949, p. 6.

1405.   "Studies Bop, Returns to Original Love, Dixieland."
        Down Beat, 21 Apr. 1950, p. 4.

1406.   "Ten Nights with the Great Eckstine." *Our World*,
        July 1952, pp. 24-29.

1407.   "Thelonious Monk--Genius of Bop." *Down Beat*, 24 Sept.
        1947, p. 2.

1408.   "Thelonious Monk's Music May Be First Sign of Bebop's
        Legitimacy." *Record Changer*, Apr. 1948, pp. 5, 20.

1409.   Tirro, F. "Silent Theme Tradition in Jazz (Be-bop)."
        Musical Quarterly 53, no. 3 (July 1967): 313-34.

1410.   Tracy, Jack. "Gillespie's Crew Great Again, But May
        Break Up." *Down Beat*, 16 June 1950, p. 1.

1411.   ————. "Tribute to Bud Powell from His Compatriots."
        Down Beat, 22 Sept. 1966, pp. 20-21.

1412.   Tristano, Lennie. "What's Right with the Beboppers."
        Metronome, July 1947, pp. 14, 31.

1413.   Weinstock, Bob. "Dizzy Gillespie--A Complete Discog-
        raphy." *Record Changer*, July 1949, pp. 8, 18.

1414.   "Where Is Small-Band Jazz Going?" *Music and Rhythm* 2,
        no. 12 (Dec. 1941): 18.

1415.   Wilder, Alec. "The State of Jazz." *House and Garden*,
        July 1950, pp. 49-50.

1416.   Williams, Martin. "Bebop and After: A Report." *Jazz*.
        Edited by Nat Hentoff and Albert McCarthy. New York:
        Rinehart, 1959, pp. 287-303.

1417.   ————. "Charlie Parker: The Burden of Innovation."
        The Jazz Tradition. New York: Oxford University
        Press, 1970, pp. 120-37.

        A critical, realistic look at Parker's life and
        troubles, musical influences, and associates. Several
        of his recordings are reviewed, and he is compared to
        other jazz musicians.

1418.   ————, ed. "Jazz Panorama." *Jazz Review* 5, no. 3
        (n.d.), 216-39.

        Contains information on Thelonious Monk.

1419.   ————. "Thelonious Monk: Modern Jazz in Search of
          Maturity." *The Jazz Tradition*. New York: Oxford
          University Press, 1970, pp. 138-55.

          Positive account of Monk's musical talent and style.
          Includes comment on several of his compositions, and
          compares him to other musicians.

1420.   Woodfin, Henry A. "Kenny Dorham." *Jazz Review* 3,
          no. 7 (Aug. 1960): 6-10.

1421.   "Yardbird Flies Home." *Metronome*, Aug. 1947, pp. 14,
          43-44.

          Contains information on Charlie Parker.

THESES AND DISSERTATIONS

1422.   Davis, Nathan T. "Charlie Parker's Kansas City
          Environment and Its Effect on His Later Life."
          Ph.D. dissertation, Wesleyan University, 1974.

1423.   Gray, James M. "An Analysis of Melodic Devices in
          Selected Improvisations of Charlie Parker." Master's
          thesis, Ohio University, 1966.

1424.   Owens, Thomas. "Charlie Parker: Techniques of Improvisa-
          tion." Ph.D. dissertation, University of California,
          Los Angeles, 1974.

E. MODERN

This category is primarily concerned with the life and music of selected individuals and groups who have achieved jazz fame since the Bop era. Also included is information on jazz styles that have emerged since Bop.

BOOKS

1425. Balliett, Whitney. *Dinosaurs in the Morning: 41 Pieces on Jazz*. Philadelphia: J.B. Lippincott, 1962.

1426. ————. *The Sound of Surprise: 46 Pieces on Jazz*. New York: E.P. Dutton, 1959.

1427. Broadcast Music, Inc. *The Many Worlds of Music*. New York: Author, 1974.

An illuminating profile of composers who write for television and motion pictures; includes Black composers Benny Golson, J.J. Johnson, Quincy Jones, and Oliver Nelson.

1428. Cole, William. *Miles Davis*. New York: William Morrow, 1974.

1429. Dexter, David. *The Jazz Story: From the 90's to the 60's*. Englewood Cliffs, N.J.: Prentice-Hall, 1964.

1430. Feather, Leonard. *The Encyclopedia of Jazz in the Sixties*. New York: Horizon Press, 1966.

1431. ————. *The Encyclopedia Yearbook of Jazz*. New York: Horizon Press, 1959.

1432. ————. *The New Edition of the Encyclopedia of Jazz*. New York: Horizon Press, 1960.

1433. ————. *The New Yearbook of Jazz*. New York: Horizon Press, 1955.

1434.   Goldberg, Joe. *Jazz Masters of the Fifties*. New
        York: Macmillan, 1966.

        Contains biographies of about ten significant jazz
        musicians from the early 1950's to the early 1960's.
        The biographies include those of Miles Davis, Ray
        Charles, John Coltrane, Art Blakey, Charles Mingus,
        Gerry Mulligan, Thelonious Monk, and others.

1435.   James, Michael. *Miles Davis*. New York: A.S. Barnes,
        1961.

1436.   ————. *Ten Modern Jazzmen: An Appraisal of the
        Recorded Work of Ten Modern Jazzmen*. London: Cassell,
        1960.

        A collection of essays which analyzes the recorded
        work of Charlie Parker, Dizzy Gillespie, Bud Powell,
        Miles Davis, Stan Getz, Thelonious Monk, Gerry Mulligan,
        John Lewis, Lee Konitz, and Wardell Gray.

1437.   Jepsen, Jorgen Grunnet. *A Discography of John Coltrane*.
        Copenhagen: Karl E. Knudsen, 1969.

1438.   ————. *A Discography of Miles Davis*. Copenhagen:
        Karl E. Knudsen, 1969.

1439.   Jones, LeRoi. *Black Music*. New York: William Morrow,
        1967.

        A description of recent events and people in the world
        of jazz, with a brief discography and a few photographs.

1440.   Kofsky, Frank. *Black Nationalism and the Revolution
        in Music*. New York: Pathfinder, 1970.

1441.   Larkin, Philip. *All What Jazz?* New York: St. Martin's,
        1970.

        Contains information on the jazz years of 1961-1968
        only. Covers the Duke Ellington "Panorama," the Parker
        "Legend," how Billie "Scores," and Aretha's "Gospel,"
        etc.

1442.   Markewich, Reese. *Inside Out: Substitute Harmony in
        Modern Jazz and Pop Music*. New York: Author, 1967.

1443.   Mingus, Charles. *Beneath the Underdog*. New York:
        Knopf, 1971.

1444. Ostransky, Leroy. *The Anatomy of Jazz.* Seattle:
       University of Washington Press, 1960.

1445. Raben, Erik. *A Discography of Free Jazz.* Copenhagen:
       Karl E. Knudsen, 1969.

       Covers Ayler, Cherry, Coleman, Sanders, Shepp, and
       Taylor.

1446. Reginald, Oscar. *Ella Fitzgerald Story.* New York:
       Stein & Day, 1971.

1447. Reisner, R.G. *The Jazz Titans, Including 'The Parlance
       of Hip' with Short Biographical Sketches and Brief
       Discographies.* Garden City, New York: Doubleday,
       1960.

1448. Rosenthal, George S., ed. *Jazzways.* Cincinnati: Jazz-
       ways, 1946.

       A collection of articles on various aspects of jazz
       by leaders in the field. List of collector's items
       included.

1449. Shapiro, Nat, and Nat Hentoff, eds. *The Jazz Makers.*
       New York: Rinehart, 1957.

       Contains information on Bessie Smith, Fats Waller,
       Art Tatum, Coleman Hawkins, Benny Goodman, Duke Elling-
       ton, Charles Parker, Fletcher Henderson, Count Basie,
       Lester Young, Billie Holiday, Roy Eldridge, Charlie
       Christian, and Dizzy Gillespie.

1450. Somosko, Vladimir, and Barry Tepperman. *Eric Dolphy:
       A Musical Biography and Discography.* Washington,
       D.C.: Smithsonian Institution Press, 1974.

1451. Simpkins, C.O. *Coltrane: A Biography.* New York:
       Herndon House, 1975.

1452. Stock, Dennis, and Nat Hentoff. *Jazz Street: A Photo-
       graphic Exploration into the World of Jazz.* Garden
       City, New York: Doubleday, 1960.

1453. Tirro, Frank. *The Jazz Combo from ODJB to the MJQ.*
       Urbana: University of Illinois Press, 1977.

1454. Williams, Martin, ed. *Jazz Panorama.* New York: Macmillan, Crowell-Collier, 1962.

Contains biographies of several great jazz musicians: Jelly Roll Morton, King Oliver, Louis Armstrong, Bix Beiderbecke, Jimmie Lunceford, Lester Young, Billie Holiday, Stan Getz, Miles Davis, Charlie Parker, Thelonious Monk, Sonny Rollins, Cannonball Adderly, Ray Charles, and Eric Dolphy.

1455. ———. *The Jazz Tradition.* New York: Oxford University Press, 1970.

With information on or about Jelly Roll Morton, Louis Armstrong, Bix Beiderbecke, Coleman Hawkins, Billie Holiday, Duke Ellington, Count Basie, Lester Young, Charles Parker, Thelonious Monk, the Modern Jazz Quartet, Sonny Rollins, Horace Silver, Miles Davis, John Coltrane, and Ornette Coleman.

1456. Wilson, John S. *Jazz, the Transition Years: 1940-1960.* New York: Appleton-Century-Crofts, 1966.

ARTICLES

1457. "About John Coltrane." *Jazz* 1, no. 1 (1960): 22.

1458. Abrahams, Richard; David N. Baker; and Charles Ellison. "The Social Role of Jazz." *Reflections on Afro-American Music.* Edited by D.R. de Lerma. Kent, Ohio: Kent State University Press, 1973, pp. 104-10.

1459. "Aftermath for Miles." *Down Beat,* 29 Oct. 1959, p. 20.

1460. "Albert Ayler Dies." *Down Beat,* 7 Jan. 1971, p. 10.

1461. Albertson, Chris. "Blood, Sweat and Tears: With Miles Davis." *Down Beat,* 17 Sept. 1970, p. 12.

1462. ———. "Cannonbass the Communicator." *Down Beat,* 8 Jan. 1970, pp. 12-13.

1463. ———. "Charles McPherson: Ornithologist." *Down Beat,* 16 May 1968, pp. 19-20.

1464. ———. "Irene Reid: I've Been There All the Time." *Down Beat,* 12 Nov. 1970, p. 15.

1465. Alletti, V. "Red Roses from Laura for Miles."
      Rolling Stone, 16 Apr. 1970, p. 20.

1466. Anderson, A. "Three Kids Making It with Jazz: Craig
      Hundley Trio." *Life*, 20 Nov. 1968, p. 75.

1467. Anderson, Lee J. "The Musings of Miles." *Saturday
      Review*, 11 Oct. 1958, pp. 58-66.

      Tells how Miles Davis came to play the trumpet and
      jazz, and comments on his personality and music. Also
      included are some of Davis' comments about other jazz
      musicians.

1468. Atkins, R. "John Coltrane and Dizzy Gillespie in
      Britain." *Jazz Monthly* 13, no. 2 (Feb. 1967): 11-12.

1469. Avakian, George. "A Gentle Gentleman of a Man." *Jazz*,
      no. 10 (Oct. 1964): 14.

      On Eric Dolphy.

1470. "Ayler, Coleman Quartets Play for Trane Funeral."
      Melody Maker, Aug. 1967, p. 3.

1471. "Band of the Year: Stan Kenton." *Metronome*, Jan. 1947,
      pp. 17-19, 44-46.

1472. Baraka, Imamu Amiri. "The Ban on Black Music." *Black
      World*, July 1971, pp. 4-11.

1473. Barber, Rowland. "The Ranking Genius of Jazz." *Compact*,
      Mar. 1963, pp. 25-26, 116-20.

1474. "Beat Me Daddy, Twenty-Seven to the Bar." *Time*, 26 May
      1967, pp. 76-77.

1475. Bennett, Richard Rodney. "Techniques of the Jazz
      Singer." *Music and Musicians* 20, no. 6 (Feb. 1972):
      30-35.

1476. Berendt, Joachim E. "Free Jazz der neue Jazz 60er
      Jahre." *Melos* 24, no. 10 (1967): 343-52.

1477. ————. "John Lewis--Konig des Coll Jazz." *Melos* 22,
      no. 12 (Dec. 1955): pp. 348-50.

1478. Berger, D. "John Coltrane." *Jazz Hot* 23, no. 8 (Aug.
      1967): 5.

1479.   ————, and A. Corneau. "Free 66." *Jazz Hot* 22, nos.
        7-8 (July-Aug. 1966): 17-27.

1480.   "Best on Wax." *Down Beat*, 23 Mar. 1951, p. 7.

        On Miles Davis.

1481.   Bianco, F. "Trionfo di Davis ad Antibes." *Musical
        Jazz*, Sept. 1963, pp. 17-19.

1482.   "Billy Shearing Opener Hits Jackpot." *Down Beat*,
        20 Oct. 1950, pp. 1, 19.

1483.   Black, Edwin. "Ramsey's Golden Touch." *Down Beat*,
        14 May 1970, p. 18.

1484.   "Blindfold Test." *Down Beat*, 13 June 1968, p. 34.

        On Miles Davis.

1485.   "Blindness Is No Handicap." *Ebony*, Aug. 1952, p. 67.

        On the musical life of Art Tatum.

1486.   Blume, August. "An Interview with John Coltrane."
        Jazz Review 2, no. 7 (1955): 25.

1487.   "Bodyguard for Miles Davis." *Melody Maker*, 27 Aug.
        1960, p. 1.

1488.   Bolognani, M. "John Coltrane: Sensibilitia o transtor-
        misco." *Musical Jazz*, Nov. 1967, pp. 37-38.

1489.   Bolton, Robert. "Clifford Brown." *Jazz Journal* 22,
        no. 5 (May 1969): 6-11.

1490.   Bourne, Mike. "Defining Black Music." *Down Beat*,
        18 Sept. 1969, pp. 14-15.

        An interview with David Baker.

1491.   ————. "George Duke: The Whole Gamut." *Down Beat*,
        28 Oct. 1971, pp. 14, 35.

1492.   ————. "Les McCann: An Appreciation." *Down Beat*,
        15 Oct. 1970, pp. 13, 37.

1493.   ————. "Rahsaan Roland Kirk: Heavy Vibrations."
        Down Beat, 1 Oct. 1970, pp. 13, 30.

1494. ————. "Youthful Time." *Down Beat*, 18 Mar. 1971,
       pp. 18-19.

       An interview with Chico Hamilton.

1495. Bowers, F. "Making a Lady of Jazz." *House and Garden*,
       Apr. 1967, p. 24.

1496. "Break Color Line: WBBM Signs Lurlean Hunter to Live
       Show." *Billboard*, 3 Aug. 1963, pp. 39-40.

1497. Bright, George. "Getting Into It--Grachan Moncur III."
       Down Beat, 28 Jan. 1965, pp. 14-15.

1498. Brown, D. "Record Review: Coltrane's Legacy." *Coda*
       2 (1971): 16.

1499. Brubeck, Dave. "Jazz Evolvement as Art Form." *Down
       Beat*, 27 Jan. 1950, p. 2.

1500. "Buck Clayton on 'Crow Jim' in Jazz." *Variety*, 21 Aug.
       1963, p. 45.

1501. Buin, Y. "Coltrane ou la mise à mort." *Jazz Hot* 23,
       no. 5 (May 1967): 14-17.

1502. Burns, J. "Miles Davis: The Early Years." *Jazz Journal*
       23, no. 1 (Jan. 1970): 2-4.

1503. Burks, J. "Miles a Lot of Different Bitches." *Rolling
       Stone*, 9 July 1970, p. 15.

1504. Byrd, Donald. "The Meaning of Black Music." *Black
       Scholar* 3, no. 10 (Summer 1972): 28-31.

1505. Calloway, Cab. "Is Dope Killing Our Musicians?"
       Ebony, Feb. 1951, pp. 22-28.

1506. "Carmen McRae: New Singer Challenges Ella, Sarah, for
       Jazz Supremacy." *Ebony*, Feb. 1956, pp. 67-70.

1507. Carno, Zita. "Art Blakey." *Jazz Review* 3, no. 1 (Jan.
       1959): 6-11.

       A musical analysis of his style; gives several
       examples.

1508. ————. "The Style of John Coltrane." *Jazz Review* 2,

no. 9 (Oct. 1959): 16-22; no. 10 (Nov. 1959): 13-18.

Includes numerous examples of Coltrane's style of 1959-1960. Among the examples are transcriptions of "Moment's Notice," "Bass Blues," "Blue Train," and "Locomotion." Both articles are excellent.

1509. "Caught in the Act." *Down Beat*, 6 Aug. 1959, p. 14. John Coltrane.

1510. "Caught in the Act." *Down Beat*, 6 July 1961, p. 42. Miles Davis.

1511. "Caught in the Act." *Down Beat*, 2 Aug. 1962, p. 31. Miles Davis.

1512. "Caught in the Act." *Down Beat*, 23 July 1970, p. 28. Miles Davis.

1513. "Caught in the Act." *Melody Maker*, 8 May 1971, p. 32. Miles Davis.

1514. "Charge Dismissed." *Down Beat*, 2 Nov. 1959, p. 11. Miles Davis.

1515. "Chronique des disques: John Coltrane." *Jazz Hot* 28, nos. 7-8 (July-Aug. 1972): 29.

1516. "Cinq personnages en quête de 'Trane." *Jazz Hot* 18, no. 1 (Jan. 1962): 16-21.

1517. "Clapton and Bruce to Join Miles!" *Melody Maker*, 6 June 1970, n.p.

1518. Clar, Mimi. "Erroll Garner." *Jazz Review* 2, no. 1 (Jan. 1959): 6-11.

1519. ————. "The Negro Church: Its Influence on Modern Jazz." *Jazz Review* 1, no. 1 (Nov. 1958): 16-18; 2, no. 1 (Jan. 1959): 6-11, 22-26; 2, no. 2 (Feb. 1959): 28-30.

An excellent series of articles which discusses specific Black church influences, e.g., melody and harmony, on modern jazz.

1520. Coleman, R. "Coltrane." *Melody Maker*, 11 July 1964, p. 6.

1521. Coltrane, John. "Coltrane on Coltrane." *Down Beat*, 29 Sept. 1960, pp. 26-27.

1522. "Coltrane: Anti-Jazz or the Wave of the Future?" *Melody Maker*, 28 Sept. 1963, p. 11.

1523. "Coltrane, Dead of a Liver Ailment." *Billboard*, 29 July 1967, p. 12.

1524. "Coltrane Dies in New York." *Melody Maker*, 22 July 1967, p. 1.

1525. "Concertizing Kenton." *Newsweek*, 1 Mar. 1948, p. 74.

1526. Cooke, Jack. "Eric Dolphy." *Jazz Monthly* 12, no. 1 (Jan. 1965): 25-40.

1527. Cook, J. "The Avant-Garde." *Jazz Monthly* 12, no. 6 (June 1966): 2-9.

1528. ————. "Miles Davis and Archie." *Jazz Monthly* 13, no. 12 (Dec. 1967): 16.

1529. ————. "Late Trane." *Jazz Monthly* 16, no. 1 (Jan. 1970): 2-6.

1530. Cooper, R. "Twenty Years Back." *Jazz Journal* 21, no. 5 (May 1968): 3-4.

1531. Cordle, O. "The Soprano Saxophone: From Bechet to Coltrane to Shorter." *Down Beat*, 20 July 1972, pp. 14-15.

1532. Coryell, Larry. "Larry Coryell Speaks on the Modern Electric Eclecticism." *Down Beat*, 30 Jan. 1975, n.p.

    On the use of electronic experimentation with gadgets and gimmicks.

1533. Coss, Bill. "John Lewis and the Orchestra." *Down Beat*, 14 Feb. 1963, p. 20.

1534. Coterrell, R. "Interlude: Miles Davis with Hank Mobley." *Jazz Monthly* 13, no. 10 (Oct. 1967): 3-4.

1535. Cox, Pat. "Tony Williams: An Interview Scenario." *Down Beat*, 28 May 1970, pp. 14-15, 33.

1536. Crawford, M. "Miles and Gil--Portrait of a Friend-ship." *Down Beat*, 16 Feb. 1961, pp. 18-19.

1537. Crawford, Marc. "Miles Davis: Evil Genius of Jazz." *Ebony*, Jan. 1961, pp. 69-72.

1538. Curon, Wystan. "The Jazz Avant-Garde." *Comment*, Apr. 1965, pp. 41-43.

1539. Cuscuna, Michael. "Doing It Right: Buddy Guy." *Down Beat*, 31 Oct. 1968, p. 19.

1540. ————. "Herbie Hancock's Declaration of Independence." *Down Beat*, 1 May 1969, pp. 18, 42.

1541. Dahlgreen, Marvin. "Drums in Perspective: The Styles and How They Developed." *Down Beat*, 3 Mar. 1960, pp. 21-23.

1542. ————. "Evolution of the Drum Solo." *Down Beat*, 30 Mar. 1961, pp. 22-26.

1543. Dameron, Tadd. "The Case for Modern Music." *Record Changer*, Feb. 1948, pp. 5, 16.

1544. Dance, Helen. "Down Patti." *Down Beat*, 19 Oct. 1967, pp. 23-24.

1545. Delmore, M. "Coltrane 1963: Vers la composition." *Jazz Hot* 19, no. 12 (Dec. 1963): 10-11.

1546. Delmoro, M. "John Coltrane est mort." *Jazz Hot* 23, no. 8 (Aug. 1967): 15-16.

1547. DeMichael, Don. "Jackson of the MJQ." *Down Beat*, 30 Mar. 1961, pp. 22-26.

1548. ————. "John Coltrane and Eric Dolphy Answer the Jazz Critics." *Down Beat*, 12 Apr. 1962, pp. 20-30.

1549. ————. "Miles Davis." *Rolling Stone*, Dec. 1969, pp. 22-26.

A historical overview of Miles Davis.

1550. ————. "The Varied Peripeties of Roy Haynes, or They Call Him Snap, Crackle." *Down Beat*, 15 Dec. 1966, pp. 18-19, 44.

1551. Dews, Angela. "Alice Coltrane." *Essence*, Dec. 1971, pp. 42-43.

A look into the life of Alice Coltrane, musician and mother.

1552. Dixon, B. "Contemporary Jazz: An Assessment." *Jazz and Pop* 6, no. 11 (Nov. 1967): 31-32.

1553. "Doctor Jazz." *Newsweek*, 27 Sept. 1965, p. 94.

1554. "Dolphins on a Wave: C. Lloyd, Prophet of New Wave Jazz." *Time*, 3 Feb. 1967, p. 38.

1555. Dorham, Kenny. "No Bells, No Beads." *Down Beat*, 19 Sept. 1968, p. 20.

1556. "Drummers Should Be Musicians, Too: Tiny Kahn." *Down Beat*, 7 Apr. 1950, p. 3.

1557. Durham, Mark. "Frank Foster's Big Band Quest." *Down Beat*, 9 Dec. 1971, pp. 16, 31.

1558. Ebert, Alan. "Still Sassy." *Essence*, Oct. 1974, pp. 42, 75-76.

An excellent article on the life and music of Sarah Vaughan; offers special insights into her experiences from a domestic point of view and as a Black female jazz artist.

1559. Edey, Mait. "Tatum: The Last Years." *Jazz Review* 3, no. 7 (Aug. 1960): 4-6.

1560. "Ella Fitzgerald: Her Vocal Versatility Continues to Amaze Musicians." *Ebony*, May 1949, pp. 45-46.

1561. Ellis, Don. "Henry (Red) Allen Is the Most Avant-Garde Trumpet Player in New York City." *Down Beat*, 28 Jan. 1965, p. 13.

1562. Eniss, J. "Miles Smiles." *Melody Maker*, 9 Jan. 1971, pp. 16-17.

1563. "Eric Joins Miles' New Rock Group." *Rolling Stone*, 25 June 1970, p. 10.

1564. "Fatha Hines Settles Down." *Ebony*, Oct. 1957, pp. 63-66.

1565. Feather, Leonard. "Ailing Jazz Has a New Doctor."
       Variety, 3 Jan. 1968, p. 153.

1566. ———. "Archie Shepp: Some of My Best Friends Are
       White." *Melody Maker*, 30 Apr. 1966, p. 6.

1567. ———. "Blindfold Test." *Down Beat*, 18 June 1964,
       p. 31.

       On Miles Davis.

1568. ———. "Coltrane, Does It Not Mean a Thing, If It
       Ain't Got That Swing?" *Melody Maker*, 16 Apr. 1966,
       p. 6.

1569. ———. "Erroll Garner: At the Summit." *Down Beat*,
       25 June 1970, pp. 12-13, 31.

1570. ———. "For Coltrane the Time Is Now." *Melody Maker*,
       19 Dec. 1964, p. 10.

1571. ———. "Giants of Jazz: The Clarinetists." *International Musician* 61, no. 1 (Jan. 1963): 14-15.

1572. ———. "Honest John." *Down Beat*, 19 Feb. 1959, p. 39.

1573. ———. "Jazz: A List of Artists Pushed Out and List
       of Those Now In with Analysis." *Show*, Oct. 1964,
       p. 58.

1574. ———. "Modern Jazz Conquers Japan." *Ebony*, Oct.
       1964, pp. 127, 128, 130-32, 134.

1575. ———. "The New Life of Ray Brown." *Down Beat*,
       Mar. 1967, pp. 24-26.

1576. ———. "The Rebirth of Gene Ammons." *Down Beat*,
       25 June 1970, pp. 12-13, 31.

       Gene Ammons: his past, present, and future music.

1577. ———. "Ronnell Bright! The Complete Accompanist."
       Down Beat, 5 Feb. 1970, pp. 17-18.

1578. ———. "Vocal Combos, Jazz, Rock'n Rollers, Folkniks."
       Show, Nov. 1964, p. 85.

1579. Fiofori, Tam. "Sun Ra's Space Odyssey." *Down Beat*,
       14 May 1970, pp. 14-17.

1580. ————. "Re-Entry: The New Orbit of Sonny Rollins."
       Down Beat, 14 Oct. 1971, pp. 14-15, 39.

1581. Flender, H. "A Comment on Social Protest Jazz."
       Variety, 4 Jan. 1967, p. 170.

1582. Fox, H. "Chasm Between Jazz and Popular Music Nar-
       rows." *Billboard*, 13 Aug. 1966, p. 80.

1583. Frost, J. "Miles Davis." *Metronome*, May 1957, p. 27.

1584. Gallagher, Joe. "Jazz Can Be Sold." *Down Beat*, 19 Feb.
       1970, p. 13.

       Lee Morgan's music today.

1585. Gardner, Barbara. "The Electrified Sonny Stitt." *Down
       Beat*, 6 Oct. 1966, pp. 16-17.

1586. ————. "The Enigma of Miles Davis." *Down Beat*, 7 Jan.
       1960, pp. 20-23.

1587. ————. "Harry Sweets Edison--In Focus." *Down Beat*,
       28 Jan. 1965, pp. 20-21.

1588. ————. "Jazzman of the Year: John Coltrane." *Down
       Beat*, Special Issue 1962, pp. 66-69.

1589. Garland, Phyl. "The Many Bags of Oliver Nelson."
       Ebony, Nov. 1968, pp. 108-12.

       A complimentary article on the arranger, composer,
       conductor, and virtuoso reedman. Tells how and where
       he lives, his income, and with whom he has worked.
       Stan Kenton and Henry Mancini praised him for his
       ability to compose symphonies, rock 'n roll, blues,
       baroque fugues, and electronic music.

1590. ————. "Requiem for Trane." *Ebony*, Nov. 1967, pp. 66-
       70, 72.

1591. Garriques, C.J. "Recapturing the Magic of Miles."
       San Francisco Examiner, 11 Oct. 1959.

1592. Gaspard, J.J. "Miles Davis." *Musica* 67, no. 10 (Oct.
       1959): 9.

1593. Gerber, A. "Giants of Jazz." *International Musician*
       45, no. 1 (Jan. 1967): 9.

1594. ————. "Huit faces de Coltrane." *Jazz* 11, no. 6
       (June 1972): 25-31.

1595. Gibson, M. "John Coltrane: The Formative Years."
       Jazz Journal 13, no. 6 (June 1960): 9-10.

1596. ————. "Miles Davis: An Appreciation." *Jazz Journal*
       12, no. 6 (June 1959): 7-8.

1597. Gitler, Ira. "Dexter Drops In." *Down Beat*, 29 May
       1969, p. 15.

1598. ————. "The Good Book." *Down Beat*, 7 Mar. 1968,
       pp. 23-24.

       The life and music of Booker Ervin.

1599. ————. "Jimmy Owens! Going Up." *Down Beat*, 25 Jan.
       1968, pp. 20-21.

       Jimmy Owens' life and musical style.

1600. ————. "Playing the Truth: Elvin Jones." *Down Beat*,
       2 Oct. 1969, pp. 12-13, 30.

       An interview with Elvin Jones.

1601. ————. "Record Reviews: Milt Jackson, Sonny Stitt."
       Down Beat, 30 July 1964, pp. 29-30.

1602. ————. "Sonny Rollins: Music's an Open Sky." *Down
       Beat*, 29 May 1969, pp. 18-19.

1603. ————. "Thad's Thing." *Down Beat*, 22 Feb. 1968,
       pp. 18-19, 39.

       The life and music of Thad Jones.

1604. ————. "Trane on the Track." *Down Beat*, 16 Oct. 1958,
       pp. 16-17.

1605. Goddet, L. "La chronique des disques: Bitches Brew."
       Jazz Hot 263, no. 2 (Summer 1970): 42.

1606. Gonda, Janos. "Problems of Tonality and Function in
       Modern Jazz Improvisation." *Jazzforschung* 3-4 (1971-
       1973): 114-205.

1607. Goodman, J. "Looking for the Black Message." *News-
       leader*, 1 Jan. 1968, pp. 26-28.

1608. Gray, Gene. "Bernard Purdie: Soul Beat Marvin." *Down Beat*, 21 Jan. 1971, pp. 18, 37.

His background, musical career, and techniques.

1609. Griggs, Georgia. "Randy Weston in Africa." *Down Beat*, 13 July 1967, pp. 16-17, 38.

1610. Grigson, L. "Directions in Modern Jazz." *Jazz Monthly* 6, no. 4 (Sept. 1961): 17.

1611. Gros-Claude, P. "Miles Davis à Wright." *Jazz* 182, no. 10 (Oct. 1970): 12-13.

1612. Gross, M. "Jazz Shipping New Beat as 'Potpourri.'" *Billboard*, 11 May 1968, p. 1.

1613. Hadlock, Dick. "Sonny Rollins' Freedom Suite." *Jazz Review* 2, no. 4 (May 1959): 10-12.

A musical analysis, including examples of the Freedom Suite.

1614. Harris, P. "Nothing But BOP? 'Stupid' Says Miles." *Down Beat*, 27 Jan. 1950, pp. 18-19.

1615. Harrison, Max. "Gil Evans and Miles Davis: Part II." *Jazz Monthly* 5, no. 2 (Feb. 1960): 10-12.

1616. ————. "Looking Back on the Modern Jazz Quartet." *The Art of Jazz*. Edited by Martin T. Williams. New York: Oxford University Press, 1959, pp. 219-31.

1617. ————, and Michael James. "A Debate on Lee Konitz." *Jazz Review* 3, no. 6 (July 1969): 10-13.

1618. Hart, Howard. "Elvin Jones: A Different Drummer." *Down Beat*, 20 Mar. 1969, pp. 20-21.

1619. Harvey, E. "Social Change and the Jazz Musician." *Social Forces* 55, no. 1 (Sept. 1976): 34-42.

1620. Hasse, John. "Roland Hanna: Inside Insight." *Down Beat*, 15 Oct. 1970, pp. 16-17, 34.

1621. Heckman, Don. "After Coltrane." *Down Beat*, 9 Mar. 1967, pp. 18-19, 40.

Jimmy Garrison discusses his musical career with and after John Coltrane.

1622. ————. "Aiming High--The Jazz Masters." *American Record Guide*, May 1967, p. 828.

1623. ————. "Caught in the Act: Gunther Schuller." *Down Beat*, 9 May 1963, p. 34.

1624. ————. "Gil Evans on His Own." *Jazz Review* 3, no. 3 (Mar.-Apr. 1960): 14-18.

       The musical career of composer-arranger Gil Evans.

1625. ————. "Jazz Trombone--Five Views." *Down Beat*, 28 Jan. 1965, pp. 17-19.

1626. ————. "The New Jazz: A Matter of Doing." *Down Beat*, 9 Feb. 1967, pp. 24-25.

1627. ————. "Ron Carter." *Down Beat*, 9 Apr. 1964, pp. 18-19.

1628. ————. "The Value of Eric Dolphy." *Down Beat*, 8 Oct. 1964, p. 17.

1629. Hendrie, A. "Tempo, Technique, and the Ballad." *Jazz Monthly* 13, no. 4 (Apr. 1967): 8-9.

1630. Hennessy, Mike. "Charles Mingus: Changed Man?" *Down Beat*, 13 May 1971, pp. 14, 31.

1631. ————. "Cherry's Catholicity." *Down Beat*, 28 July 1966, pp. 14-15.

1632. ————. "Coltrane: Dropping the Ball and Chain from Jazz." *Melody Maker*, 14 Aug. 1965, p. 6.

1633. ————. "Don Byas! Emphatic Expatriate." *Down Beat*, 27 July 1967, pp. 23, 26.

       Information on his European musical career.

1634. ————. "Forty-Seven Minutes of Magnificent Coltrane." *Melody Maker*, 31 July 1965, p. 8.

1635. ————. "Organic Groove." *Down Beat*, 5 Feb. 1970, pp. 16, 39.

       Life and musical career of Richard "Groove" Holmes.

1636. Hentoff, Nat. "An Afternoon with Miles Davis." *Jazz Review* 1, no. 2 (Dec. 1958): 9-13.

1637. ————. "Caught in the Act." *Down Beat*, 6 Oct. 1954, p. 32.

1638. ————. "Counterpoint." *Down Beat*, 30 Dec. 1953, p. 8.

1639. ————. "Doctor Digs Jazz." *Holiday*, May 1965, pp. 109-10.

1640. ————. "Introducing Ray Bryant." *Jazz Review* 3, no. 3 (Mar.-Apr. 1960): 18-20.

1641. ————. "Jazz Reviews: Modern Jazz Quartet." *Down Beat*, 4 Nov. 1953, p. 15.

1642. ————. "Jazz Revolution." *Reporter*, 20 May 1965, p. 42.

1643. ————. "John Coltrane: Challenge Without End." *International Musician* 51, no. 3 (Mar. 1962): 12-13.

1644. ————. "John Lewis." *Down Beat*, 20 Feb. 1957, pp. 15-16.

1645. ————. "John Lewis: Success with Integrity." *International Musician* 50, no. 6 (June 1961): 16-17.

1646. ————. "The Modern Jazz Quartet." *High Fidelity*, Mar. 1955, pp. 36-38.

1647. ————. "New Directions in Jazz." *International Musician* 59, no. 9 (Sept. 1960): 14, 35.

1648. ————. "New Jazz, Black, Angry and Hard to Understand." *New York Times Magazine*, 25 Dec. 1966, pp. 10-11, 36-39.

1649. ————. "The Post-Bop Legitimacy of Modern Jazz." *Reporter* 18 (6 Feb. 1958): 39.

1650. ————. "The Third Stream." *International Musician* 60, no. 10 (Oct. 1961): 24-25.

1651. ————. "The Truth Comes Marching In." *Down Beat*, 17 Nov. 1966, pp. 16-18, 40.

An interview with Albert and Don Ayler.

1652. "Here's My Theory." *Melody Maker*, 1 Oct. 1960, p. 3.

Miles Davis.

1653. Hess, J.B., et al. "Miles Davis: La volonté de puissance."
       Jazz Magazine, Mar. 1971, pp. 28-33.

1654. Hickock, Larry. "No Ordinary Joe--Joe Farrell." *Down
       Beat*, 28 Mar. 1974, pp. 17-19.

       Farrell discusses the growing use of the soprano
       saxophone, his career, and musical influences.

1655. "Hierarchy of the Jazz Anarchy: Symposium." *Esquire*,
       Sept. 1965, pp. 123-25.

1656. Hodes, Art. "Looking at Red." *Down Beat*, 10 Aug. 1967,
       pp. 18-19, 40.

       Contains historical information on the musical career
       of Theodore (Red) Saunders.

1657. Hoefer, George. "Early J.J." *Down Beat*, 28 Jan. 1965,
       pp. 16, 33.

1658. ————. "Early Miles." *Down Beat*, 6 Sept. 1967,
       pp. 16-19.

       The life and music of Miles Davis to 1948.

1659. Holly, Ha. "Anthony Band Solid Hit in First West Coast
       Date." *Down Beat*, 17 Nov. 1950, p. 8.

1660. Hundley, C. "Jazz Is My Bag!" *Seventeen*, Jan. 1960,
       p. 40.

1661. Hunt, D.C. "Coleman, Coltrane and Shepp: The Need for
       an Educated Audience." *Jazz and Pop*, no. 10 (Oct.
       1968): 18-21.

1662. Idestram-Almquist, D. "In Memoriam." *Orkester Journal-
       en*, Sept. 1967, pp. 6-7.

       John Coltrane.

1663. ————. "Miles Davis." *Orkester Journalen*, Jan. 1964,
       pp. 12-13.

1664. "Impressions of a John Coltrane Concert." *Variety*,
       16 Mar. 1968, p. 65.

1665. "Impulse, Mrs. Coltrane in Legacy Agreement." *Down
       Beat*, 5 Sept. 1968, p. 13.

1666. "In Tribute: Eric Dolphy 1928-1964." *Down Beat*, 27 Aug. 1964, p. 10.

1667. Ioakmidis, D. "Sonny Rollins et John Coltrane." *Jazz Hot* 18, no. 12 (Dec. 1962): 30-34.

1668. ————. "Sonny Rollins et John Coltrane en parallels." *Jazz Hot* (Sept. 1967): 24-27.

1669. "Is Miles Quitting?" *Melody Maker*, 31 July 1971, p. 4.

1670. James, Michael. "New Ebb, Old Flow." *Jazz Monthly* 14, no. 6 (June 1968): 7-8.

1671. Jasper, Bobby. "Elvin Jones and Philly Joe Jones." *Jazz Review* 2, no. 2 (Feb. 1959): 6-9.

1672. "Jazz Action Movement Blends Jazz with Rock." *Billboard*, 27 July 1968, p. 16.

1673. "Jazz and Race." *Commonweal* 81, no. 1 (8 Jan. 1965): 482-84.

1674. "Jazz and Revolutionary Black Nationalism." *Jazz* 5, no. 7 (1966): 34.

1675. "Jazz and the Liberation of Worship." *Christian Century* 86, no. 18 (16 Apr. 1969): 499.

1676. "Jazz at Tanglewood." *Record Changer*, July-Aug. 1950, pp. 31, 46, 47.

1677. "Jazz Goes to Church." *Ebony*, Apr. 1966, pp. 76-80; July 1968, p. 16.

1678. "Jazz Trumpeter M. Davis Reported in Satisfactory Condition on Oct. 21 After Breaking Both His Legs in Auto Accident in NYC." *New York Times*, Oct. 22, 1966.

1679. Jepsen, Jorgen Grunnet. "John Lewis Diskografi." *Orkester Journalen*, Jan. 1959, p. 39.

1680. Jewell, D. "Don't Give Me That Jazz." *Twentieth Century* 174, no. 1028 (Winter 1966): 31-36.

1681. "John Coltrane." *Jazz and Pop* (Sept. 1967): 26.

1682. "John Coltrane, 1926-1967, Saxophonist." *British Book Year*, 1968, p. 588.

1683. "John Coltrane and the Jazz Revolution: The Case of Albert Ayler." *Jazz* 1, no. 2 (1960): 24-25.

1684. "John Coltrane Dies." *Down Beat*, 24 Aug. 1967, pp. 12-13.

   On the life and music of John Coltrane.

1685. "John Coltrane! In Memoriam." *Down Beat*, 7 Sept. 1967, pp. 15-17.

   Contains the reactions of Coltrane's friends to his death.

1686. "John Lewis, Music Master." *Ebony*, Mar. 1960, pp. 110-14.

1687. Johnson, Brooks. "Herbie Hancock: Into His Own Thing." *Down Beat*, 21 Jan. 1971, pp. 14-15, 34.

1688. ————. "Toms and Tomming: A Contemporary Report." *Down Beat*, 16 June 1966, p. 24.

1689. Jones, John. "Chick Corea." *Down Beat*, 27 Mar. 1974, pp. 15-18.

   Corea discusses his theories and ideas on music, his piano playing with Miles Davis, his influences, and his involvement in record production.

1690. Jones, LeRoi. "A Coltrane Trilogy." *Metro* 78, no. 12 (Dec. 1961): 34-36.

1691. ————. "Apple Cores: A Few Notes on Avant-Garde." *Down Beat*, 26 Jan. 1967, p. 10.

1692. ————. "Caught in the Act: John Coltrane-Cecil Taylor-Art Blakey." *Down Beat*, 27 Feb. 1964, p. 34.

1693. ————. "Introducing Wayne Shorter." *Jazz Review* 2, no. 10 (Nov. 1959): 22-25.

   Life, music, and musical influences of Wayne Shorter.

1694. ————. "Jazz and the White Critic: A Provocative Essay on the Situation of Jazz Criticism." *Down Beat*, 15 Aug. 1963, pp. 16-17.

1695. ————. "Voice from the Avant-Garde: Archie Shepp." *Down Beat*, 14 Jan. 1965.

1696. Jones, M. "It May Be What Jazz Needs, the Psychedelic Touch." *Melody Maker*, 9 Sept. 1967, p. 6.

1697. ————. "Miles Is Taking a Chance." *Melody Maker*, 8 Oct. 1960, pp. 8-9.

1698. Jones, Shelby. "Bobby Bryant's Hattiesburg Happenings." *Down Beat*, 17 Sept. 1970, pp. 16-17.

1699. "Judge Finds Miles Not Guilty." *Melody Maker*, 24 Oct. 1959, p. 1.

1700. "Just Punch a Button and Blow Wind: A Talk with Ornette Coleman." *Encounter* 25, no. 11 (Nov. 1965): 39-42.

1701. Kart, Larry. "The Coltrane Legacy." *Down Beat*, 13 May 1971, p. 22.

1702. ————. "Miles Davis: Caught in the Act." *Down Beat*, 7 Aug. 1969, p. 28.

1703. Kennard, D. "It Do Mean a Thing (Avant-Garde)." *Jazz Journal* 20, no. 6 (June 1967): 18-19.

1704. Kenton, Stan. "Sure, I Helped to Wreck the Dance Biz, Says Kenton." *Down Beat*, 19 May 1950, p. 1.

1705. "Kenton Chances Blasting a Path to Prostration." *Down Beat*, 2 June 1948, p. 10.

1706. "Kenton Grabs Early Poll Lead." *Down Beat*, 1 Dec. 1950, pp. 1, 19.

1707. "Kenton's Music 'Greatest Ever.'" *Down Beat*, 24 Mar. 1950, pp. 1, 16, 18.

1708. "Kenton Quits Music Business." *Down Beat*, 14 Jan. 1949, p. 1.

1709. "Kenton Readies Ork for Concert Tour." *Down Beat*, 4 Nov. 1949, p. 2.

1710. "Kenton, Shearing Poll Winners: All-Star Band Gets New Faces." *Down Beat*, 29 Dec. 1950, pp. 1, 14-15.

1711. "Kenton Unveils Ork at Preview Concert." *Down Beat*,
       Mar. 1950, p. 5.

1712. "Kenton Winds Up 1st 'Innovations' Tour." *Down Beat*,
       14 July 1950, p. 5.

1713. King, B. "Introducing the High-Life." *Jazz Monthly*
       12, no. 7 (July 1966): 3-8.

1714. Kingston, M. "Form in Jazz, If Any." *Jazz Journal* 20,
       no. 3 (Mar. 1967): 6-7.

1715. Kinsolving, L. "Demurrer on Jazzy Lord's Suppers."
       Christian Century, 22 July 1966, pp. 803-4.

1716. Klee, Joe H. "Horace Silver's United States of Mine."
       Down Beat, 1 Apr. 1971, pp. 16-17.

1717. ————. "Leon Thomas: Avant-Garde with Roots." *Down
       Beat*, 10 Dec. 1970, pp. 18-19.

1718. Knox, K. "Sounds from the Avant-Garde: The Aesthetic
       Problem." *Jazz Monthly* 12, no. 2 (Feb. 1967): 10-12.

1719. Koechlin, P. "Coltrane à Paris." *Jazz Hot* 21, no. 9
       (Sept. 1965): 10.

1720. ————. "L'Ambre de Coltrane sous le soleil de Parker."
       Jazz Hot 20, no. 1 (Jan. 1964): 10.

1721. ————. "Miles Davis." *Musica* 126, no. 9 (Sept. 1964):
       60-61.

1722. Kofsky, Frank. "The Avant-Garde Revolution: Origins
       and Directions." *Jazz* 5, no. 1 (1966): 14-19.

1723. ————. "Brief Interview with John Coltrane." *Jazz
       and Pop* 6, no. 9 (Sept. 1967): 23-31.

1724. ————. "Interview with John Coltrane." *Black National-
       ism and the Revolution in Music*. New York: Path-
       finder, 1966, pp. 224-43.

1725. ————. "John Coltrane." *Jazz and Pop* 7, no. 3 (Mar.
       1968): 22-23.

1726. Kolodin, I. "Miles Ahead or Miles' Head?" *Saturday
       Review*, 12 Sept. 1959, pp. 60-61.

1727. Kopulos, Gordon. "John Coltrane: Retrospective Perspective." *Down Beat*, 22 July 1971, pp. 14-15, 40.

1728. ———. "Needed Now: Sonny Rollins." *Down Beat*, 24 July 1971, pp. 12-13, 30.

1729. Korall, Burt. "Background Music." *Down Beat*, 7 Mar. 1968, p. 14.

1730. ———. "The Davis Phenomenon." *Saturday Review*, 10 Feb. 1968, pp. 50-51.

1731. ———. "I've Talked Enough: Interview with Sonny Rollins, John Coltrane and Ornette Coleman." *Melody Maker*, 15 Sept. 1962, pp. 8-9.

1732. ———. "The Roots of the Ducky." *Down Beat*, 13 July 1967, pp. 21-22.

    The life and musical career of Sonny Greer.

1733. Kosner, Edward. "Miles Davis Benefit: 'My Present to Africa.'" *New York Post*, 7 May 1961, p. 7.

1734. Kunstadt, Len. "Some Early West Coast Jazz History." *Record Research* 3, no. 3 (July 1964): 14-17.

1735. Laird, P. "Science and Twentieth Century Music." *Twentieth Century* 147, no. 12 (Nov. 1960): 457-67.

1736. Lee, Robert Charles. "The Afro-American Foundations of the Jazz Idiom." *Jazz Forum* 6, no. 15 (1972): 84-86.

1737. Lees, Gene. "In Walked Ray." *Down Beat*, 31 Aug. 1961, pp. 18-20.

1738. ———. "Jazz Composer: A Study in Symbiosis." *High Fidelity*, Aug. 1963, pp. 55-79.

1739. ———. "L'Homme Coltrane." *Jazz Magazine*, Nov. 1961, pp. 34-35.

1740. ———. "View of the Third Stream." *Down Beat*, 13 Feb. 1964, pp. 16-17.

1741. Lehman, G. "Coast Group Set Up to Keep Jazz Alive." *Billboard*, 18 May 1968, p. 20.

1742. Lewis, John. "The Golden Age/Time Future." *Esquire*, Jan. 1959, pp. 112, 115.

1743. Lifton, Lloyde. "Miles Davis Solo on Godchild." *Down Beat*, 10 July 1969, p. 42.

1744. "Liturgy and Headlines: Jazz Masses." *America*, 21 Jan. 1967, p. 79.

1745. Litweiler, John. "A Man with an Idea." *Down Beat*, 5 Oct. 1967, pp. 23, 26, 41.

   A discussion of Richard Abrams, his music, and his philosophy.

1746. ————. "The Legacy of Albert Ayler." *Down Beat*, 1 Apr. 1971, pp. 14-15, 29.

1747. ————. "Lockjaw Davis: Time to Overhaul the Jazz Business Machine." *Melody Maker*, 6 May 1967, p. 6.

1748. ————. "Needs and Acts and Cecil Taylor in Wisconsin." *Down Beat*, 14 Oct. 1971, pp. 16-17, 40.

1749. ————. "Shepp: An Old Schoolmaster in a Brown Suit." *Down Beat*, 7 Nov. 1974, p. 11.

   Shepp discusses his views on Black blues, jazz artists, and African musical influences.

1750. Lorentz, D. "Listen Dammit!" *Jazz Report* 5, no. 5 (1967): 17-18.

1751. "Louis, Shearing on Same Bill Enrich Bop City Till." *Down Beat*, 7 Oct. 1949, p. 2.

1752. Lucraft, H. "Miles and the Band at the Bowl." *Melody Maker*, 25 July 1970, p. 14.

1753. Lyons, Ken. "Dollars and Sense." *Down Beat*, 8 May 1975, pp. 12-14.

   Milt Jackson discusses his feelings on jazz and his belief that jazz has never been properly promoted.

1754. Lystedt, Lars. "Art Farmer: Ambivalent Expatriate." *Down Beat*, 19 Feb. 1970, pp. 18, 32.

1755. Lyttelton, H. "Miles Davis in England: Boor or Business-man?" *Metro* 77, no. 12 (Dec. 1960): 53.

1756. Madin, M. Arif. "The School of Jazz." *Jazz Review* 2, no. 1 (Jan. 1959): 17-19.

1757. Maremaa, Thomas. "Berklee Jazz: Black and Rootey." *Rolling Stone*, May 1971, pp. 16-17.

1758. Marne, Geoffrey. "The Modern Jazz Quartet." *International Musician* 62, no. 1 (Jan. 1964): 8-9, 39-40.

1759. Martin, Terry. "Blowing Out in Chicago." *Down Beat*, 6 Apr. 1967, pp. 20-21, 47.

   Life and music of Roscoe Mitchell.

1760. ————. "The Chicago Avant-Garde." *Jazz Monthly* 14, no. 3 (Mar. 1968): 12-18.

1761. Massaquoi, H.J. "Billy Mo: The Satchmo of Germany." *Ebony*, July 1967, pp. 68-73.

1762. Mathieu, Bill. "Milford Graves Speaks Words." *Down Beat*, 3 Nov. 1966, pp. 23, 44.

1763. McLarney, Bill. "Better Carter: The 'In' Singer." *Down Beat*, 28 July 1966, pp. 18-19, 39.

1764. ————. "Bill Harris: Acoustic Maverick." *Down Beat*, 27 June 1968, pp. 21-22.

   Bill Harris' musical career, style, and influences.

1765. ————. "Jazz: Art or Entertainment?" *Jazz* 6, no. 7 (July 1967): 25.

1766. ————. "Roy Brooks: Unsung Hero." *Down Beat*, 10 Aug. 1967, pp. 15-17.

1767. ————. "Telling It Like It Is." *Down Beat*, 18 May 1967, pp. 17-18, 42.

   An interview with Roland Kirk.

1768. ————. "Urge to Merge: The Harold Land-Bobby Hutcherson Quintet." *Down Beat*, 5 Feb. 1970, pp. 14-15.

1769. McMillan, Lewis, Jr. "Jo Jones: Percussion Patriarch." *Down Beat*, 18 Mar. 1971, pp. 16-17, 38.

1770. ———. "Kenny Burrell: Man with a Mission." *Down Beat*, 10 June 1971, pp. 12-13.

1771. ———. "Mary Lou Williams: First Lady of Jazz." *Down Beat*, 27 May 1971, pp. 16-17.

1772. McNamara, Helen. "Buddy Tate: Still Keeping Up." *Down Beat*, 29 Apr. 1971, pp. 16-17.

1773. ———. "Ed Thigpen: On the Move." *Down Beat*, Mar. 1967, pp. 18-19.

1774. McRae, B. "A. B. Basics: A Column for the Newcomer to Jazz." *Jazz Journal* 20, no. 1 (Jan. 1967): 11.

1775. ———. "John Coltrane--The Impulse Years." *Jazz* 10 (July 1971): 26.

1776. Meadows, Elliot. "About Time." *Down Beat*, 10 Dec. 1970, pp. 20, 34.

1777. ———. "Grady Tate: He'd Rather Sing." *Down Beat*, 13 May 1971, pp. 18, 29.

1778. ———. "Make Room for Billy Harper." *Down Beat*, 24 June 1971, pp. 16-17.

1779. ———. "Many-Sided Harold Mabern." *Down Beat*, 28 Oct. 1971, pp. 15, 36.

1780. ———. "Spotlight on Larry Ridley." *Down Beat*, 18 Feb. 1971, pp. 16-17.

1781. ———. "The World of Tommy Flanagan." *Down Beat*, 20 Oct. 1970, pp. 8, 37.

1782. Mehegan, John. "The ABC of the New Jazz." *Saturday Review*, 10 Nov. 1956, pp. 34-35.

1783. "Merci Miles!" *Jazz Magazine*, Dec. 1960, p. 22.

1784. Merriam, A.P., and R.W. Mack. "Jazz Community." *Social Forces* 38, no. 3 (Mar. 1960): 211-22.

1785. "Miles: Appraisal of Today's Jazz Scene." *Down Beat*, 2 Nov. 1955, pp. 13-14.

1786. "Miles and Leo." *Metronome*, July 1947, p. 19.

1787. "Miles and Miles of Trumpet Players." *Down Beat*,
       21 Sept. 1955, p. 33.

1788. "Miles an Manne." *Jazz Magazine* 154, no. 5 (May 1968):
       15.

1789. "Miles au Pion." *Jazz Magazine* 7, no. 7 (July 1961):
       15.

1790. "Miles and the Fifties." *Down Beat*, 2 July 1964,
       pp. 66-68.

1791. "Miles: A View from the Top." *Melody Maker*, 20 Apr.
       1968, p. 11.

1792. "Miles Back in Action." *Down Beat*, 30 Dec. 1965, p. 14.

1793. "Miles Davis." *International Musician* 59, no. 2 (Feb.
       1961): 20-21.

1794. "Miles Davis." *Melody Maker*, 14 Oct. 1967, p. 21.

1795. "Miles Davis." *Orkester Journalen* 26, no. 12 (Dec.
       1958): 10-11.

1796. "Miles Davis." *Rolling Stone*, 13 Dec. 1969, pp. 23-26.

1797. "Miles Davis Acquitted of Charges He Assaulted N.Y.C.
       Ptl." *New York Times*, 12 Jan. 1960, p. 4.

1798. "Miles Davis Acquitted on Dope Charge." *Melody Maker*,
       27 Jan. 1951, p. 6.

1799. "Miles Davis Approved for Bay Concert." *Down Beat*,
       20 July 1961, pp. 13-14.

1800. "Miles Davis Arrested on Narcotics Charge." *Melody
       Maker*, 30 Sept. 1950, p. 1.

1801. "Miles Davis's Band Is a Laboratory." *Melody Maker*,
       12 Sept. 1959, p. 12.

1802. "Miles Davis: Conception in Search of a Sound." *Jazz*
       4 (1965): 8-11.

1803. "Miles Davis: Concert with Septet, Filmore East." *New
       York Times*, 19 June 1970, p. 3.

1804. "Miles Davis Concert Review." *Jazz Monthly* 6, no. 12
       (Dec. 1960): 14-15.

1805. "Miles Exonerated." *Down Beat*, 18 Feb. 1960, p. 12.

1806. "Miles Flies." *Down Beat*, 31 Mar. 1960, p. 13.

1807. "Miles--Henderson Joins the Sextet." *Melody Maker*,
       25 Mar. 1967, p. 6.

1808. "Miles Hits the Mood of Today." *Melody Maker*, 24 Oct.
       1970, p. 39.

1809. "Miles Davis Is a Genius." *Melody Maker*, 1 Oct. 1960,
       pp. 2-3.

1810. "Miles Davis Is the End." *New Haven Register*, 27 Aug.
       1961.

1811. "Miles Davis Quintet." *Down Beat*, 8 Aug. 1957, p. 31.

1812. "Miles Davis Plays to the Press." *Melody Maker*,
       10 Sept. 1960, p. 1.

1813. "Miles Davis: Shot by Unknown Assailant While Sitting
       in His Car." *New York Times*, 10 Oct. 1969, p. 1.

1814. "Miles Davis Takes New Bride of Many Talents." *Down
       Beat*, 14 Nov. 1968, pp. 10-11.

1815. "Miles Davis Talks about Birdland, Europe, Britain."
       Melody Maker, 1 Feb. 1964, p. 16.

1816. "Miles Davis Times Three: The Evolution of a Jazz
       Artist." *Down Beat*, 30 Aug. 1962, pp. 16-19.

1817. "Miles Davis to Retire?" *Down Beat*, 6 July 1961, p. 13.

1818. "Miles Was Waiting for Diz with a Trumpet and a Union
       Card." *San Francisco Chronicle*, 26 Jan. 1958.

1819. "Miles Davis Wows 'em at Vanguard!" *Billboard*, 21 Nov.
       1960, p. 17.

1820. Millstein, Gilbert. "On Stage: Miles Davis." *Horizon*,
       May 1961, pp. 100-101.

1821. Mingus, Charles. "An Open Letter to Miles Davis."
       Down Beat, 30 Nov. 1955, pp. 12-13.

1822. "Mingus in Europe: Part II--Or Get It Straight." *Down Beat*, 18 June 1964, p. 10.

1823. "Mingus Sharply Criticized for Tour Behavior." *Down Beat*, 18 June 1964, p. 10.

1824. Mitchell, Charles. "Bim, Bang Boing, Slam Pop, Z-i-i-ing!: The Anatomical Signatures of Airto." *Down Beat*, 7 Nov. 1974, pp. 10-12.

Airto discusses his childhood and interest in percussion; also his recording sessions with Miles Davis, Weather Report, "Return to Forever," as well as his own recordings.

1825. ————. "The Bass-ic Expansions of Stanley Clarke." *Down Beat*, 27 Mar. 1975.

Bassist for "Return to Forever," Clarke discusses his thoughts on musicianship, the fusion of rock and jazz, and his recordings.

1826. Mitchell, Sammy. "The Magic of Carmen McRae." *Down Beat*, 12 Dec. 1968, pp. 18, 41.

1827. "Mixed Reaction on Kenton Band's First N.Y. Job." *Down Beat*, 15 Mar. 1942, p. 2.

1828. "More Miles." *Down Beat*, 17 Aug. 1958, p. 24.

1829. Morgan, R. "Jazz: The Happy Sound Is Dying." *Esquire*, Apr. 1963, pp. 148-50.

1830. Morgenstern, Dan. "'Bags' Groove." *Down Beat*, 27 Nov. 1958, pp. 17, 48.

1831. ————. "Coleman Hawkins, 1904-1969." *Down Beat*, 26 June 1969, pp. 13-14.

1832. ————. "Flexible Chico." *Down Beat*, 15 June 1967, pp. 18-19.

1833. ————. "Gene Ammons: Here to Stay." *Down Beat*, 2 Apr. 1970, p. 18.

1834. ————. "George Freeman: Fire Is the Essence." *Down Beat*, 12 June 1971, pp. 14-15.

1835. ————. "In His Own Right." *Down Beat*, 14 July 1966, pp. 26-27.

1836. ———. "Johnny Hodges 1906-1970." *Down Beat*,
       25 June 1970, pp. 7-8.

1837. ———. "Little Jazz: The Fire Still Burns." *Down
       Beat*, 4 Feb. 1971, pp. 14-15, 33.

1838. ———. "Mellow McDuff." *Down Beat*, 1 May 1969, pp.
       19, 43.

       Concerns Jack McDuff.

1839. ———. "Miles in Motion." *Down Beat*, 3 Sept. 1970,
       pp. 16-17.

       On the current musical style of Miles Davis.

1840. ———. "Phil Upchurch." *Down Beat*, 26 June 1969,
       p. 18.

1841. ———. "The Poll Winner as Teacher, Alan Dawson."
       Down Beat, 22 Sept. 1966, pp. 27-29.

1842. ———. "Richard Davis: The Complete Musician."
       Down Beat, 2 June 1966, pp. 16-17.

1843. ———. "Toward Completeness." *Down Beat*, 1 Dec.
       1966, pp. 19-21.

       Life and music of Freddie Hubbard.

1844. ———. "Why Is This Man So Happy?" *Down Beat*,
       1 June 1967, pp. 16-17.

       Life and musical career of Clark Terry.

1845. "Mostly Modernists: Miles Davis." *Saturday Review*,
       25 Oct. 1969, p. 75.

1846. "Moving with Miles." *Melody Maker*, 6 June 1964, p. 12.

1847. "Music or Militancy: A New Breed Assumes Dominance."
       Commonweal 84 (14 Mar. 1969): 733-34.

1848. "Musician of the Year: Lee Konitz." *Jazz 1950*. Edited
       by Barry Ulanov and George Simon. New York: Metro-
       nome, 1950, p. 11.

1849. "Musician of the Year: Lennie Tristano." *Metronome*,
       Jan. 1948, p. 19.

1850. "My Best on Wax." *Down Beat*, 23 Mar. 1951, p. 7.

     Miles Davis.

1851. Nelson, Don. "Miles Davis Scores at Benefit." *New York Daily News*, 20 May 1961.

1852. ———. "Jazz and Copyright: A Study in Improvised Protection." *Northwestern University Law Review*, May-June 1972, pp. 216-44. Reprint. *Bulletin of the Copyright Society of the U.S.A.*, Dec. 1972, pp. 83-111.

1853. "New Jazz." *Newsweek*, 12 Dec. 1966, pp. 101-4.

1854. "New Jazz." *Vogue*, 1 Feb. 1966, p. 177.

1855. "New Trends?" *Second Line* 14 (1963): 10-11.

1856. Newton, F. "Bossa Nova." *New Statesman*, 21 Dec. 1962, pp. 910-11.

1857. "Newport Revisited." *High Fidelity*, Sept. 1967, pp. 21-23.

1858. "No, Jazz Isn't Dead." *New Republic*, 26 Oct. 1968, pp. 34-36.

1859. Nolan, Herb. "The Essence of George Benson." *Down Beat*, 7 June 1973.

     Benson discusses his past history, the impact of Wes Montgomery on his style, and his discovery of fellow guitarist Earl King.

1860. Norris, John. "Heard and Seen." *Coda* 9, no. 42 (11 Nov. 1971): 42.

1861. "Notes pour Miles." *Jazz Magazine* 9, no. 7 (7 July 1963): 22-25.

1862. "Now It's Miles the Mikado." *Melody Maker*, 8 Aug. 1956, p. 9.

1863. O'Brien, N.C. "Miles Davis." *Jazz Journal* 9, no. 8 (Aug. 1956): 9.

1864. O'Kuley, Faith. "Dollar Brand--African Wayfarer." *Down Beat*, 4 Apr. 1968, pp. 18, 45.

1865.   "Oscar Peterson Is One of Finest Things in Years: Mix."
        Down Beat, 21 Apr. 1950, p. 5.

1866.   "Oscar Pettiford Now on Cell Kick." *Down Beat*, 29 Dec.
        1950, p. 20.

1867.   Page, Ben S. "Open Bags." *Down Beat*, 30 Apr. 1970,
        pp. 18-19, 37.

        An interview with Milt Jackson.

1868.   Palmer, Bob. "Pharoah Sanders." *Rolling Stone*, Apr.
        1970, pp. 42-44.

1869.   Panassie, Hugues. "A Tribute to Tiny Grimes." *Down
        Beat*, 26 June 1969, p. 17.

1870.   "Paying the New Jazz Dues." *Nation*, 22 June 1964,
        p. 635.

1871.   Pease, Sharon A. "John Lewis Piano Style." *Down Beat*,
        8 Feb. 1956, pp. 46-47.

1872.   Pekar, Harvey. "Notes on Tristano." *Jazz Review* 3,
        no. 6 (July 1960): 13-15.

1873.   Peterson, O. "3rd Thoughts on the 'New Thing.'" *Jazz
        Monthly* 14, no. 6 (June 1968): 2-6.

1874.   Pleasants, Henry. "Bel Canto in Jazz and Pop Singing."
        Music Educators Journal 59, no. 9 (May 1973): 54-56.

1875.   ————. "Plenty of Horn." *Reporter*, 2 Jan. 1964,
        pp. 39-40.

1876.   "Poll-Topper Miles Has Been at a Standstill Since Back
        in 1950." *Melody Maker*, 3 Feb. 1952, p. 11.

1877.   Postgate, J. "The Black and White Show--1970-80: A
        Speculation on the Future of Jazz." *Jazz Monthly* 14,
        no. 12 (Dec. 1970).

1878.   ————. "Random Reflections." *Jazz Monthly* 14, no. 3
        (Mar. 1968): 30-31.

1879.   Postif, F. "John Coltrane: Une interview." *Jazz Hot*
        22, no. 1 (Jan. 1962): 12-14.

1880. Quinn, Bill. "Donald Byrd: Campus Catalyst." *Down Beat*, 14 Oct. 1971, pp. 19, 38.

1881. ———. "Groupless Leader." *Down Beat*, 15 June 1967, pp. 20-22.

   Eddie Harris' musical style, technique, and career.

1882. ———. "Lou's Blues." *Down Beat*, 6 Feb. 1969, pp. 15-16, 35.

1883. ———. "Max Roach: Highlights." *Down Beat*, 2 Mar. 1968, pp. 19-21.

1884. ———. "Quotet: Most Underrated Jazz Musicians on the Current Scene." *Down Beat*, 7 Mar. 1968, p. 15.

1885. ———. "Sassy '67." *Down Beat*, 27 July 1967, pp. 18-20.

   On Sarah Vaughan.

1886. ———. "The Testimony of Bunky Green." *Down Beat*, 15 Dec. 1966, pp. 20-22, 42.

   Green's life history, personality, and musical style.

1887. ———. "The Thumb's Up." *Down Beat*, 27 June 1968, pp. 17-18, 44-45.

   The life and music of Wes Montgomery.

1888. ———. "Top Side Underground." *Down Beat*, Feb. 1967, pp. 14-15, 38.

   The life and music of Marion Brown.

1889. ———. "Well Rounded 'Ball.'" *Down Beat*, 16 Nov. 1967, pp. 17-19.

   Life and music of Julian (Cannonball) Adderly.

1890. "Reed Man Eric Dolphy Dies in Berlin." *Down Beat*, 13 Aug. 1964, p. 8.

1891. Reisner, R.G. "The Titans XIII, Miles Davis." *Village Voice*, 25 June 1958.

1892. "Revolution, Coltrane, and the Avant-Garde." *Jazz* 4 (1965): 13-16.

1892a. "Rex Stewart Dist." *Down Beat*, 19 Oct. 1967, p. 13.

1893. Rivelli, P. "Alice Coltrane: Interview." *Jazz and Pop* 7, no. 9 (Sept. 1968): 26-30.

1894. ————. "Jazz Is Alive." *Jazz* 6, no. 6 (June 1967): 9-13.

1895. Roach, Max. "What Jazz Means to Me." *Black Scholar* 3, no. 10 (Summer 1972): 3-6.

1896. Robinson, Stanley G. "The Modern Touch." *Los Angeles Sentinel*, 9 July 1964.

1897. "Rock Is a White Man's Word, Says Miles." *Melody Maker*, 17 Oct. 1970, p. 25.

1898. "Rock Is a White Man's Word, Says Miles." *Rolling Stone*, 24 Dec. 1970, p. 54.

1899. "Rollins and Davis Renewed." *Saturday Review*, 30 Oct. 1965, p. 91.

1900. Rolontz, B. "Miles Davis Group Is Strong as Ethel Ennis Debuts Well." *Billboard*, 28 July 1958.

1901. Ropulos, Gordon. "John Coltrane: Retrospective Perspective." *Down Beat*, 22 July 1971, pp. 14-15, 40.

1902. Rorem, Ned. "Is New Music New?" *American Record Guide*, May 1966, pp. 776-79.

1903. Rozek, Michael. "A Matter of Values--A Conversation with Lenny White." *Down Beat*, 24 Apr. 1975, pp. 15-17.

       White discusses the importance of communication in music.

1904. "Rub Down." *New Statesman*, 3 Nov. 1967, pp. 610-11.

1905. Russell, George, and Martin Williams. "Ornette Coleman and Tonality." *Jazz Review* 3, no. 5 (June 1960): 6-11.

       A dialogue between Russell and Williams that leads to a discussion of the theoretical implications of Ornette Coleman's tonal practices.

1906. Rust, B. "Half a Century of Jazz." *Gramophone* 44, no. 5 (May 1967): 571.

1907. Saal, Herbert. "Miles of Music." *Newsweek*, 23 Mar. 1970, pp. 99-100.

1908. Saltonstall, R. "New Surge for a Tired Old Idiom:
       Charles Lloyd and Jazz." *Life*, 9 June 1967, p. 15.

1909. "Sarah Vaughan." *Metronome*, July 1946, pp. 21, 48-49.

1910. Schonfield, V. "Rule Britannia? Britain Taking Avant-
       Garde Lead." *Down Beat*, 11 July 1968, pp. 24-25.

1911. Schuller, Gunther. "Jazz and Classical Music." *The
       New Edition of the Encyclopedia of Jazz*. Edited by
       Leonard Feather. New York: Bonanza, 1960, pp. 497-99.

1912. ―――. "John Lewis on the Modern Jazz Beachhead."
       High Fidelity, Oct. 1960, pp. 54-56, 134-35.

1913. ―――. "Sonny Rollins and the Challenge of Thematic
       Improvisation." *Jazz Review* 1, no. 1 (Nov. 1958):
       6-12.

       An analysis of Sonny Rollins' improvisation. Includes
       examples. An excellent article.

1914. "Self-Portrait of the Artist." *Down Beat*, 6 Mar. 1968,
       p. 17.

1915. Shaughnessy, Ed. "About 'Face'! Zutty Singleton."
       Down Beat, 12 June 1969, p. 40.

1916. Shaw, Arnold. "The Dilemma of Jazz (Commercialization)."
       Jazz 4, no. 4 (1965): 8-11.

1917. Shaw, R.B. "Miles Above." *Jazz Journal* 13, no. 11
       (Nov. 1960): 15-16.

1918. Siders, Harvey. "Hamp's New Blues." *Down Beat*, 17 Oct.
       1968, pp. 16-17, 41.

1919. ―――. "Jazz from 9 till 2 Only." *Down Beat*, 26 Jan.
       1967, pp. 20-22.

1920. ―――. "Jimmy Smith! A New Deal for the Boss." *Down
       Beat*, 15 Oct. 1970, pp. 14-15.

1921. ―――. "Keeping Up with Quincy Jones." *Down Beat*,
       27 Nov. 1969, pp. 13, 21.

1922. ―――. "The Natural." *Down Beat*, 19 Oct. 1967, pp.
       16-18.

       Erroll Garner's life and music.

1923. ———. "Oliver's New Twist." *Down Beat*, 23 July 1970, p. 7.

1924. ———. "Quincy's Got a New/Old Bag." *Down Beat*, 26 Nov. 1970, pp. 13, 31.

1925. ———, et al. "Quotet (Jazz)." *Down Beat*, 11 Jan. 1968, p. 25.

1926. Slater, Jack. "Pointer Sisters: They Update the Past." *Ebony*, Dec. 1973, pp. 103-8, 112-13.

Discusses the musical history of the Pointer Sisters up to the present.

1927. Smith, Arnold Jay. "The Acoustic Colors of Ron Carter." *Down Beat*, 27 Mar. 1975.

Carter discusses his influences, his preference for acoustic rather than electric bass, his encounters with Miles Davis, and the bass as a solo instrument.

1928. ———. "Profile." *Down Beat*, 24 Apr. 1975.

Woody Shaw talks about jazz today and why many jazz musicians are geared toward making money rather than music.

1929. ———. "Slide Down the Middle of the Road." *Down Beat*, 22 May 1975.

Garnett Brown describes himself as a middle-of-the-road trombonist; also gives his opinion on other jazz musicians' styles.

1930. Smith, C.E. "Jazz Parallels: Third Stream, Pop-Pop, Op-Op." *Jazz* 5, no. 10 (1966): 20-22.

1931. Smith, V. "Phenomenon of Parallel Sound (Jazz or Blue-Grass)." *Music Journal* 25, no. 9 (Dec. 1967): 56.

1932. "Some Notes on 'Lift to the Scaffold!'" *Jazz Monthly* 7, no. 2 (Feb. 1962): 45.

On Miles Davis.

1933. "Sound of the Sixties." *Time*, 21 May 1965, pp. 84-86.

1934. "Sounds in the Square." *Jazz Monthly* 13, no. 3 (Mar. 1967): 18.

1935. "Soundings (Jazz)." *Jazz and Pop* 7, no. 1 (Jan. 1968): 13.

1936. Spellman, A.B. "Deeper Than Jazz: Afro-American Music." *New Republic*, 11 May 1968, pp. 37-38.

1937. —————. "John Coltrane, 1926-1967." *Nation*, 14 Aug. 1967, pp. 119-20.

1938. —————. "Trane and 7: A Wild Night at the Gate." *Down Beat*, 30 Dec. 1965, p. 15.

1939. "Stan Kenton's Band Will Devastate 'em and Nothing Can Be Done about It." *Down Beat*, 1 Apr. 1942, p. 9.

1940. "Stan Kenton Ork Set for New York Debut at Door." *Down Beat*, 1 Nov. 1941, p. 1.

1941. "Stan Kenton Turns Minneapolis 'Innovations' into Music Appreciation Session." *Down Beat*, 21 Apr. 1942, p. 9.

1942. Stebbins, R.A. "Theory of the Jazz Community." *Sociological Quarterly* 9, no. 2 (Summer 1968): 318-31.

1943. Stearns, Marshall W. "Main Trends in Jazz Today." *Musical America* 81, no. 1 (Jan. 1961): 22-23.

1944. —————. "New Directions in Jazz." *Yale Review* 49, no. 3 (Autumn 1959): 154-60.

1945. Stenbeck, L. "Quo Vadis, Miles?" *Orkester Journalen* 28, no. 1 (Jan. 1960): 8-9.

1946. Stewart, C. "The Year That Was." *Jazz* 6, no. 1 (Jan. 1967): 8-13.

1947. Stewart, Rex. "Flow Gently, Sweet Rhythm." *Down Beat*, 15 June 1967, pp. 23-25, 52-53.

Reflections of John Kirby.

1948. —————. "Genius in Retrospect, Art Tatum." *Down Beat*, Oct. 1966, pp. 17-19, 42.

1949. —————. "My Man, Big Sid." *Down Beat*, 17 Nov. 1966, pp. 20-22, 40.

Life and musical career of Sid Catlett.

1950. Stewart-Baxter, S. "Miles Davis." *Jazz Journal* 9, no. 11 (Nov. 1956): 7.

1951. Deleted.

1952. Stratton, Bert. "Miles Ahead in Rock Country." *Down Beat*, 14 May 1970, p. 19.

Miles Davis in Ann Arbor concert.

1953. ———. "Stuff Smith Dies." *Down Beat*, 16 Nov. 1967, p. 13.

1954. "Tadd Dameron." *Metronome*, Aug. 1947, pp. 24, 35.

1955. Taggart, J., ed. "Poems for John Coltrane: An Anthology." *Jazz Monthly* 16, no. 10 (Oct. 1970): 31.

1956. Teranet, A., et al. "Special Coltrane." *Jazz Hot* 26, no. 10 (Oct. 1970): 6-25.

1957. Tesser, Neil. "Freddie Hubbard: Without Music, Life Would Be Dull." *Down Beat*, 31 Jan. 1974, pp. 12-13.

1958. ———. "The Cool School." *Ebony*, Feb. 1955, pp. 74-80.

1959. ———. "'Cut Out the Lass': Ahmad Jamal." *Down Beat*, 17 Jan. 1974, pp. 14-15.

1960. "The Jazz Fan: 1967." *Jazz Magazine*, Aug. 1967, pp. 36-42.

1961. "The Jazz Scene." *Jazz* 6, no. 4 (Apr. 1967): 20-24.

1962. "The Miles Davis Sextet All Play Miles' Way." *San Francisco Sunday Chronicle*, 7 June 1959.

1963. "The New Jazz." *International Music* 56, no. 10 (Oct. 1967): n.p.

1964. "The New Miles Davis Sextet." *Down Beat*, 25 Apr. 1963, p. 17.

1965. "The Real Miles Davis." *Melody Maker*, 17 Sept. 1960, pp. 2-3.

1966. "The St. Louis Sound." *Jazz Monthly* 14, no. 4 (Apr. 1968): 2-6.

1967. "The Singular Trumpet of Miles Davis." *Hi-Fi/Stereo Review*, Dec. 1965, p. 86.

1968. "The Slugging of Miles." *Down Beat*, 1 Oct. 1959, pp. 11-12.

1969. "The State of British Jazz." *Melody Maker*, 10 Feb. 1968, pp. 8-9.

1970. "The Survival of Jazz." *International Musician* 46, no. 1 (Jan. 1968): 5.

1971. "They'll Say Jazz Is Dead, Again!" *Melody Maker*, 30 Dec. 1967, p. 6.

1972. Thiele, Bob. "Mingus Ho-Hum." *Jazz* 3, no. 10 (Oct. 1964): 20-21.

1973. Thorne, Francis. "An Afternoon with John Lewis." *Jazz Review* 3, no. 3 (Mar.-Apr. 1960): 6-9.

In addition to his life and musical career, Lewis discusses the origin of the Modern Jazz Quartet.

1974. Thomas, J.C. "Sun Ra's Space Probe." *Down Beat*, 13 June 1968, pp. 19-20.

Sun Ra's musical philosophy.

1975. Tolnay, Thomas. "Art Blakey's Jazz Message." *Down Beat*, 18 Mar. 1971, pp. 14-15.

1976. ————. "'Jazz Will Survive!' J.J. Johnson." *Down Beat*, 28 May 1970, pp. 16-17.

J.J. Johnson discusses the state of jazz today and its future.

1977. Toomajian, S. "Caught in the Act." *Down Beat*, 16 Nov. 1967, p. 47.

1978. "Top Tenorists Evaluate Coleman Contribution." *Down Beat*, 20 Oct. 1950, p. 3.

1979. Townley, Ray, and Eric Nemeyer. "The Herculean Tenor of Joe Henderson." *Down Beat*, 16 Jan. 1975, n.p.

Henderson discusses his saxophone influences and the overdue recognition that he is now receiving.

1980.   ————. "Lester Who?" *Down Beat*, 31 Jan. 1974, pp. 11-
         12.

1981.   ————. "The Mysterious Travelling of an Austrian
         Mogul." *Down Beat*, 30 Jan. 1975.

         Joe Zawinul discusses his experiences and influences
         from Cannonball Adderly and Miles Davis to his band of
         today, Weather Report.

1982.   ————. "The Two-Fisted Rubato of Sir Roland Hanna."
         Down Beat, 10 Apr. 1975, p. 18.

         Hanna discusses his musical philosophy and feel for
         the piano.

1983.   Tynan, Kenneth. "The Antic Arts: Miles Apart."
         Holiday, Feb. 1963, pp. 101-8.

         The story of Miles Davis' life, his musical influ-
         ences and attitudes toward music, and some of his
         current escapades.

1984.   "Unmasking of Miles Davis." *Saturday Review*, 27 Nov.
         1971, pp. 67-69.

1985.   Vartan, E. "Miles Davis, le solitaire." *Jazz Magazine*,
         Mar. 1960, pp. 20-25.

1986.   "Vibe Tribe: Vibraharp Players." *Newsweek*, 15 May
         1967, p. 105.

1987.   Vitet, Bernard. "Miles Davis--Un styliste en constant
         évolution." *Jazz Hot* 26, no. 4 (Apr. 1960): 10-13.

1988.   Voce, S. "Basic Trane'ing." *Jazz Journal* 20, no. 8
         (Aug. 1967): 10.

1989.   Walcott, Ronald. "Ellison, Gordone and Tolson: Some
         Notes on the Blues, Style and Space." *Black World*,
         Dec. 1972, pp. 4-29.

1990.   Walker, M. "John Coltrane (Discography)." *Jazz
         Monthly* 12, no. 8 (Aug. 1966): 11-13.

1991.   "Way Out of the Muddle: Rock Music Influence on Jazz
         Idiom." *Time*, 11 Aug. 1967, p. 36.

1992.   Webber, A.C. "A Pride of Prejudices." *Second Line*,
         May-June 1968, pp. 58-59.

1993. Weisenberg, Charles M. "The State of Jazz Education."
Down Beat, 19 Sept. 1968, pp. 16-17, 38.

An interview with Oliver Nelson.

1994. Welch, Jane. "Cal Massey's Odyssey." *Down Beat*, 4 Feb.
1971, pp. 20, 33.

1995. ————. "Pharoah Sanders: I Play for the Creator."
Down Beat, 13 May 1971, pp. 15, 32.

1996. Welding, P. "Times for Revolution (Interview with Don
Ellis)." *Down Beat*, 20 Apr. 1967, pp. 25-29.

1997. Wells, Dickie. "Rehearsal Time: An Inside View."
Down Beat, 15 Apr. 1971, p. 19.

Dickie Wells tells of a typical band rehearsal.

1998. ————. "West Coast Sounds." *Jazz Journal* 20, no. 11
(Nov. 1967): 26-27.

1999. "What Made Miles Davis Go Pop?" *Melody Maker*, 13 June
1970, pp. 20-21.

2000. "Where's the Melody?" *American Record Guide*, May 1961,
pp. 774-75.

2001. "Who's Prompting What?" *Down Beat*, 25 July 1968, pp.
34-35.

2002. Wiedemann, Erik. "Milt Jackson Diskografi." *Orkester
Journalen* 23, no. 5 (May 1955): 43.

2003. Williams, Martin. "Bash It." *Down Beat*, 11 July
1968, pp. 22-23.

2004. ————. "Caught in the Act: Sonny Rollins-John Lewis."
Down Beat, 5 July 1962, p. 38.

2005. ————. "Closing Chorus for the MJQ." *Saturday Review*,
14 July 1962, pp. 34-35.

2006. ————. "Coltrane, Coleman Up to Date." *Jazz* 5, no.
11 (Nov. 1966): 4-5.

2007. ————. "The Funky Hard Bop Regression." *The Art of
Jazz*. New York: Oxford University Press, 1959,
pp. 233-37.

2008. ———. "Early MJQ: An Appreciation." *Kulchur* 4, no. 2 (Spring 1964): 94-97.

2009. ———. "Extended Improvisation and Form: Some Solutions." *Jazz Review* 1, no. 2 (Dec. 1958): 13-16.

2010. ———. "Introducing Eric Dolphy." *Jazz Review* 3, no. 5 (June 1960): 16-18.

       A short article that includes some information on Eric Dolphy's musical influences.

2011. ———. "Jazz Pianists and Brubeck." *Saturday Review*, 28 Sept. 1958, p. 78.

2012. ———. "John Coltrane: Man in the Middle." *Down Beat*, 14 Dec. 1967, pp. 15-17.

       Coltrane's life, musical style, and influence on jazz.

2013. ———. "John Lewis and the Modern Jazz Quartet." *Evergreen Review* (Mar.-Apr. 1962): 112-25.

2014. ———. "Legacy of John Coltrane." *Saturday Review*, 16 Sept. 1967, p. 64.

2015. ———. "Miles Davis: A Man Walking." *The Jazz Tradition*. New York: Oxford University Press, 1970, pp. 175-94.

       Contains information on Miles' personal approach to modern jazz, his life and musical career, and reviews of several of his compositions.

2016. ———. "Ornette Coleman: Ten Years After." *Down Beat*, 8 Jan. 1970, pp. 9, 33.

2017. ———. "Pharoah's Tale." *Down Beat*, 16 May 1968, pp. 21-22.

       Pharoah Sanders' background, influences, musical career, and style.

2018. ———. "Two Revues of Third Stream Music." *Jazz Panorama*. New York: Macmillan, Crowell-Collier, 1962, pp. 302-5.

2019. Williams, R. "Jazz Record: Live in Seattle." *Melody Maker*, 17 Apr. 1971, p. 28.

2020. Wilmer, Valerie. "The Advantages of Gregariousness." *Down Beat*, 9 Mar. 1967, pp. 22-23.

2021. ————. "Bill Coleman--No Back Home Blues." *Down Beat*, 6 Oct. 1966, pp. 19-20.

2022. ————. "Billy Higgins--Drum Love." *Down Beat*, 21 Mar. 1968, pp. 27-30.

2023. ————. "Controlled Freedom--The Thing This Year." *Down Beat*, 23 Mar. 1967, pp. 16-17.

   Life and music of Sonny Murry.

2024. ————. "Conversation with Coltrane." *Jazz Journal* 15, no. 1 (Jan. 1962): 1-2.

2025. ————. "Ed Blackwell--Well-Trained Drummer." *Down Beat*, 3 Oct. 1968, pp. 18-19, 38.

2026. ————. "Gettin' Out There." *Down Beat*, 4 May 1967, pp. 18-19, 43.

   Life and musical career of Charles Moffett.

2027. ————. "Lockjaw Speaks Out." *Down Beat*, 7 Sept. 1967, pp. 23-25.

   Eddie (Lockjaw) Davis gives his opinions, theories, and thoughts on life, music, and people.

2028. ————. "Little Giant, Big Feeling." *Down Beat*, 18 May 1967, pp. 18-19.

   Life and music of Johnny Griffin.

2029. ————. "Oliver Jackson: The Versatile Swinger." *Down Beat*, 14 Dec. 1967, pp. 26-27.

2030. ————. "Playing from the Heart." *Down Beat*, 25 Jan. 1968, pp. 27-28.

   Life and musical career of Al Grey.

2031. ————. "Randy Weston: The Beat Is Universal." *Down Beat*, 4 Sept. 1969, pp. 16-17, 30.

2032. ————. "Roy Draper: Problems, Promise, and Poems." *Down Beat*, 4 Feb. 1971, pp. 18-19.

2033.   ————. "What Charles Tolliver Can Use." *Down Beat*,
        20 Feb. 1969, pp. 16-17.

2034.   ————. "When You Lose an 'Elder Brother' (Interview
        with McCoy Tyner)." *Melody Maker*, 19 Aug. 1967,
        p. 8.

2035.   ————. "The Youngest 40-Year-Old in Jazz." *Down
        Beat*, 23 Feb. 1967, pp. 20-21.

        Life and music of Tom McIntosh.

2036.   Wilson, John S. "Connie Kay." *Down Beat*, 5 Mar. 1959,
        pp. 20-21, 40.

2037.   ————. "Meet Professor Carter." *Down Beat*, 2 Apr.
        1970, pp. 19, 32.

        Information on Benny Carter.

2038.   Winick, C. "How High the Moon--Jazz and Drugs."
        Antioch Review 21, no. 2 (Spring 1961): 53-68.

2039.   Wiskirchen, G. "Jazz on Campus." *Down Beat*, 9 Feb.
        1967, p. 36.

2040.   Woodfern, Henry. "Whither Albert Ayler?" *Down Beat*,
        17 Nov. 1966, p. 19.

2041.   Woods, Stuart. "Tony Williams." *Jazz and Pop* 9, no. 1
        (Jan. 1972): 16-20.

2042.   "Woody Hits Road After NYC Bow." *Down Beat*, 2 June
        1950, p. 16.

2043.   "Woody's New Band." *Metronome*, June 1948, pp. 15, 27.

2044.   Zwerin, Michael. "Different Drummers, or the Case of
        the Paranoid Percussionist." *Down Beat*, 11 Dec.
        1969, pp. 13, 32.

2045.   ————. "Dues Paid." *Down Beat*, 8 Feb. 1968, pp. 18-
        20, 40-41.

2046.   ————. "Miles Davis--A Most Curious Friendship."
        Down Beat, 10 Mar. 1966, pp. 18-19.

2047.   ————. "The Real Nina Simone." *Down Beat*, 11 Jan.
        1968, pp. 16-17.

THESES AND DISSERTATIONS

2048. Cole, William. "The Story of John Coltrane." Ph.D.
      dissertation, Wesleyan University, 1974.

2049. Howlett, Felicity A. "The Piano Style of Art Tatum."
      Ph.D. dissertation, Cornell University.

2050. Owens, Thomas. "Improvisation of the Modern Jazz
      Quartet." Master's thesis, University of California,
      Los Angeles, 1965.

2051. Stewart, Milton Lee. "Structural Development in the
      Jazz Improvisational Technique of Clifford Brown."
      Ph.D. dissertation, University of Michigan, 1973.

2052. Woodson, Craig DeVere. "Solo Jazz Drumming: An
      Analytical Study of the Improvisational Techniques
      of Anthony Williams." Master's thesis, University
      of California, Los Angeles, 1973.

II
Reference Materials

A. BIBLIOGRAPHIES-DICTIONARIES-ENCYCLOPEDIAS

2053.   Case, Brian, and Stan Beitt. *The Illustrated Encyclo-
        pedia of Jazz*. New York: Harmony Books, 1978.

        Primarily a pictorial essay on jazz to the 1970's.
        Contains new and old photographs.

2054.   Collier, Graham. *Jazz: A Student's and Teacher's Guide*.
        New York: Cambridge University Press, 1978.

        Bibliography and discography. A selected list of
        entries that is not in-depth on any particular area.

2055.   Gold, Robert S. *A Jazz Lexicon*. New York: Knopf,
        1967.

        Contains a discussion of words and phrases used in
        the jazz world. Included are entries on "parts of
        speech," origins, and definitions of each term. The
        author then chronologically lists passages quoting the
        terms in context and points out differences in meaning
        over time.

2056.   Gregor, Carl, Duke of Mecklenburg. *International Jazz
        Bibliography: Jazz Books from 1917 to 1969*. Graz:
        Universal Edition, 1969.

        One of the first attempts to compile a comprehensive
        list of books on jazz. Contains 1,562 unannotated
        entries, some lacking complete bibliographic informa-
        tion. For the most part books are arranged in alpha-
        betical order by author. Good for making scholars
        aware of the number of books published in jazz.

2057.   ————. *1970 Supplement to International Jazz Bibliog-
        raphy and International Drum and Percussion Bibliog-
        raphy*. Graz: Universal Edition, 1971.

        Contains 429 titles, books, and pamphlets published
        between 1968 and 1970 as well as some items omitted from

the first volume. This supplement contains fourteen
categories, including biographies, discographies,
history, and theory. The drum and percussion entries
total 358. The entries cover a wide range of styles,
including jazz.

2058.   ———. *1971/72/73 Supplement to International Jazz
          Bibliography and Selective Bibliography of Some Back-
          ground Literature and Bibliography of Two Subjects
          Previously Excluded*. Graz: Universal Edition, 1975.

          Lists new titles published between 1971 and 1973
          plus additional entries omitted from the original
          volume and 1970 supplement. Some entries are incom-
          plete.

2059.   Haselgrove, J.R., and D. Kennington, eds. *Reader's
          Guide to Books on Jazz*. 2 vols. London: Library
          Association, County Libraries Section, 1960.

          Both editions cover general background, theory,
          biographies, criticism, discographies, and more.
          Second volume is more detailed than the first.

2060.   Hoffman, Daniel G. "From Blues to Jazz: Recent
          Bibliographies and Discographies." *Midwest Folklore*
          5, no. 2 (Summer 1955): 107, 144.

          Contains a wide range of information on several
          blues/jazz styles and personalities. The listings
          are selective, but valuable because of broad coverage
          of information and artists.

2061.   Horn, David. *The Literature of American Music in Books
          and Folk Music Collections: A Fully Annotated Bib-
          liography*. Metuchen, New Jersey: Scarecrow, 1977.

          A detailed listing of 1,696 books considered essen-
          tial for a comprehensive library on American music:
          folk, country, blues, rock, musical stage, soul, jazz.
          Excellent annotations.

2062.   Jackson, Edgar, and Leonard Hibbs. *Encyclopedia of
          Swing*. London: Decca Records, 1961.

          Designed to promote the company's interest rather
          than promote scholarship on the topic. Contains a
          selected list of recordings of many different artists.

2063.   Kennington, David. *The Literature of Jazz: A Critical

Guide. London: Library Association, 1970. Reprint. Chicago: American Library Association, 1972.

Provides access to a cross section of jazz literature. Includes entries on jazz history, biographies, analysis and theory, and reference and periodical literature. The author provides a short annotated bibliography at the end of each chapter.

2064. Kinkle, Roger D. *The Complete Encyclopedia of Popular Music and Jazz, 1900-1950.* 4 vols. New Rochelle, New York: Arlington House, 1974.

Includes biographies as well as lists of compositions and recordings organized by year from 1900 to 1950. Also includes excellent indexes.

2065. Lee, Bill. *Jazz Dictionary.* New York: Charles Hansen, 1979.

Covers a wide range of terms commonly used in jazz, including some historical ones. The book also contains a chart of jazz periods and styles, a list of outstanding jazz musicians from 1900 to 1978, and the Down Beat Poll Winners from 1937 to 1978.

2066. Loade, Wolfgang. *Jazz Lexicon.* Stuttgart: G. Hatze, 1953.

Dictionary of jazz terms and phrases.

2067. Markewich, Reese. *The Definitive Bibliography of Harmonically Sophisticated Tonal Music.* Riverdale, New York: Markewich, 1970.

Contains several listings of interest to serious jazz performers, but is not a definitive listing of materials on the subject.

2068. ————. *Bibliography of Jazz and Pop Tunes Showing the Chord Progressions of Other Compositions.* Riverdale, New York: Markewich, 1970.

An alphabetical list of tune titles. Each title is followed by a list of other compositions based on the same chord progressions.

2069. ————. *Jazz Publicity: Bibliography of Names and Addresses of International Critics and Magazines.* Riverdale, New York: Markewich, 1973.

2070.   ———. *Jazz Publicity II: Newly Revised and Expanded*
         Bibliography of Names and Addresses of Hundreds of
         International Jazz Critics and Magazines. Riverdale,
         New York: Markewich, 1974.

2071.   ———. *The New Expanded Bibliography of Jazz Composi-*
         tions Based on the Chord Progressions of Standard
         Tunes. Riverdale, New York: Markewich, 1974.

         Includes the name of the composer, publisher, and
         recorder of numerous standard tunes. An expansion of
         item 2068.

2072.   Merriam, Alan P. *A Bibliography of Jazz*. Philiadelphia:
         American Folklore Society, 1954. Rev. ed. New York:
         Da Capo, 1974.

         This first book-length bibliography of jazz literature
         contains 3,324 entries, each coded to one of thirty-two
         subject categories. A thorough listing that includes
         a subject index with jazz artists' names as well.

2073.   ———, and Robert J. Benford. *A Bibliography of Jazz*.
         Philadelphia: American Folklore Society, 1954.
         Reprint. New York: Da Capo, 1970.

         Contains an extensive unannotated list of books and
         articles as well as jazz periodicals.

2074.   Moon, Pete. *A Bibliography of Jazz Discographies*
         Published Since 1960. Edited by Barry Witherden.
         London: British Institute of Jazz Studies, 1969.

         Devoted primarily to single artist discographies.
         The bibliography is arranged alphabetically by artist
         with details of compiler, source, and format.

2075.   Morgenstern, Dan, Ira Gitler, and Jack Bradley. *Bird*
         and Diz: A Bibliography. New York: New York Jazz
         Museum, 1973.

         Lists books and articles on Gillespie and Parker as
         well as discographies on each artist.

2076.   Ortiz, Nestor R. *Diccionario del jazz*. Buenos Aires:
         Ricordi americana, 1959.

         Contains jazz terms and phrases.

2077.   Panassie, Hugues, and Madeleine Gautier. *Dictionnaire*
         du jazz. Paris: Laffont, 1954.

         Includes entries for bands, instruments, styles, and

technical terms as well as such useful information as song titles.

2078.   Reisner, Robert George. *The Literature of Jazz: A Selective Bibliography*. 2nd, rev. ed. New York: New York Public Library, 1959.

Arranged in four sections: books on jazz, background books, selective magazine references in non-jazz periodicals, and international magazines devoted to jazz.

2079.   Ruecker, Norbert. *Jazz Index: Bibliography of Jazz Literature in Periodicals*. Frankfurt: Ruecker, 1978.

Contains a list of periodicals regularly indexed as well as a list of publishers arranged alphabetically.

2080.   Tenot, Frank. *Dictionnaire du jazz*. Les dictionnaires de l'homme du XXe siècle. Paris: Larousse, 1967.

Contains brief biographies on jazz artists as well as entries for jazz terms.

2081.   Voigt, John. *Jazz Music in Print*. Winthrop, Massachusetts: Flat Nine Music, 1975.

Contains names and addresses of transcribers and publishers of hundreds of jazz tunes.

2082.   ————. *Jazz Music in Print*. 2nd ed. Boston: Hornpipe Music, 1978.

Updates and expands on volume one.

B.   BIOGRAPHIES-AUTOBIOGRAPHIES

COLLECTIVE

2083.   Balliett, Whitney. *New York Notes: A Journal of Jazz.*
New York: Houghton Mifflin, 1976.

Presents highly edited versions of the author's
columns arranged in chronological order. Gives the
reader a random sampling of such New York jazz scene
giants as Charles Parker, Art Tatum, Sonny Greene,
Eubie Blake, and Duke Ellington.

2084.   Blesh, Rudi. *Combo: Eight Lives in Jazz, U.S.A.*
Philadelphia: Chilton, 1971.

Provides biographical portraits of Louis Armstrong,
Sidney Bechet, Jack Teagarden, Lester Young, Billie
Holiday, Gene Krupa, Charlie Christian, and Eubie Blake.
The portraits of Blake and Krupa contain information
collected in interviews whereas the portrait of
Christian includes information provided by Ralph
Ellison. The book also includes a discography and
general and music index.

2085.   Brask, Ole. *Jazz People.* New York: Abrams, 1976.

Focuses on the contributions and careers of the most
significant musicians throughout the history of jazz.
Includes a discussion of "early giants," "giants of
the golden age," and "modern masters" as well as jazz
vocalists and "keepers of the flame." Each musician is
summarized in a brief biography and statement on style.
The text is by Dan Morgenstern.

2086.   Charters, Samuel. *Jazz: New Orleans, 1885-1957: An
Index to the Negro Musicians of New Orleans.* Belleville, New Jersey: W.C. Allen, 1958; London: Jazz
Journal, 1959. Rev. ed. *Jazz: New Orleans, 1885-
1963.* New York: Oak, 1963.

Presents biographical portraits of musicians (both famous and not so famous) who performed in New Orleans from 1885 to 1931. Sketches include information on artists' lives and deaths, musical careers, and groups in which they performed. In addition, the book contains a selected discography and indexes of musicians, bands, and tune titles.

2087.   Chilton, John. *Who's Who of Jazz: Storyville to Swing Street*. Philadelphia: Chilton, 1972.

Biographical information on over one thousand American jazz musicians before 1920.

2088.   Edwards, Carlos V. *The Giants of Bebop*. Urbana: University of Illinois Press, 1962.

Discusses Charles Parker, Thelonious Monk, Dizzy Gillespie, Bud Powell, Charles Mingus, and others.

2089.   Feather, Leonard B. *The Encyclopedia of Jazz*. New York: Bonanza, 1960.

Consists primarily of a biographical dictionary supplemented with historical and stylistic information.

2090.   ————. *The Encyclopedia of Jazz in the Sixties*. New York: Bonanza, 1965.

Expands on *The Encyclopedia of Jazz*, with emphasis on activities in the early sixties and several new names among the one thousand biographies listed.

2091.   ————. *The Encyclopedia of Jazz in the Seventies*. New York: Horizon Press, 1970.

Contains 1,400 biographies in this third installment in a chronological series of reference books on jazz-men. Introduction by Quincy Jones.

2092.   ————. *The Pleasures of Jazz: Leading Performers on Their Lives, Their Music, Their Contemporaries*. Introduction by Benny Carter. New York: Horizon Press, 1970.

Relates jazz to European and American musical trends and influences since 1950. Author focuses on the careers and activities of forty-two performers representative of the new sounds, the old masters, band and combo leaders, and vocalists.

2093. ————. *From Satchmo to Miles*. New York: Stein & Day, 1972; London: Quarter Books, 1976.

Presents biographies of thirteen musicians important to the development of jazz: Louis Armstrong, Duke Ellington, Billie Holiday, Ella Fitzgerald, Count Basie, Lester Young, Charlie Parker, Dizzy Gillespie, Norman Granz, Oscar Peterson, Ray Charles, Don Ellis, and Miles Davis. The biographies had been published previously between 1953 and 1972 in journals or booklets.

2094. Feather, Leonard G., and Ira Gitler. *The Encyclopedia of Jazz in the Seventies*. New York: Horizon Press, 1976.

Extends the previous editions through 1975. Contains 1,400 biographies.

2095. Gitler, Ira. *Jazz Masters of the Forties*. New York: Macmillan, 1966.

Contains bio-musical assessments of several out-standing musicians of the Bop era such as Charles Parker, Dizzy Gillespie, Bud Powell, J.J. Johnson, Oscar Peterson, Kenny Clarke, Max Roach, Dexter Gordon, Lennie Tristano, Lee Konitz, and Tadd Dameron. There are selected discographies at the end of each chapter and an index.

2096. Gleason, Ralph. *Jam Sessions: An Anthology of Jazz*. New York: G.P. Putnam's, 1958; London: Jazz Book Club, 1961.

Includes thirty-five essays covering several basic areas such as: the background of jazz, blues, and spirituals; the jazz revival, e.g., in New Orleans; jazz personalities, e.g., Fats Waller, Earl Hines, Dizzy Gillespie, Django Reinhardt, Nat King Cole, and Erroll Garner; and modern jazz.

2097. ————. *Celebrating the Duke, and Louis, Bessie, Billie, Bird, Carmen, Miles, Dizzy, and Other Heroes*. Garden City, New York: Doubleday, 1973.

Collects Gleason's reviews on music and musicians, with a foreword by Studs Terkel.

2098. Goldberg, Joe. *Jazz Masters of the Fifties*. New York: Macmillan, 1965.

Contains bio-musical portraits of Gerry Mulligan,

Thelonious Monk, Art Blakey, Miles Davis, Sonny Rollins, the Modern Jazz Quartet, Charles Mingus, Paul Desmond, Ray Charles, John Coltrane, Cecil Taylor, and Ornette Coleman, with selected discographies after each portrait. A sequel to *Jazz Masters of the Forties*.

2099.   Green, Benny. *The Reluctant Art: Five Studies in the Growth of Jazz*. London: MacGibbon & Kee, 1962; New York: Horizon Press, 1963; London: Jazz Book Club, 1964.

Discusses Bix Beiderbecke, Benny Goodman, Lester Young, Billie Holiday, and Charlie Parker, and how they altered the course of jazz.

2100.   Green, Stanley. *Kings of Jazz*. Cranbury, New Jersey: A.S. Barnes, 1976.

Consists of short bio-musical assessments of such artists as Louis Armstrong, Duke Ellington, Charles Parker, and Benny Goodman.

2101.   Hadlock, Richard. *Jazz Masters of the Twenties*. New York: Macmillan, 1965.

Presents a series of bio-musical essays on the importance of several musicians to the development of jazz in the 1920's. Personalities covered are Louis Armstrong, Earl Hines, Bix Beiderbecke, and several Chicago musicians (Goodman, Fats Waller, James P. Johnson, Jack Teagarden, Fletcher Henderson, Don Redman, Bessie Smith, and Eddie Lang). In each case, musicians' style and influence are discussed. The author does not explain his criteria for inclusion.

2102.   Horricks, Raymond, et al. *Jazz Masters of the 50's*. London: Jazz Book Club, 1968.

Contains essays written mostly by British authors on sixteen jazz musicians: Thelonious Monk, Miles Davis, J.J. Johnson, Gerry Mulligan, Bud Powell, Gil Evans, Milt Jackson, John Lewis, Max Roach, Art Blakey, Jimmy Guiffre, Dave Brubeck, Charles Mingus, Gigi Gryce, Sonny Rollins, and Quincy Jones. The format is bio-musical with some critical information and an index included.

2103.   James, Michael. *Ten Modern Jazzmen: An Appraisal of the Recorded Work of Ten Modern Jazzmen*. London: Cassell, 1960.

Discusses Charles Parker, Dizzy Gillespie, Bud Powell, Miles Davis, Stan Getz, Thelonious Monk, Gerry Mulligan, John Lewis, Lee Konitz, and Wardell Gray.

2104. Jones, LeRoi. *Black Music*. New York: William Morrow, 1967.

Comments in essays and reviews on the performance of several musicians: Thelonious Monk, Ray Haynes, Sonny Rollins, John Coltrane, Cecil Taylor, Archie Shepp, and others. The book contains some excellent sociological and philosophical views concerning the importance of this music as a reflection of black life.

2105. Jorgenson, John, and Erik Wiedemann. *Mosaik Jazz-Lexicon*. Hamburg: Mosaik, 1966.

Includes approximately 1,800 biographies of jazz musicians, singers, orchestra leaders, and composers, plus a limited number of entries on individual orchestras. There are no entries for styles, instruments, or clubs.

2106. Jost, Ekkehard. *Free Jazz*. Graz: Universal Edition, 1974.

Suggests an important approach to jazz scholarship of the 1960's and 70's. Attempts to analyze the magic of several of the "free" jazz musicians. In addition to Ayler, Coleman, Coltrane, Cherry, Mingus, and Shepp, the book includes some information on the music of Sun Ra and the Association for the Advancement of Creative Musicians (e.g., Richard Abrams, Lester Bowie, Joseph Jarman) as well as numerous musical examples. Serious jazz scholars might be interested in using this book along with the outstanding transcriptions of John Coltrane by Andrew White as a way of expanding their understanding of jazz since 1960.

2107. Ramsey, Fredric, and Charles E. Smith, eds. *Jazz Men*. New York: Harcourt, Brace, 1939; London: Jazz Book Club, 1950; London: Sidgwick & Jackson, 1957. Reprint. St. Clair Shores, Michigan: Scholarly Press, 1972.

Includes several outstanding articles on analytical and historical jazz topics. The book is divided into four basic style sections: New Orleans, Chicago, New York, and "Hot Jazz Today." The definition and development of these styles is told through the contributions and careers of outstanding jazz personalities. Among

the writers contributing to this excellent volume are
William Russell, E. Simms Campbell, Wilder Hobson, and
the authors.

2108. Reisner, Robert G. *The Jazz Titans, Including the
Parlance of Hip with Short Biographical Sketches
and Discographies.* Garden City, New York: Doubleday,
1960.

Contains thirty-three jazz portraits, among which are
Louis Armstrong, King Oliver, Count Basie, Duke Elling-
ton, Benny Goodman, Charles Parker, Dizzy Gillespie,
Thelonious Monk, and Miles Davis.

2109. Rockmore, Noel. *Preservation Hall Portraits.* Baton
Rouge: Louisiana State University Press, 1968.

Portraits, in black and white, of fifty New Orleans
musicians as well as members of the Eureka Brass Band.
Pictures are by Noel Rockmore and text by Larry Borenstein and Bill Russell.

2110. Shapiro, Nat, and Nat Hentoff, eds. *The Jazz Makers.*
New York: Rinehart, 1957; New York: Grove, 1958;
London: Davies, 1958.

Offers twenty-one biographical essays by George
Avakian, Leonard Feather, George Hoefer, Orrin Keepnews,
Bill Simon, Charles E. Smith, and John S. Wilson, in
addition to those by the authors. The essays, most
bio-musical in content, cover Jelly Roll Morton, Baby
Dodds, Louis Armstrong, Jack Teagarden, Fatha Hines,
Bix Beiderbecke, Pee Wee Russell, Bessie Smith, Fats
Waller, Art Tatum, Coleman Hawkins, Benny Goodman,
Duke Ellington, Charlie Parker, Fletcher Henderson,
Count Basie, Lester Young, Billie Holiday, Roy Eldridge,
Charlie Christian, and Dizzy Gillespie.

2111. Spellman, A.B. *Four Lives in the Bebop Business.* New
York: Pantheon Books; London: MacGibbon & Kee, 1967;
New York: Schocktor, 1970.

Discusses bio-musical and career development of
Ornette Coleman, Jackie McLean, Herbie Nichols, and
Cecil Taylor.

2112. Stewart, Rex. *Jazz Masters of the Thirties.* New York:
Macmillan, 1972.

Written by the former Duke Ellington and Fletcher
Henderson cornetist, this book contains numerous por-

traits of musicians of the twenties and thirties. The
author relies on his own experiences and knowledge of
the musicians that he discusses. Contains biographical
portraits of several of Ellington's musicians (e.g.,
Joe Nanton and Harry Carney) as well as profiles of
Fletcher Henderson, Coleman Hawkins, John Kirby, Benny
Carter, Art Tatum, and many more. Hsio Wen Shih
provides the portrait of Count Basie. Interesting and
informative.

2113. Terkel, Louis, and Milly Hawk. *Giants of Jazz.* New
       York: Cromwell, 1975.

Presents bio-musical sketches of such outstanding
jazz musicians as Armstrong, Ellington, Goodman, and
Parker.

2114. Williams, Martin, ed. *The Art of Jazz: Essays on the
       Nature and Development of Jazz.* New York: Oxford
       University Press, 1959; London: Cassell, 1960; London:
       Jazz Book Club, 1962.

Covers several blues-jazz musicians and styles.
Among the blues-boogie woogie musicians discussed in
essays by some of the best writers on blues-jazz are
Sonny Terry, Bessie Smith, Meade Lux Lewis, Jimmy
Yancey, and Cripple Clarence Lofton. Jazz personalities
covered include Jelly Roll Morton, King Oliver, James P.
Johnson (jazz ragtime), Bix Beiderbecke, Duke Ellington,
Billie Holiday, Art Tatum, Charlie Christian, and the
Modern Jazz Quartet. Some of the articles contain
musical analysis.

2115. ————. *Jazz Panorama from the Pages of "The Jazz
       Review."* New York: Crowell-Collier, 1962; London:
       Jazz Book Club, 1965.

An excellent collection of thirty-nine essays by
critics and musicians that appeared in *The Jazz Review.*
Devoted primarily to individual personalities, with
historical, analytical, and personal points of view as
well. Among the outstanding blues-jazz personalities
covered are: Jelly Roll Morton, King Oliver, Miles
Davis, Sonny Rollins, Ray Charles, and Lightnin
Hopkins. Some of the articles, such as Gunther
Schuller's, include musical analyses and examples.

2116. ————. *Jazz Masters of New Orleans.* New York: Mac-
       millan, 1967.

Presents bio-musical portraits of Buddy Bolden, Jelly

Roll Morton, Joe "King" Oliver, Sidney Bechet, Zutty
Singleton, Kid Ory, Bunk Johnson, Red Allen, the
Original Dixieland Jazz Band, and the New Orleans
Rhythm Kings. Only biographical information is pro-
vided on Louis Armstrong. Discographies are included
at the end of each portrait.

2117. ————. *The Jazz Tradition*. New York: Oxford Univer-
         sity Press, 1970.

Consists of essays, most written between 1959 and
1967, on sixteen artists. The author analyzes a
selection of each artist's individual recordings,
without musical examples. The artists covered are:
Jelly Roll Morton, Louis Armstrong, Bix Beiderbecke,
Coleman Hawkins, Billie Holiday, Duke Ellington, Count
Basie, Lester Young, Charles Parker, Thelonious Monk,
John Lewis, Sonny Rollins, Horace Silver, Miles Davis,
Ornette Coleman, and John Coltrane.

2118. Wilmer, Valerie. *Jazz People*. Indianapolis: Bobbs-
         Merrill; London: Allison and Busby, 1971.

Analyzes the music of Buck Clayton, Lockjaw Davis,
Art Farmer, Jimmy Heath, Babs Gonzales, Jackie McLean,
Howard McGhee, Clark Terry, Archie Shepp, Joe Turner
and Randy Weston, Cecil Taylor, Thelonious Monk, and
Billie Higgins. The author combines data obtained from
interviews with her own assessments in musical portraits
of these musicians.

INDIVIDUAL

LOUIS ARMSTRONG

2119. Armstrong, Louis. *Swing That Music*. London: Longmans,
         Green, 1937.

Covers the first thirty-six years of Armstrong's
life in this first autobiography of a Black jazz
musician. An interesting music section contains ten
musical examples, an original song ("Swing That Music"),
and individual improvisations by several swing musicians
(e.g., Benny Goodman, Tommy Dorsey, Bud Freeman, Red
Norvo, and Louis). Introduction is by Rudy Vallee and
music section is edited by Horace Gerlach.

2120. ————. *Satchmo: My Life in New Orleans*. New York:
Prentice-Hall, 1954; London: Davies, 1955; London:
Jazz Book Club, 1957; New York: New American Library,
1961.

Portrays the early life and music of Louis Armstrong.
Takes his career through his New Orleans stage to the
time he joined King Oliver in Chicago. A good presentation.

2121. ————. *Louis Armstrong, A Self-Portrait*. New York:
Eakins Press, 1971.

In this interview with Richard Meryman, Armstrong
describes his life until he left Chicago for New York
in 1928. He discusses his New Orleans childhood, the
Chicago jazz scene with King Oliver, and his experiences
with Fletcher Henderson. In addition, he talks about
an entertainer's life and his survival in the music
world.

2122. Eaton, Jeanette. *Trumpeter's Tale: The Story of Young
Louis Armstrong*. New York: William Morrow, 1955.

Appeals particularly to young jazz fans.

2123. Goffin, Robert. *Horn of Plenty: The Story of Louis
Armstrong*. Translated by James Bezov. New York:
Allen, Towne and Heath, 1947.

Details the life and musical career of Armstrong up
to 1946. Contains good information on early musical
influences on Armstrong.

2124. Jones, Max, and John Chilton. *Louis: The Louis Armstrong Story, 1900-1971*. Boston: Little, Brown;
London: Studio Vista, 1971.

Gives a good picture of the life and musical contributions of Armstrong. Coverage of the Armstrong musical
style, drugs, and racism is particularly interesting.

2125. Jones, Max; John Chilton; and Leonard Feather. *Salute
to Satchmo*. London: IPC, 1970.

Contains a tribute by Feather as well as other musicians
to Armstrong on his seventieth birthday. The main text
is concerned with Louis the man--public reaction to him,
his personality, his life. The book includes a list
of films and an index. A good book for learning how
and why people admired Armstrong.

2126.   McCarthy, Albert J.   *Louis Armstrong*.   London: Cassell,
         1960; New York: Barnes, 1961.

         Concerns Armstrong's style up to 1959 and gives
         special attention to the middle years.   The author dis-
         cusses the stylistic characteristics that made Armstrong
         great.   He includes quotations from other musicians
         and a discography.

2127.   Panassie, Hugues.   *Louis Armstrong*.   Paris: Nouvelles
         éditions latines, 1969; New York: Scribner's, 1971.

         Consists of a biography presented in three parts:
         the life of Armstrong; a general description of Arm-
         strong's jazz style; and a chronological survey and
         discography of Armstrong's recordings from 1923 to
         1968.   The book also contains numerous photographs.

COUNT BASIE

2128.   Horricks, Raymond.   *Count Basie and His Orchestra: Its
         Music and Musicians*.   New York: Citadel Press; London:
         Gollancz, 1957; London: Jazz Book Club, 1958.   Re-
         print. Westport, Connecticut: Negro Universities
         Press, 1971.

         Presents a penetrating view of Basie as band leader
         and musician as well as discussing musicians who made
         up the Basie band from 1936 to 1950.   After opening with
         a portrait of Basie as a leader, the author gives an
         illuminating account of the evolution and development
         of the band's musical style in its first twenty years.
         He also comments on Basie as a pianist and on the style
         and contributions of some of his most famous sidemen--
         Buck Clayton, Dickie Wells, Lester Young, Jimmy Rushing,
         and several more from the 1950's.   Biographical sketches
         are provided along with a complete discography by Alun
         Morgan.

DANNY BARKER

2129.   Buerkle, Jack V., and Danny Barker.   *Bourbon Street
         Black: The New Orleans Black Jazz Man*.   New York:
         Oxford University Press, 1973.

         A sociological study of early New Orleans jazz per-
         formers including some background information on the
         life and music of Danny Barker.

SIDNEY BECHET

2130.   Bechet, Sidney. *Treat It Gentle.* New York: Hill &
         Wang, 1960.

         Autobiography of an outstanding New Orleans jazz
         clarinetist and soprano saxophonist. Provides good
         information on Bechet's early career and influences
         and on the socio-musical makeup of early New Orleans
         jazz.

2131.   Mouly, R. *Sidney Bechet, notre ami.* Paris: La table
         ronde, 1959.

         Contains an excellent discography and some interesting
         facts about Bechet and his early influences. However,
         the book also contains some inaccuracies.

BIX BEIDERBECKE

2132.   Berton, Ralph. *Remembering Bix: A Memoir of the Jazz
         Age.* New York: Harper & Row, 1974.

         Written by the brother of Vic Berton, the drummer
         who recorded with the Wolverines in 1924 and 1927, this
         book is more concerned with spotlighting Berton's
         contribution than with Beiderbecke himself. Offers
         little or no new information on Bix.

2133.   James, Burnett. *Bix Beiderbecke.* London: Cassell,
         1959. Reprint. New York: Barnes, 1961.

         Primarily a bio-musical study that gives a short but
         insightful account of Bix's life, style, and contribu-
         tions (with reference to his recordings). A selected,
         fully detailed discography that lists all the Micro-
         groove collections released in Britain is also provided.

2134.   Sudhalter, Richard M., and Philip R. Evans. *Bix: Man
         and Legend.* New Rochelle, New York: Arlington House;
         London: Quarter Books, 1974.

         Perhaps the best-written and best-researched biography
         to date on Beiderbecke. The authors, with William Deun-
         Myatt, separate fact from fiction in assessing the
         achievements of Beiderbecke. Including much informa-
         tion gathered from Beiderbecke's friends and colleagues
         as well as anecdotes from other sources, they cover his
         life, the formation and recordings of the Wolverines,

his membership in the Goldkette and Whitman bands, his fascination with the piano and the music of the European tradition, and his physical and psychological problems. The book also features a unique "Diary" of Bix's life and a 78-rpm discography with music notations to differentiate takes.

2135. Waring, Charles, and George Garlick. *Bugles for Beiderbecke*. London: Sidgwick & Jackson, 1958; London: Jazz Book Club, 1960.

Offers a study of Beiderbecke that is arranged in three parts: his life and career; his musical expertise, compositions, and contributions; and a comprehensive, fully detailed discography.

BUDDY BOLDEN

2136. Marquis, Donald M. *In Search of Buddy Bolden, First Man of Jazz*. Baton Rouge: Louisiana State University Press, 1977.

Contains much new information on Bolden. In this excellent, well-researched book, the author disproves or confirms statements by previous researchers about Bolden as well as speculating on what Bolden might have sounded like.

CAB CALLOWAY

2137. Calloway, Cab. *Of Minnie the Moocher and Me*. New York: Crowell, 1970.

A combined autobiography-documentary covering many of the high points of Calloway's career. The book, done with Bryant Rollins, also contains information on some of the great musicians who performed for Calloway.

JOHN COLTRANE

2138. Cole, Bill. *John Coltrane: A Musical Biography*. New York: Schirmer Books, 1976.

Assesses Coltrane's life and music. In this bio-musical study, the author includes information on

Coltrane's musical influences (e.g., Miles Davis and Thelonious Monk) along with several transcriptions.

2139. Simpkins, Cuthbert O. *Coltrane: A Biography*. New York: Herndon House, 1975.

Presents new information and photographs from Coltrane's early life. The many quotations help to create a warm and positive work. While the book does not contain transcriptions, references are made to Coltrane's musical style.

2140. Thomas, J.C. *Chasin' the Trane: The Music and Mystique of John Coltrane*. Garden City, New York: Doubleday, 1975.

Includes biographical information along with comments and recollections of musicians who knew and admired Coltrane. The book is interesting for the insight it provides into Coltrane as a person and musical innovator as well as the opinions other musicians held of him.

2141. Turner, Richard. "John Coltrane: A Biographical Sketch." *The Black Perspective in Music* 3, no. 1 (Spring 1975): 3-17.

Contains information on Coltrane's life, the groups with which he performed, and his musical influences and style.

LEE COLLINS

2142. Collins, Lee. *Oh, Didn't He Ramble: The Life Story of Lee Collins, as Told to Mary Collins*. Edited by Frank J. Gillis and John W. Miner. Urbana: University of Illinois Press, 1974.

Presents a vivid portrait of Collins' early life, his life in Chicago, and his two European tours of 1951 and 1954. The book also contains short portraits of many of the New Orleans musicians with whom Collins performed and a discography of commercial and private recordings. This unique biography is based on memoirs, first edited by Miner, that Collins began writing about 1943. After the musician's death in 1960, Gillis completed the manuscript.

EDDIE CONDON

2143.   Condon, Eddie. *We Called It Music: A Generation of
        Jazz.* Narration by Thomas Sugrue. New York: Henry
        Holt, 1967. Reprint. Westport, Connecticut: Green-
        wood, 1970.

        Draws a vivid picture of the events and personalities
        in Chicago and New York jazz in the 1920's and 1930's.
        Numerous musicians give firsthand accounts of jazz
        during this era, including some interesting and insight-
        ful anecdotes about Condon. An extensive discography
        of Condon is also presented.

2144.   Condon, Eddie, and Hank O'Neal. *The Eddie Condon Scrap-
        book of Jazz.* New York: St. Martin's, 1973; London:
        Hale, 1974.

        Primarily an album of Condon's recollections, clip-
        pings, posters, and letters rather than a detailed
        bio-musical study.

MILES DAVIS

2145.   Cole, Bill. *Miles Davis: A Musical Biography.* New
        York: William Morrow, 1974.

        Provides an interesting study of the musical career
        of Miles Davis. The author discusses Davis' musical
        influences and style as well as the rejection of that
        style in the late 1960's. He also comments on the
        succession of musicians who performed with Davis,
        though there are occasional mistakes--e.g., in the
        personnel listed for the "Bitches Brew" album. Thirteen
        transcriptions and an excellent bibliography are in-
        cluded.

2146.   James, Michael. *Miles Davis.* New York: Barnes; London:
        Cassell, 1961.

        Studies Davis' musical development from about 1945
        with Charles Parker to 1959 as demonstrated in selected
        recordings. The author elaborates on Davis' strengths
        and weaknesses. A selected bibliography is included,
        but no index.

BABY DODDS

2147.   Dodds, Warren "Baby." *The Baby Dodds Story, as Told
        to Larry Gara.* Los Angeles: Contemporary Press,
        1959.

        Describes Dodds's life in New Orleans as well as the
        revival of New Orleans jazz in the 1940's. The author
        discusses his association with Louis Armstrong, King
        Oliver, Jelly Roll Morton, and Bunk Johnson. The in-
        formation on the styles and the role of the drummer
        in New Orleans jazz makes this a particularly useful
        autobiography.

JOHNNY DODDS

2148.   Lambert, G.E. *Johnny Dodds.* New York: Barnes; London:
        Cassell, 1971.

        In addition to biographical information, includes a
        good discussion of Dodds's role in his recordings with
        King Oliver, Louis Armstrong's Hot Five and Hot Seven,
        and his own Washboard Band as well as his contributions
        at other sessions. His contributions to jazz are also
        discussed. The selected discography lists 78's and
        Microgroove recordings. No index.

ERIC DOLPHY

2149.   Simasko, Vladimir, and Barry Tepperman. *Eric Dolphy:
        A Musical Biography and Discography.* Washington:
        Smithsonian Institution Press, 1974.

        Evaluates Dolphy's contributions to jazz and analyzes
        his musical development as demonstrated in his recordings.
        In this short but valuable study, the author also codes
        each composition to indicate whether or not Dolphy
        performs a solo and includes a list of composer credits.

DORSEY BROTHERS

2150.   Sanford, Herb. *Tommy and Jimmy: The Dorsey Years.* New
        Rochelle, New York: Arlington House; London: Ian
        Allan, 1972.

Presents a detailed account of the separate and combined careers of the Dorsey Brothers, from the Goldkette
and Whitman Orchestras through the Swing era. With
information compiled from anecdotes, personal recollections, and other research, the author reflects on the
Dorsey Brothers' accomplishments and critical reception.
A 1935 itinerary, index, and list of musicians who
worked with the Dorseys are also included.

DUKE ELLINGTON

2151.   Arnaud, Noel. *Duke Ellington.* Paris: Messager boetus,
        1950.

Discusses Ellington's early life and music and rise
to fame. The book also comments on some of Ellington's
musicians and his relationship with artists like Billy
Strayhorn and Paul Gonzales.

2152.   Dance, Stanley. *The World of Duke Ellington.* New
        York: Scribner's, 1970; London: Macmillan, 1971.

Presents an excellent insight into Ellington, the
man and his music, through interviews with Duke and
his musicians. Among the twenty-six musicians
interviewed are Billy Strayhorn, Mercer Ellington, and
Thomas L. Whaley. The interviews are supplemented by
the author's assessment of their musicianship. Of
particular importance to some researchers will be
Mercer Ellington's attitude to his father. The book
also contains descriptions of five important events
in the musical career of Ellington. They are: the
Monterrey Festival of 1961, the Sacred Concerts of
1965 and 1968, the Latin American Tour of 1968, and
Duke's seventieth birthday celebration at the White
House in 1969. Also included are a chronology of
Ellington's life, a limited discography, and an index.

2153.   Ellington, Edward Kennedy. *Music Is My Mistress.*
        Garden City, New York: Doubleday, 1973; London:
        Allen, 1974.

Presents musicians' views of Ellington as well as
Ellington's views of himself rather than a history of
the Ellington band or a treatise on his approach to
musical composition. The book contains excellent information on Ellington's life, early childhood in
Washington, D.C., and foreign tours. A list of his

honors and a catalog of his compositions in copyright order are also included.

2154. Gammond, Peter, ed. *Duke Ellington: His Life and Music.* New York: Roy; London: Phoenix House, 1958; London: Jazz Book Club, 1959. Reprint. New York: Da Capo, 1977.

Offers contributions by fifteen authors on Ellington. Among the areas covered are his musical style (piano playing and composition); an analysis of his recordings; and biographical sketches of most of his musicians. A fully detailed, chronological discography is included.

2155. Jewell, Derek. *Duke: A Portrait of Duke Ellington.* New York: W.W. Norton, 1977.

Contains little or no new information, but is well-presented and researched. The book contains interesting insights into the personality of Ellington with a positive, humanistic approach.

2156. Lambert, G.E. *Duke Ellington.* London: Cassell, 1959; New York: Barnes, 1961.

Assesses Ellington and describes his recordings, many in detail, to 1958. The author suggests ways Ellington tailored his talents to fit the personnel in his band instead of making the band adjust to his arranging and compositional skills. A selected discography is included.

2157. Montgomery, Elizabeth Rider. *Duke Ellington: King of Jazz.* Champaign, Illinois: Garrard, 1972.

Gives a positive portrayal of the man and his music, but provides no new information.

2158. Ulanov, Barry. *Duke Ellington.* New York: Creative Age Press, 1946; London: Musicana Press, 1947.

Accounts for Duke's life and music to about 1945. The book is particularly informative on the sociological conditions surrounding the development of jazz to this date, especially as it related to Duke. Brief comments on several of Ellington's more popular recordings are also included.

ELLA FITZGERALD

2159.   Reginald, Oscar. *Ella Fitzgerald Story*. New York:
        Stein & Day, 1971.

        Discusses Fitzgerald's life and musical career,
        including information on musicians with whom she per-
        formed or associated. The biography is positive and
        informative not only in its account of her career
        but also for its insight into the music of several
        other prominent artists.

POPS FOSTER

2160.   Foster, Pops. *Pops Foster: The Autobiography of a
        New Orleans Jazzman, as Told to Tom Stoppard*.
        Berkeley: University of California Press, 1971.

        Presents an accurate picture of the music and
        musicians of New Orleans from 1899 to 1919. Details
        of Foster's life and music are presented from his early
        New Orleans beginnings through his life in New York and
        his travels with Louis Armstrong. The introduction by
        Bertram Turetzky contains some information on his bass
        technique. A chronological list of the groups that he
        performed with, a discography by Ross Russell, and an
        index are also included.

DIZZY GILLESPIE

2161.   Gillespie, Dizzy, and Al Frazer. *To Be or Not to Bop:
        The Autobiography of Dizzy Gillespie*. Garden City,
        New York: Doubleday, 1978.

        Details many large and small points about Gillespie's
        life and musical career, particularly his attitude
        toward Bop. This interesting self-portrait discusses
        his relationship with other jazz personalities such as
        Charles Parker.

2162.   James, Michael. *Dizzy Gillespie*. London: Cassell,
        1959; New York: Barnes, 1961.

        A bio-musical assessment of the life and music of
        Gillespie to 1957. The author analyzes the evolution
        of his style and notes Gillespie's importance in the

development of modern jazz. A selected discography, 1939-1957, is included.

BABS GONZALES

2163.   Gonzales, Babs. *I Paid My Dues: Good Times ... No Bread*. East Orange, New Jersey: Expubidence Publishing, 1967.

Deals primarily with Gonzales' extramusical activities, with little information on his musical style. The book does provide insight into some followers of Bebop.

BENNY GOODMAN

2164.   Connor, D. Russell, and Warren W. Hicks. *B.G. on the Record: A Bio-discography of Benny Goodman*. New Rochelle, New York: Arlington House, 1969.

Extends and revises *B.G. off the Record*, with bio-musical information on Goodman to 1968. Particularly interesting are the authors' critical comments on some of Goodman's recordings. A chronological, fully detailed discography of all Goodman recordings is included along with tune titles and indexes to radio and television programs and films.

2165.   Goodman, Benny, and Irving Kolodin. *The Kingdom of Swing*. New York: Stackpole; London: Allen, 1939. Reprint. New York: Frederick Ungar, 1961.

Discusses the elements of "Swing style" and details the life and music of Goodman to 1939.

JOHN HAMMOND

2166.   Hammond, John. *John Hammond on Record: An Autobiography*. New York: Summit Books, 1977.

Details Hammond's involvement with figures from the worlds of music and civil rights. This autobiography, written with Irving Townsend, has much to say about the recording industry and Hammond's forty years in it, discovering and promoting new talent.

HAMPTON HAWES

2167.   Hawes, Hampton. *Raise Up Off Me: An Autobiography of
        the Black Jazz Pianist.* New York: Coward, McCann &
        Geoghegan, 1974.

        Discusses the many difficulties Hawes faced in his
        life.

COLEMAN HAWKINS

2168.   McCarthy, Albert J. *Coleman Hawkins.* London: Cassell,
        1963.

        Provides biographical information and analyzes
        Hawkins' recordings in three sections (1924-1939;
        1939-1949; and 1950-1962) to illustrate the development
        of his saxophone style. A selected discography is
        included.

TED HEATH

2169.   Heath, Ted. *Listen to My Music: An Autobiography.*
        London: Muller, 1957.

        Life of the British jazz band director whose band
        included many of the leading British jazz musicians
        in the 1940's and 1950's.

FLETCHER HENDERSON

2170.   Allen, Walter C. *Hendersonia: The Music of Fletcher
        Henderson and His Musicians: A Bio-discography.*
        Highland Park, New Jersey: Author, 1973.

        Details Henderson's musical career with biographical
        and discographical materials. The discographies in-
        clude all known recordings featuring Henderson as a
        performer or conductor as well as all known sessions
        recorded with Henderson musicians. The author also
        offers a chronological list of Henderson's compositions,
        a catalog of his arrangements, biographical rosters of
        his musicians and vocalists, tune titles, and more. An
        excellent portrait of the life and music of Fletcher
        Henderson.

EARL HINES

2171.   Dance, Stanley. *The World of Earl Hines*. New York:
           Scribner's, 1977.

           Discusses the career of Fatha Hines, drawing on per-
           sonal interviews as well as the author's friendship
           with Hines. The book contains some important informa-
           tion on the people who performed with Hines but has few
           references to his style.

BILLIE HOLIDAY

2172.   Chilton, John. *Billie's Blues: A Survey of Billie
           Holiday's Career, 1933-1959*. New York: Stein & Day;
           London: Quarter Books, 1975.

           Approaches Holiday's life without sentimentality.
           In this well-researched study, the author comments on
           Holiday's musical style and how Holiday incorporated
           her life experiences into it. Buck Clayton wrote the
           Foreword.

2173.   Holiday, Billie. *Lady Sings the Blues*. Garden City,
           New York: Doubleday, 1956; New York: Popular Library;
           London: Barrie Books, 1958; New York: Lancer Books,
           1965; London: Barrie and Jenkins; London: Sphere
           Books, 1973.

           Stresses Holiday's life and the problems in her musical
           career rather than her musical style. The book does
           deal with her start in jazz, her experiences with the
           Artie Shaw and Count Basie bands, and the so-called true
           account of her problem with drugs.

2174.   Kuehl, Linda, and Ellie Schokert. *Billie Holiday
           Remembered*. New York: New York Jazz Museum, 1973.

           A brief but interesting series of recollections about
           Holiday.

BUNK JOHNSON

2175.   Sonnier, Austin M. *Willie Geary "Bunk" Johnson: The
           New Iberia Years*. Boston: Crescendo, 1977.

           Provides biographical information, particularly in

regard to the early musical influences of Johnson and the
most significant bands with which he performed.

MAX KAMINSKY

2176. Kaminsky, Max. *My Life in Jazz*. New York: Harper &
       Row, 1963; London: Deutsch, 1964.

       Comments on the author's associations with Armstrong,
       the Dorseys, and Artie Shaw as well as Chicago jazz
       musicians of the 1920's and 1930's.

GEORGE LEWIS

2177. Bethell, Tom. *George Lewis: A Jazzman from New Orleans*.
       Berkeley: University of California Press, 1977.

       Surveys Lewis' career, musical associations, and
       musical accomplishments with perception and detail.

2178. Stuart, Jay Allison. *Call Him George*. London: Peter
       Davies, 1961; London: Jazz Book Club, 1963.

       Presents biographical information provided by Lewis
       himself. The biography also discusses early New
       Orleans.

WINGY MANONE

2179. Manone, Wingy, and Paul Vandervoort. *Trumpet on the
       Wing*. Garden City, New York: Doubleday, 1948. Re-
       print. London: Jazz Book Club, 1964.

       Covers Manone's career from his early life in New
       Orleans, St. Louis, New York, and Chicago to his
       comedian/musician life in Hollywood. The Foreword is
       by Bing Crosby.

GLENN MILLER

2180. Flower, John. *Moonlight Serenade: A Bio-discography
       of the Glenn Miller Civilian Band*. New Rochelle,
       New York: Arlington House, 1972.

       Combines biographical and discographical materials

in an informative, well-researched portrait of Miller's life and music. The author provides a diary of the Miller band schedule from 1935 to 1963 with full discographical and broadcast detail. He also includes indexes of tune titles and band personnel.

2181. Simon, George T. *Glenn Miller and His Orchestra.* New York: Crowell; London: W.H. Allen, 1974.

Presents a positive and detailed view of Miller with material drawn from personal association with him as well as from material gathered from interviews. The author, Miller's first drummer, divides Miller's life into four stages: The Early Years, 1904 to 1935; The Band that Failed, 1935 to 1938; The Band that Made It, 1938 to 1942; and The Armed Forces Band, 1942 to 1944. Little information on the musical style of Miller is offered.

CHARLES MINGUS

2182. Mingus, Charlie. *Beneath the Underdog: His World as Composed by Mingus.* Edited by Nel King. New York: Knopf; London: Weidenfeld and Nicolson, 1971.

Assesses Mingus' life and music and also comments on his musical influences.

JELLY ROLL MORTON

2183. Lomax, Alan. *Mister Jelly Roll: The Fortunes of Jelly Roll Morton, New Orleans Creole and "Inventor of Jazz."* New York: Grosset & Dunlap, 1950; London: Cassell, 1952; New York: Grove Press, 1956; London: Pan Books, 1959. 2nd ed. Berkeley: University of California Press, 1973.

Based on interviews with Morton at the Library of Congress in 1938. This biography is particularly interesting for Jelly Roll's own assessment of his life as well as for Mabel Morton's comments on Jelly Roll and their life together. An appendix lists Morton's compositions, recordings, and tunes.

2184. Williams, Martin. *Jelly Roll Morton.* London: Cassell, 1962; New York: Barnes, 1963.

Analyzes Morton's piano solos, pre-Pepper and Red
Hot Pepper recordings, duets, trios, and quartets,
primarily as word analysis rather than detailed tran-
scriptional analysis. The author also discusses the
roots of and influences on Morton's style.

RED NICHOLS

2185.   Johnson, George. *The Five Pennies: The Biography of
        Jazz Band Leader Red Nichols.* New York: Dell, 1959.

        Details Nichols' career, including groups he led and
        musicians with whom he associated.

KING OLIVER

2186.   Allen, Walter C., and Brian A.L. Rust. *King Joe
        Oliver.* Belleville, New Jersey: Author, 1955;
        London: Jazz Book Club, 1957; London: Sidgwick &
        Jackson, 1958.

        Comments on Oliver the man as well as on his composi-
        tions. This book, a combined biography and discography
        by two of the best jazz discographers, fully details
        all the recordings that Oliver made. The 1934-1935
        Oliver band itinerary and an index of recorded titles
        are included.

2187.   Williams, Martin. *King Oliver.* London: Cassell, 1960;
        New York: Barnes, 1961.

        Approaches Oliver's life in two sections: the first
        deals with his experiences from New Orleans to New
        York; the second part assesses his "Creole Jazz Band,"
        "Dixie Syncopators," 1929-1930 Victor Recording Orches-
        tra, and musical style.

ORIGINAL DIXIELAND JAZZ BAND

2188.   Brunn, H.O. *The Story of the Original Dixieland Jazz
        Band.* Baton Rouge: Louisiana State University Press,
        1960; London: Sidgwick & Jackson; London: Jazz Book
        Club, 1963.

        Attempts to prove that the Original Dixieland Jazz
        Band created jazz. In a rather biased approach and

based primarily on material from LaRocca, the author
does not mention how musicians like LaRocca listened
to and copied the style of Black musicians like King
Oliver. Since it fails to detail the Black influence
on the Original Dixieland Jazz Band, this book cannot
be taken as an accurate assessment of the Band's music
and influence.

CHARLES PARKER

2189. Harrison, Max. *Charlie Parker*. London: Cassell, 1960;
New York: Barnes, 1961.

A short bio-musical portrait of Parker's life that
presents little new information. A selected discography
is included.

2190. Reisner, R.G. *Bird: The Legend of Charlie Parker*.
New York: Citadel Press, 1962; London: MacGibbon &
Kee, 1963; London: Jazz Book Club, 1965.

Compiles recollections of Parker from those who knew
him both personally and as a musician.

2191. Russell, Ross. *Bird Lives: The High Life and Hard Times
of Charlie (Yardbird) Parker*. New York: Charterhouse; London: Quarter Books, 1973.

Considered by many the best biography on Parker to
date, this book is rich with material on Parker as a
man and musician. Russell (who was the owner of Dial
Records) conducted painstaking research into Parker's
life and so provides a vivid picture of Parker, from
his beginnings as a Kansas City musician and his infatu-
ation with Lester Young to his many experiences in New
York. Russell also offers some musical examples as
well as commenting on several of Parker's performances
and the influence of the blues on his musical style.

DJANGO REINHARDT

2192. De Launay, Charles. *Django Reinhardt, souvenirs.
Précedés d'un inédit de Jean Cocteau*. Paris:
Editions jazz-hot, 1954.

Includes an extensive discography.

BUDDY RICH

2193.   Balliett, Whitney. *Super Drummer: A Profile of Buddy
        Rich*. Indianapolis: Bobbs-Merrill, 1968.

        Contains good photographs in a description of the
        life and music of Rich.

ARTIE SHAW

2194.   Blandford, Edmund L. *Artie Shaw: A Bio-discography*.
        Hastings, Sussex: Castle Books, 1973.

        Compiles a picture of Shaw drawn from books and
        articles about him. The author does not assess Shaw's
        music but does include a discography.

2195.   Shaw, Artie. *The Trouble with Cinderella: An Outline
        of Identity*. New York: Farrar, Straus and Young,
        1952; London: Jarrolds, 1955; New York: Collier, 1963.

        An interesting self-portrait of the man more than
        his music.

WILLIE SMITH

2196.   Smith, Willie "The Lion." *Music on My Mind: The
        Memoirs of an American Pianist*. Garden City, New York:
        Doubleday, 1964; London: MacGibbon & Kee, 1965;
        London: Jazz Book Club, 1966; New York: Da Capo,
        1975.

        Details the life and musical career of Smith. A list
        of his compositions and a discography, 1920 to 1961,
        are included. Foreword is by Duke Ellington.

JACK TEAGARDEN

2197.   Smith, Jay D., and Len Guttridge. *Jack Teagarden: The
        Story of a Jazz Maverick*. London: Cassell, 1960;
        London: Jazz Book Club, 1962.

        A positive portrayal of the life and music of this
        outstanding trombonist. A selected discography of LP's
        only covering the years 1928 to 1958 is included.

FATS WALLER

2198. Fox, Charles. *Fats Waller*. London: Cassell, 1960;
       New York: Barnes, 1961.

       Contains a short biographical sketch of Waller as
       well as an assessment of his music based on selected
       recordings. There is also a selected discography.

2199. Kirkeby, W.T. *Ain't Misbehavin': The Story of Fats
       Waller*. London: Davies, 1966; London: Jazz Book
       Club, 1967.

       A narrative account of Waller's life, written in
       collaboration with Duncan P. Schiedt and Sinclair
       Traill. The author bases his account on his personal
       acquaintance with Waller from 1937 to 1943, when he was
       his manager.

DICKY WELLS

2200. Wells, Dicky. *The Night People: Reminiscences of a
       Jazzman*. Boston: Crescendo; London: Hale, 1971.

       A detailed account, as told to Stanley Dance, of
       Wells's life and association with such musicians as
       Fletcher Henderson, Count Basie, and Ray Charles
       from his successful years to his decline in Paris in
       the 1950's. Foreword is by Count Basie.

PAUL WHITEMAN

2201. Whiteman, Paul, and M.M. McBride. *Jazz*. New York:
       Sears, 1926.

       Treats Whiteman's career and contributions to jazz
       romantically.

C. DISCOGRAPHIES

SCIENCE OF DISCOGRAPHY

2202. Black, Douglas C. *Matrix Numbers: Their Meaning and History*. Melbourne: Australia Jazz Quarterly, 1946.

Contains a brief introduction to the significance of matrix numbers and their usefulness to collectors. Also provides notes on different matrix number series, such as Decca, Okeh, Columbia, Brunswick, and Victor. A good manual for the beginning discographer.

2203. Langridge, Derek. *Your Jazz Collection*. London: Archon Books, 1970.

Discusses collecting and literature relating to it, with much of the book devoted to classifying and indexing both literature and recordings.

2204. Taubman, Howard, ed. *The New York Times Guide to Listening Pleasure*. New York: Macmillan, 1968.

Concentrates on classical music, with some limited attention to jazz. Essentially this is a how-to guide for the novice record collector.

COLLECTIVE JAZZ DISCOGRAPHIES

2205. Allen, Walter C., ed. *Studies in Jazz Discography, I*. Newark: Institute of Jazz Studies, Rutgers, The State University of New Jersey, 1971.

These are the edited proceedings of three conferences-- the first two Conferences on Discographical Research (June, 1968 and 1969) and the Conference on Preservation and Extension of the Jazz Heritage (July, 1969). Papers from the discographical research conferences discuss

discographical goals and methods, problems of dating
and performer identification, and issues in jazz and
social science. These papers also concern historical
aspects of discography, archival practices of record
companies, the research value of Black newspapers, and
uninvestigated areas in discographical studies. Papers
from the third conference cover areas such as the
function of a jazz archive, the collection and preservation of material, jazz education and the community, and
general related topics.

2206. Avakian, George. *Jazz from Columbia: A Complete Jazz
   Catalog.* New York: Columbia Records, 1956.

   Arranged by style/category, this list contains approximately 150 entries. Each style/category is preceded
   by a short introductory essay. Discographical information is confined to the album release numbers.

2207. Blackstone, Orin. *Index to Jazz.* 4 vols. Fairfax,
   Virginia: Record Changer, 1945-48. 2nd ed. Vol. 1
   only. New Orleans: Privately printed, 1949.

   Frequently omits dates and matrix numbers.

2208. Bruyninckx, Walter. *50 Years of Recorded Jazz: 1917-
   1967.* Mechelen, Belgium: Author, 1968.

   Contains full discographical information, arranged
   alphabetically by artist.

2209. Carey, David A., and Albert J. McCarthy. *The Directory
   of Recorded Jazz and Swing Music.* Vols. 1-4. Fording-
   bridge and Hampshire: Delphic Press, 1949-1952. Vols.
   5-6. London: Cassell, 1955-1957.

   Contains broad, comprehensive listings for recorded
   jazz (particularly Bebop and Swing) through 1957, when
   publication ceased. Also has listings in spirituals,
   gospels, and "race records."

2210. Cherrington, George, and Brian Knight. *Jazz Catalogue:
   A Discography of All British Jazz Releases Complete
   with Full Personals and Recording Dates.* 10 vols.
   London: Jazz Journal, 1960-1971.

   Itemizes British releases from numerous jazz labels,
   such as Bluenote, Prestige, and Riverside. Also lists
   some blues and gospel recordings. Arrangement is alphabetical by artist with separate listings of collections
   at the back of each section.

2211. Cooper, David E. *International Bibliography of Discog-
       raphies: Classical and Jazz and Blues, 1962-1972: A
       Reference Book for Record Collectors, Dealers, and
       Libraries.* Littleton, Colorado: Libraries Unlimited,
       1975.

       Deals in the first section with classical music and
       in the second with blues and jazz. A carefully organized
       and categorized bibliography.

2212. Culloz, Maurice. *Guide des disques de jazz.* Paris:
       Buchet/Chastel, 1971.

       Contains over 1,000 selected jazz, spiritual, gospel,
       and blues recordings.

2213. DeLaunay, Charles. *Hot Discography.* Paris: Hot jazz,
       1936.

       Organizes artists according to broad, chronologically
       arranged stylistic categories. DeLaunay, one of the
       foremost jazz discographers, is selective here. In
       subsequent discographies he expands his coverage.

2214. ————. *Hot Discography.* 2nd ed. Paris: Hot jazz,
       1938.

2215. ————. *Hot Discography.* 3rd ed. Edited by Hot Jazz.
       New York: Commodore Music Shop, 1940.

2216. ————. *New Hot Discography: The Standard Dictionary
       of Recorded Jazz.* Edited by Walter Schaap and George
       Avakian. New York: Criterion, 1948.

2217. ————. *Hot discographie encyclopédique avec la col-
       laboration de Kurt Mohr.* 3 vols. Paris: Jazz
       disques, 1951-52.

2218. Evensmo, Jan. *The Tenor Saxophonists of the Period
       1930-1942.* Vol. 1. Oslo: Evensmo, 1969.

       Offers separate discographies of Chu Barry, Herschel
       Evans, Coleman Hawkins, Ben Webster, and Lester Young.
       The compiler comments on each solo on the recordings.

2219. Fox, Charles; Peter Gammond; and Alun Morgan. *Jazz on
       Record: A Critical Guide.* London: Hutchinson, 1960.

       Contains blues and jazz entries arranged alphabetically
       by artist. The entries include artist's name, date, and

instrument; significance in the development of the style; and an assessment of the artist's recordings and stylistic evolution. Although English recordings constitute the majority of entries, many American labels are also included, along with a full name index. Alexis Korner provides additional material.

2220.   Harris, Rex, and Brian Rust. *Recorded Jazz: A Critical Guide*. Harmondsworth: Penguin, 1958.

Provides biographical information and stylistic comments for each of the more popular jazz musicians or groups covered. Recordings from both American and British LP's and EP's of the 1950's are included.

2221.   Harrison, Max; Alun Morgan; Ronald Atkins; Michael James; and Jack Cooke. *Modern Jazz: The Essential Records*. London: Aquarius Books, 1975.

Assesses what these British critics selected as the two hundred best postwar jazz recordings. Critical essays on each of the recordings are arranged according to eight chronological styles/categories. Although one thousand artists are covered, Parker, Coleman, Coltrane, Monk, and Rollins dominate the book. Each entry has complete discographical information as well as the later available British and American record numbers.

2222.   Jasen, David A. *Recorded Ragtime 1897-1958*. Hamden, Connecticut: Archon, 1973.

A comprehensive discography, containing record label numbers as well as date of the recording.

2223.   *Jazz Records, 1897-1942*. Rev. ed. London: Storyville Publications, 1970.

Lists all known American and British recordings in the ragtime, jazz, and swing styles made up to the Petrillo band. Arrangement is alphabetical by artist or band, with composers' names given for ragtime numbers. There is a ninety-page artist index in this revised edition.

2224.   *Jazz on LP's: A Collector's Guide to Jazz on Decca, Brunswick, Capitol, London and Felsted Long Playing Records*. Rev. ed. London: Decca Records, 1956.

Recordings are listed first, followed by stylistic

assessments. Entries include date of the recording
and names of the personnel involved.

2225.   *Jazz on 78's: A Guide to the Many Examples of Classic
        Jazz on Decca, Brunswick and London 78 R.P.M. Records*.
        London: Decca Records, 1954.

        Contains general stylistic critiques rather than
        assessments of individual recordings. The booklet lists
        78's only, including recording personnel and date.

2226.   Jepsen, Jorgen Grunnet. *Jazz Records: A Discography*.
        Copenhagen: Karl E. Knudsen, 1963.

        Includes discographies of many of jazz's outstanding
        performers.

2227.   ————. *Jazz Records: A Discography*. 8 vols. Copen-
        hagen: Karl E. Knudsen, 1963-1970.

        First published to continue the Carey and McCarthy
        work, volumes 5 through 8 (covering 1942-1962) were
        issued first, followed by volumes 1 through 3 (1965)
        and 4 (1967). The listings, arranged alphabetically by
        artist or band and chronologically within entries,
        include blues, rhythm and blues, and gospel. Cross-
        references are good, but the index is limited.

2228.   Lange, Horst H. *Die Deutsche Jazz-Discographie: Eine
        Geschichte des Jazz auf Schallplatten von 1902 bis
        1955*. Berlin: Bore & Bock, 1955.

        Offers good cross section of listings on jazz to 1955.

2229.   McCarthy, Albert J. *Jazz Discography I: An International
        Discography of Recorded Jazz, Including Blues, Gospel
        and Rhythm and Blues for the Year January-December
        1958*. London: Cassell, 1960.

        Attempts to provide a list of new releases and U.S.
        reissues for the one year. Mostly jazz entries.

2230.   McCarthy, Albert, ed. *Jazz on Records, 1917-1967*.
        2nd ed. New York: Oak, 1969.

        Contains alphabetically arranged biographical articles
        with selective discographies for each artist. Also
        included are general articles, surveys of musical ap-
        peals (e.g., "Post-War Reeds"), and geographical sur-
        veys of blues.

2231.   McCarthy, Albert; Alun Morgan; Paul Oliver; and Max
        Harrison. *Jazz on Record: A Critical Guide to the
        First 50 Years, 1917-1967.* New York: Oak; London:
        Hanover Books, 1968.

        Extends the discography by Fox, Gammond, Morgan, and
        Korner. It includes entries on blues and jazz repre-
        senting both American and British labels as well as a
        second section in which artists who do not appear in
        the first work are discussed. These artists are
        treated in categories, as follows: geographical blues,
        piano blues, ragtime, New Orleans jazz, big bands,
        post-war pianists, progressives, spirituals, and songs.
        A name index is included.

2232.   Panassie, Hugues. *Discographie critique des meilleurs
        disques de jazz.* Paris: Laffont, 1958.

        Contains valuable comments on a wide range of jazz
        recordings up to 1957.

2233.   Ramsey, Frederic. *A Guide to Longplay Records.* New
        York: Long Player Publications, 1954.

        An annotated guide of about four hundred entries to
        individual artists and bands. The book contains short
        discussions of select available recordings as well as
        artist and title indexes.

2234.   Ruppli, Michel. *Prestige Jazz Records 1949-1969: A
        Discography.* Copenhagen: Karl E. Knudsen, 1972.

        Includes original blues, gospel, and jazz recordings
        as well as all reissues made by Prestige during this
        period. The original recordings are arranged in chrono-
        logical order of recording session. Reissues from other
        labels are also included and listed chronologically
        by original recording date.

2235.   Rust, Brian. *Jazz Records A-Z, 1897-1942.* 2 vols.
        4th ed. New Rochelle, New York: Arlington House,
        1972.

        Contains listings of all jazz recordings to 1942.
        The arrangement is alphabetical by artist or orchestra,
        with the orchestra's personnel, place and date of
        recording, song titles, matrix numbers, and label and
        issue numbers, plus notes relating to each recording
        given in each entry. Updated in a variety of sources,
        including *Jazz Journal* and *Storyville*; similar to
        Jepsen's discography.

2236. ───. *The Dance Bands*. London: Ian Allan, 1972.

Lists mainly British bands from 1919 to 1944, with many rare photographs.

2237. ───. *The American Dance Band Discography, 1917-1942*. 2 vols. New Rochelle, New York: Arlington House, 1975.

Provides complete data for the recordings of 2,000 bands, including some biographical sketches. Rust does not cover Black bands, however. The book contains a complete index.

2238. Schleman, Hilton. *Rhythm on Record: A Who's Who and Register of Recorded Dance Music*. London: Melody Maker, 1936.

Includes dance bands and brief biographical sketches on each band leader. This volume preceded DeLaunay's works.

2239. Smith, Charles Edward. *The Jazz Record Book*. New York: Smith and Durrell, 1942.

Provides a short historical and musical overview of jazz to 1942, with contributions from Frederic Ramsey, Charles Payne, and William Russell. The areas covered are Chicago, New York, blues and boogie-woogie, bands, and (then) contemporary. Full discographical details are included.

2240. Stagg, Tom, and Charlie Crump. *New Orleans, The Revival: A Tape and Discography of Negro Traditional Jazz Recorded in New Orleans or by New Orleans Bands, 1937-1972*. Dublin: Bashall Eaves, 1973.

Primarily lists New Orleans Black musicians, including brass bands. First releases, reissues, and unissued recordings are included as well as private tapes and taped interviews. In fact, much of the book consists of unissued recordings. The entries are arranged alphabetically by band leader or group name.

2241. Testoni, Gian Carlo. *Enciclopedia del jazz*. 2nd ed. Milan: Messaggerie musicali, 1954.

Contains brief biographies and detailed discographies of recordings issued in Italy from 1920 to 1950.

2242.   Traill, Sinclair, and Gerald Lascelles. *Just Jazz.*
        Vols. 1-2. London: Davies, 1957-1958; Vol. 3. London:
        Landsborough, 1959; Vol. 4. London: Souvenir Press,
        1960.

        Each volume contains a collection of essays and an
        annual discography. Some British recordings are in-
        cluded.

2243.   Van Eyle, William. *Jazz Pearls.* Oudkarged, Holland:
        Van Eyle, 1975.

        Surveys 3,102 jazz recordings listed chronologically.

2244.   Wilson, John S. *The Collector's Jazz: Traditional and
        Swing.* Philadelphia: Lippincott, 1958.

        Discusses and assesses individual jazz personalities
        and groups.

2245.   ———. *The Collector's Jazz: Modern.* Philadelphia:
        Lippincott, 1959.

        Covers several outstanding musicians, such as Parker,
        Miles Davis, and Charles Mingus. Similar to the *Tradi-
        tional and Swing* collection.

                    INDIVIDUAL DISCOGRAPHIES

LOUIS ARMSTRONG

2246.   Jepsen, Jorgen Grunnet. *A Discography of Louis Arm-
        strong.* 3 vols. Copenhagen: Karl E. Knudsen, 1968.

        Chronologically lists Armstrong's recording sessions
        with his band. Full details are given for sessions
        throughout his career, e.g., band name, personnel,
        location, date, matrix and take numbers, titles, and
        original release and LP issue numbers.

2247.   Lover, William C. "Louis Armstrong Discography."
        Jazz 1, no. 12 (Dec. 1943): 18-22.

        Itemizes Armstrong's recordings to 1943, including
        some reprints. Discographical information is provided.

2248. McCarthy, Albert J. "Louis Armstrong: Discography."
       Record Changer, July-Aug. 1950, pp. 37-42.

    Contains complete listings to 1950, including many
reprints and discographical information.

COUNT BASIE

2249. Scherman, Bo, and Carl A. Hoellstrom. *A Discography
       of Count Basie*. Vol. 1. Copenhagen: Karl E.
       Knudsen, 1969.
       Jepsen, Jorgen Grunnet. *A Discography of Count Basie*.
       Vol. 2. Copenhagen: Karl E. Knudsen, 1969.

    Continues the Jepsen series of fully detailed,
comprehensive Armstrong discographies. Volume 1 covers
1929 to 1950 and Volume 2 covers 1951 to 1968.

SIDNEY BECHET

2250. Mauerer, Hans J. *A Discography of Sidney Bechet*.
       Copenhagen: Karl E. Knudsen, 1969.

    Covers Bechet's entire career and includes recordings
of Bechet's own group as well as those he made with
others from 1921 to 1964. Each recording session is
coded to indicate who supervised the recording session
or the record label. There are artist and title indexes.

JOHN COLTRANE

2251. Jepsen, Jorgen Grunnet. *A Discography of John Coltrane*.
       Copenhagen: Karl E. Knudsen, 1969.

    Provides full discographical details on recording
sessions throughout Coltrane's career.

MILES DAVIS

2252. Jepsen, Jorgen Grunnet. *A Discography of Miles Davis*.
       Copenhagen: Karl E. Knudsen, 1969.

    Lists recording sessions of Miles Davis to 1969 with
full discographical details.

2253.   Aasland, Benny H. *The "Wax" Works of Duke Ellington*.
        Stockholm: Aasland, 1954.

        A comprehensive list of Ellington's works, including
        some reprints, with complete discographical informa-
        tion.

2254.   Bakker, Dick. *Duke Ellington on Microgroove, 1923-
        1942*. Alphen aan den Rijn, Holland: Micrography,
        1974.

        Lists all recordings made during this period, including
        broadcast and films. Personnel are not included in the
        body of this work but are given in a table, with a key,
        in the introduction.

2255.   Massagli, Luciano; Liborio Rusatori; and Giovanni M.
        Volonte. *Duke Ellington's Story on Records*. 9 vols.
        Milan: Musica jazz, 1966-1975.

        Covers the Ellington career from 1923 to 1955. This
        outstanding discography includes complete information
        on commercial recordings, sound tracks, concerts, and
        radio and television performances. In addition, the
        authors provide a structural analysis of each piece,
        e.g., the number of bars comprising the theme, the suc-
        cessions of choruses, and the contribution of specific
        soloists in order of entry. Each volume has indexes
        of titles (with composers), personnel (with dates of
        each musician's stay in the band and references to
        solos) and Microgroove releases (with contents). The
        volumes cover the following dates: vol. 1: 1923-31;
        vol. 2: 1932-38; vol. 3: 1939-42; vol. 4: 1943-44;
        vol. 5: 1945; vol. 6: 1946; vol. 7: 1947-50; vol. 8:
        1951-52; vol. 9: 1953-55.

2256.   San Filippo, Luigi. *General Catalog of Duke Elling-
        ton's Recorded Music*. Palermo: Centro studi di
        musica contemporanea, 1964; 2nd ed., 1966.

        Lists 1,472 titles covering the years 1924 to 1965,
        but not as comprehensive as the Massagli discography.
        The entries are listed in chronological order with a
        title index. In addition to complete discographical
        information, the author provides information on V-discs,
        films, and radio and television transcriptions.

DIZZY GILLESPIE

2257. Jepsen, Jorgen Grunnet. *A Discography of Dizzy Gilles-
        pie.* 2 vols. Copenhagen: Karl E. Knudsen, 1969.

        An in-depth, chronological listing of Gillespie's
        recording sessions to 1969 with full discographical
        information.

BENNY GOODMAN

2258. Connor, D. Russel, and Warren W. Hicks. *BG: On the
        Road. A Bio-discography of Benny Goodman.* New
        Rochelle, New York: Arlington House, 1969.

        Expands and updates *BG: Off the Road*, which Connor
        published privately in 1958. Contains a tremendous
        amount of data about Goodman's recordings and musicians.

BILLIE HOLIDAY

2259. Bakker, Dick M. *Billie and Teddy on Microgroove,
        1932-1944.* Alphen aan den Rijn, Holland: Micrography,
        1975.

        Consists of a discography of the microgroove reissues
        of Billie Holiday and Teddy Wilson. Some of these
        recordings were originally made on the Brunswick, Okeh,
        Vocalion, and Commodore labels. The entries provide
        details of personnel, location, date, and LP reissue
        numbers. Artist and title indexes are included.

2260. Jepsen, Jorgen Grunnet. *A Discography of Billie Holiday.*
        Copenhagen: Karl E. Knudsen, 1969.

        Offers complete discographical information on recording
        sessions throughout Billie Holiday's musical career.

MILT JACKSON AND THE M.J.Q.

2261. Wilbraham, Roy. *Milt Jackson: A Discography and Biog-
        raphy, Including Recordings Made with the M.J.Q.*
        London: Wilbraham, 1968.

        Provides a short biographical sketch of Jackson as
        well as an index to each of his compositions. The
        entries are arranged chronologically.

STAN KENTON

2262. Pirie, Christopher A., and Siegfried Mueller. *Artistry in Kenton: The Bio-discography of Stan Kenton and His Music*. 2 vols. Vienna: Siegfried Mueller, 1969.

Details all of Kenton's recordings from 1937 to 1953. A biographical narrative with comments on each session is also included, along with an itinerary, an alphabetical title index of first recordings, an artist index, and a list of arrangers.

2263. Venudor, Pete, and Michael Sparke. *The Standard Kenton Directory*. Amsterdam: Pete Venudor, 1968.

Covers a wide range of Kenton's recordings from 1937 to 1949. Also included is an index of all titles in the Kenton band book, recorded or not, as well as information on Kenton on film.

JACKIE McLEAN

2264. Wilbraham, Roy. *Jackie McLean: A Discography with Biography*. London: Wilbraham, 1967.

Contains a short biographical sketch of McLean and an index of each of his compositions. The entries are arranged chronologically.

GLENN MILLER

2265. Flower, John. *Moonlight Serenade: A Bio-discography of the Glenn Miller Civilian Band*. New Rochelle, New York: Arlington House, 1972.

A detailed chronological discography.

CHARLES MINGUS

2266. Wilbraham, Roy. *Charles Mingus: A Biography and Discography*. London: Wilbraham, 1967.

Lists each of Mingus' compositions chronologically along with a short biography.

THELONIOUS MONK

2267.   Jepsen, Jorgen Grunnet. *A Discography of Thelonious
        Monk and Bud Powell.* Copenhagen: Karl E. Knudsen,
        1969.

        Details the recordings of Monk and Powell.

JELLY ROLL MORTON

2268.   Davies, John R.T., and Laurio Wright. *Morton's Music.*
        London: Storyville Publications, 1968.

        Treats Morton's work in three sections: piano rolls,
        commercial discs, and Library of Congress recordings.
        In the commercial and Library of Congress sections, the
        author provides information on personnel, venue and
        date titles, matrix and catalog numbers, and notes.
        Also provided is information on master disposition
        dates for Victor and Columbia, including original
        disposition instructions and charge of intent and cur-
        rent disposition of each title.

HOT LIPS PAGE

2269.   Demeusy, Bertrand; Otto Fluckiger; Jorgen Grunnet
        Jepsen; and Kurt Mohr. *Hot Lips Page.* Basel: Jazz
        Publications, 1961.

        Based on DeLaunay's *New Hot Discography*, this discog-
        raphy includes brief biographical notes and information
        on Page's recordings with his band as well as on other
        bands with which he performed from 1935 to 1954.

CHARLES PARKER

2270.   Jepsen, Jorgen Grunnet. *A Discography of Charlie
        Parker.* Copenhagen: Karl E. Knudsen, 1968.

        Itemizes Parker's recordings, in-depth and chrono-
        logically, including full discographical details.

2271. Koch, Lawrence. "A Numerical Listing of Charlie Parker's
       Recordings." *Journal of Jazz Studies* 2, no. 2 (June
       1975): 86-95.

       A comprehensive listing of Parker's recordings with
       some discographical details.

2272. Koster, Piet, and Dick M. Bakker. *Charlie Parker.*
       Vol. 1, 1940-1947; vol. 2, 1948-1950. Alphen aan den
       Rijn, Holland: Micrography, 1974-75.

       Complete discographical information is given in the
       first two volumes of a projected four-volume discog-
       raphy of commercial releases, private recordings, and
       broadcasts. The third volume is scheduled to cover the
       years 1951 to 1954, while the fourth will cover addi-
       tions, corrections, and omissions.

2273. Williams, Tony. "Charlie Parker Discography." *Disco-
       graphical Forum* 2, no. 1 (Nov. 1968): 8-20.

       Provides comprehensive and accurate discographical
       information.

BUD POWELL (see item 2267)

BUDDY RICH

2274. Cooper, David J. *Buddy Rich Discography.* London:
       Blackburn, Lancs, Cooper, 1974.

       Lists Rich's recordings from 1938 to 1973, with de-
       tails of personnel, dates, locations, titles, and
       release numbers as well as brief biographical sketches.

SONNY ROLLINS

2275. Blancq, Charles Clement, III. "Melodic Improvisation
       in American Jazz: The Style of Theodore 'Sonny'
       Rollins, 1952-1962." Ph.D. dissertation, Tulane
       University, 1977.

       Studies in detail the improvisational techniques
       used by Rollins as exemplified in selected recordings.
       The author is expanding on Gunther Schuller's article
       on thematic motifs in some of Rollins' music. A
       valuable scholarly effort.

FATS WALLER

2276.   Davies, John R.T.   *The Music of Thomas "Fats" Waller,*
        with Complete Discography.   London: Jazz Journal,
        1950.   Rev. ed by R.T. Cooke.   London: Friends of
        Fats (Thomas "Fats" Waller Appreciation Society),
        1953.

        Contains approximately six hundred recordings made
        by Waller between 1922 and 1943 as a soloist, accom-
        panist, session man, and band leader.   The entries,
        arranged chronologically, provide full details of
        personnel, date, place (when possible), matrix number,
        title, and release number.   The revised edition provides
        details of more sessions, record notes, and an index.
        Both editions list piano roll titles.

LESTER YOUNG

2277.   Jepsen, Jorgen Grunnet.   *A Discography of Lester Young.*
        Copenhagen: Karl E. Knudsen, 1968.

        Fully details Young's recordings.

D. HISTORIES-SURVEYS

2278. Balliett, Whitney. *Dinosaurs in the Morning: 41 Pieces
on Jazz.* Philadelphia: Lippincott; Toronto: McClel-
land, 1962; London: Phoenix House, 1964; London: Jazz
Book Club, 1965.

Continues the same format as *The Sounds of Surprise:
46 Pieces on Jazz.* Essays in this volume originally
appeared in *The New Yorker* between 1957 and 1962. The
pieces (historical essays, interviews, descriptions,
and portraits) deal with musicians representing blues
and ragtime as well as new and old jazz styles. They
contain no musical examples but do offer insightful
approaches to appreciation and criticism.

2279. ————. *The Sounds of Surprise: 46 Pieces on Jazz.*
New York: Dutton, 1959; London: Kimber, 1960; London:
Jazz Book Club, 1962; Harmondsworth: Penguin, 1963.

Collects the author's essays from *The Saturday Review,
Reporter* (1954-56), and *The New Yorker* (1957-59). The
articles present interesting bio-musical and sociological
views concerning jazz musicians who performed in New
York in the 1950's. Among the artists discussed are
Duke Ellington, the Modern Jazz Quartet, Charles Mingus,
Red Allen, Ben Webster, Sid Catlett, and Sidney Bechet.

2280. ————. *Ecstasy at the Onion: Thirty-One Pieces on
Jazz.* Indianapolis: Bobbs-Merrill, 1971.

Presents additional essays by the author from *The
New Yorker* from 1967 to 1971. There are five pieces
on Duke Ellington, seven critical reviews, and a selected number of portraits on some of the jazz musicians
who appeared in New York during these years. Among the
musicians discussed are Ray Charles, Elvin Jones, the
Modern Jazz Quartet, Red Norvo, Bobby Short, and Charles
Mingus. The three books by Balliett are excellent for
their perceptive jazz appreciation and criticism.

2281. Berendt, Joachim Ernest. *Der Jazz: Eine Zeit kritische
       Studie*. Stuttgart, 1950.

       Offers a good interpretation of jazz and jazz his-
       tory but contains little new information.

2282. —————. *The Jazz Book from New Orleans to Rock and
       Free Jazz*. New York: Hill & Wang, 1966.

       Surveys, from the European point of view, jazz
       styles and periods through the mid-sixties. The author
       makes some interesting and perceptive points on "free"
       jazz but does not go into depth on any style.

2283. Blesh, Rudi. *Shining Trumpets: A History of Jazz*.
       New York: Knopf; London: Cassell, 1949. 2nd rev.
       ed. New York: Knopf, 1958. Reprint. New York:
       Da Capo, 1975.

       Stands as one of the most influential and well-
       researched early works on jazz history, with only one
       major flaw: the author's claim that jazz was born in
       New Orleans. This claim permeated most jazz histories
       at the time. The topics covered range from the African
       roots of jazz and the development of sacred-secular
       Black music of the South through the swing style of
       jazz. Forty-seven transcriptions supplement the good
       analyses of the performances of several New Orleans
       musicians. A selected discography and an index are
       included.

2284. —————. *This Is Jazz: A Series of Lectures Given at
       the San Francisco Museum of Art*. San Francisco,
       1943; London: Jazz Music Books, 1945.

       Focuses on the historical and musical development
       of New Orleans jazz, with critiques of the Chicago and
       Big Band styles of jazz. The lectures were scholarly
       but tainted by the author's dislike for all jazz
       styles except for New Orleans. These lectures preceded
       Shining Trumpets and contain much of the material that
       subsequently appeared in that book.

2285. Budds, Michael J. *Jazz in the Sixties: The Expansion
       of Musical Resources and Techniques*. Iowa City;
       University of Iowa Press, 1978.

       Discusses such topics as color and instrumentation,
       texture and volume, melody and harmony, meter and
       rhythm, and structural design. Includes a bibliography
       and discography.

2286. Buerkle, Jack V., and Danny Barker. *Bourbon Street Black: The New Orleans Black Jazz Man*. New York: Oxford University Press, 1973.

Provides a glimpse into the lives of many New Orleans musicians. Although the book is more sociological than musical, it does offer some good background information on music unions, music apprenticeships, the role of religion in jazz, and more.

2287. Charles, Philippe, and Jean Louis Comolli. *Free Jazz/ Black Power*. Paris: Ed. champ. libre, 1971.

Argues that the so-called free jazz style is an outgrowth of the Black awareness movement. Contains some information on Ornette Coleman, John Coltrane, and others. This study is both interesting and perceptive.

2288. Charters, Samuel B., and Leonard Kunstadt. *Jazz: A History of the New York Scene*. Garden City, New York: Doubleday, 1962.

Studies the history of New York jazz to the 1950's to show its importance in the overall development of jazz. Particular attention is given to the first thirty years as the authors detail the roles of such personalities as James Reese Europe, the ODJB, Mamie Smith, Paul Whiteman, Don Redman, Fletcher Henderson, Chick Webb, Benny Goodman, Duke Ellington, Dizzy Gillespie, Charles Parker, and Thelonious Monk. In this well-researched and concise book, the authors also describe other styles that were then developing.

2289. Coeroy, André, and André Schaegger. *Le jazz*. Paris, 1926.

One of the first critical works on jazz. Useful and insightful remarks, particularly for its time.

2290. Dance, Stanley. *The World of Swing*. New York: Scribner's, 1974.

Contains informative interviews with musicians of the Swing era, such as members of the Basie, Ellington, and Goodman bands.

2291. Dauer, Alfons M. *Der Jazz: Seine Ursprunge und seine Entwicklung*. Eisenach, German Democratic Republic, 1958.

Includes nearly one hundred pages of musical examples transcribed by the author from recordings of early jazz

and African music. The information on African roots
of jazz is especially valuable.

2292.   ────. *Jazz: Die magische Musik: Ein leitfaden Durch
          der Jazz.* Bremen, Federal Republic of Germany, 1961.

   Surveys jazz history and style but is sometimes
   lacking in documentation.

2293.   Fernett, Gene. *Swing Out: Great Negro Dance Bands.*
          Midland, Michigan: Pendell, 1970.

   Discusses twenty-five Black bands--the band leader,
   significant musicians in the group, and the group's
   musical style. The book also includes dates and places
   of birth of fifty-four musicians, the theme songs of
   the band, and some excellent photographs. Highly
   recommended.

2294.   ────. *A Thousand Golden Horns: The Exciting Age of
          America's Greatest Dance Bands.* Midland, Michigan:
          Pendell, 1966.

   Treats the work of some Swing as well as some pseudo-
   jazz bands from 1925 to 1945.

2295.   Ferstl, Erich. *Die Schule des Jazz.* Munich, 1963.

   Geared to the concerns of jazz critics and historians
   and the musically literate reader interested in performing jazz. This book is not concerned with stylistic
   subdivisions.

2296.   Finkelstein, Sidney. *Jazz: A People's Music.* New
          York: Macmillan, 1968.

   Surveys jazz to the beginning of Bop from a sound
   analytical point of view.

2297.   Fox, Charles. *Jazz in Perspective.* London: Barrier
          Jenkins, 1969.

   Traces the roots of jazz and the personalities involved in its development. The book uses many musical
   examples to illustrate the growth and evolution of
   jazz. Originally written for a B.B.C. radio series,
   this text is introductory.

2298.   Goffin, Robert. *Jazz: From the Congo to the Metropoli-
          tan.* Garden City, New York: Doubleday, 1944. Re-
          print. New York: Da Capo, 1975.

Traces the development of jazz from New Orleans to
the 1960's. The author, known for his ability to dis-
tinguish technically between hot and commercial jazz,
draws informative and perceptive portraits of several
musicians, particularly Louis Armstrong and Benny
Goodman. He argues that each continent will eventually
develop an indigenous jazz style. The introduction is
by Arnold Gingrich.

2299. ————. *Aux frontières du jazz*. Paris: Du sagittaire,
1932.

Includes some important information. However, the
book is permeated with mistakes.

2300. Gridley, Mark. *Jazz Styles*. Englewood Cliffs, New
Jersey: Prentice-Hall, 1978.

Contains biographies and word analyses of numerous
jazz musicians, e.g., Duke Ellington, Miles Davis,
John Coltrane. The analyses are based on recordings.
Good for the general student.

2301. Grossman, William L., and Jack W. Farrell. *The Heart
of Jazz*. New York, 1956.

Discusses the Dixieland jazz of the 1940's with an
appeal to maintain tradition.

2302. Harris, Rex. *Jazz*. 3rd ed. Harmondsworth: Penguin,
1954.

Comments insightfully on the origins and early history
of jazz, specifically on its African roots, although
some of the author's conclusions are questionable.
There is no musical analysis, but a chart illustrates,
in the author's opinion, the origins and development
of jazz to 1950.

2303. Hentoff, Nat. *Jazz Is*. New York: Random House, 1976.

Talks about jazz life, the players, and their music.
While not a comprehensive history, the book does provide
important information on the political economy of jazz
and the new frontiers in jazz.

2304. ————, and Albert J. McCarthy, eds. *Jazz: New
Perspectives on the History of Jazz by Twelve of the
World's Foremost Jazz Critics and Scholars*. New York:
Rinehart, 1959. Reprint. New York: Da Capo, 1974.

Presents critical and scholarly essays on the history

and development of jazz, on different jazz styles, and on individual jazz musicians.

2305.   Hobson, Wilder. *American Jazz Music*. New York: W.W. Norton, 1939; London: Dent, 1941; London: Jazz Book Club, 1956.

Examines the roots of jazz historically (through the Swing era) and analytically (by treating the technical features of jazz and Swing). A selected discography of thirty records illustrates the author's view of the development of jazz. A good index is included.

2306.   Hodeir, Andre. *Jazz: Its Evolution and Essence*. Translated by W. David Noakes. New York: Da Capo, 1956.

Emphasizes modern jazz styles. This study ranks among the first good works in jazz analysis and criticism.

2307.   Kofsky, Frank. *Black Nationalism and the Revolution in Music*. New York: Pathfinder, 1970.

Correctly assesses the creative and social forces affecting Black jazz musicians as well as the sociological forces shaping the nationalistic movement in jazz. The author, one of the first White critics to treat this subject accurately, presents a controversial and penetrating commentary on LeRoi Jones's *Blues People* as well as an illuminating critique of critics' attitudes toward Black musicians, particularly creative and innovative musicians. The second part of the book deals with the music of several outstanding artists as a reflection of Black nationalism. The author gives special attention to the music of Coltrane, Coleman, and Cecil Taylor and also acknowledges the contributions of Albert Ayler, Elvin Jones, and McCoy Tyner. There is an analysis of Tyner and Coltrane as well as an attempt to relate the nationalistic jazz movement to the career of Malcolm X.

2308.   Longstreet, Stephen. *Sportin' House: A History of New Orleans Sinners and the Birth of Jazz*. Los Angeles: Sherbourne Press, 1965.

Attempts to view sociologically life in New Orleans and its relationship to the development of jazz. The book does not contain any new information nor does it rank as an outstanding scholarly work. It is emotional in approach and frequently inaccurate.

2309. Malson, Lucien. *Histoire du jazz*. Lausanne: Editions
        rencontre, 1967.

        Traces the development of jazz from the early New
        Orleans style to the 1960's. The book, though short,
        does contain some excellent photographs, especially
        those depicting the roots of jazz in Black culture,
        to supplement the historical information.

2310. Martinez, Raymond J. *Portraits of New Orleans Jazz:
        Miscellaneous Notes*. New Orleans: Hope Publications,
        1971.

        Discusses elements important to the development of
        jazz in New Orleans. There is information on Story-
        ville, New Orleans funerals, and Congo Square; also
        on L.M. Gottschalk, Louis Armstrong, King Oliver, Jelly
        Roll Morton, and George McCullum. Of particular im-
        portance is the information on Mardi Gras Indians.
        This is a brief but valuable study.

2311. McCarthy, Albert. *The Dance Band Era: The Dancing
        Decades from Ragtime to Swing: 1910-1950*. Phila-
        delphia: Chilton; London: Studio Vista, 1971.

        Introduces and discusses British and European dance
        bands along with a selected number (mostly White) of
        such American dance bands as Paul Whiteman, Jean Gold-
        kette, Ben Pollack, Casa Loma, and Benny Goodman.
        The book contains some excellent photographs.

2312. ————. *Big Band Jazz*. London: Barrie & Jenkins,
        1974.

        Surveys the development of Big Band jazz, with
        reference to the outstanding personalities involved.
        This comprehensive and well-illustrated volume covers
        the contributions of such artists as James Reese Europe,
        Wilbur Sweatman, Fletcher Henderson, Count Basie, Benny
        Goodman, and Duke Ellington as well as many less well-
        known big band leaders. The book contains numerous
        photographs, an extensive name index, a list of refer-
        ences, and bibliographical and discographical informa-
        tion. An informative and thorough contribution to
        jazz studies.

2313. ————. *The Trumpet in Jazz*. London: Citizen Press,
        1943.

        Traces the evolution of jazz through the selected
        recordings of trumpeters from Armstrong to the Swing era.

2314.   McRae, Barry. *The Jazz Cataclysm*. Cranbury, New
        Jersey: A.S. Barnes; London: Dent, 1967.

        Attempts to analyze and survey developments in jazz
        styles from the so-called Cool era to "free" jazz of
        the late 1960's. Particular attention is given to the
        contributions and styles of Ornette Coleman, John
        Coltrane, and Sonny Rollins. The author's views are
        colored by his obvious prejudice for modern jazz, with
        jazz of the Cool era excepted.

2315.   Morgan, Alun, and Raymond Herricks. *Modern Jazz: A
        Survey of Developments Since 1939*. London: Jazz
        Book Club, 1956.

        Champions the music of Duke Ellington in a compre-
        hensive survey of jazz.

2316.   Newton, Francis. *The Jazz Scene*. New York: Da Capo,
        1960.

        Serves as a comprehensive introduction to jazz as
        well as a critique of jazz styles and performers.

2317.   Osgood, Harry O. *So This Is Jazz*. Boston: Little,
        Brown, 1926.

        Approaches jazz history from a biased viewpoint by
        failing to consider the contributions of musicians
        like Jelly Roll Morton, King Oliver, Sidney Bechet,
        and many other Black musicians. Instead the focus is
        on such artists as Paul Whiteman and Zez Confrey. Although
        the book should not be considered a serious or authorita-
        tive work on jazz history, it does contain some good in-
        formation on Paul Whiteman, Freddie Gofe, and George
        Gershwin. The author also suggests an origin for the
        word "jazz" and discusses Black folk music.

2318.   Ostransky, Leroy. *The Anatomy of Jazz*. Tacoma:
        University of Washington Press, 1964.

        Details problems in jazz composition and performing
        and provides good information on the history of jazz
        as music.

2319.   Panassie, Hugues. *The Real Jazz*. Translated by Anne
        Sorelle Williams. New York: Smith and Durrell, 1942.
        2nd ed., rev. New York: Barnes, 1960; London: Jazz
        Book Club, 1967.

        Devoted primarily to an assessment of selected groups
        of musicians according to the instruments they play.

2320.   ———. *Histoire du vrai jazz*. Paris: R. Laffont,
         1959.

         Extols the virtues of traditional jazz over the
         emerging jazz trends of the time.

2321.   Ramsey, Frederic. *Chicago Documentary: Portrait of
         a Jazz Era*. London: Jazz Music Books, 1944.

         Treats the history of jazz in Chicago in the 1920's.
         The book lacks detail and overlooks several key
         Chicago jazz musicians.

2322.   Russell, Ross. *Jazz Style in Kansas City and the
         Southwest*. Berkeley and Los Angeles: University of
         California Press, 1971.

         Recognizes the importance of Kansas City in the develop-
         ment of jazz. In addition to sociological information
         (e.g., on the Prendergast's Machine and on the musical
         preferences of the Black population), the author dis-
         cusses individual artists and bands such as Buster
         Smith, Bennie Moten, Count Basie, Andy Kirk, Harlan
         Leonard, Jay McShann, and Charles Parker. He also
         treats territorial bands (Jack Teagarden and the Texas
         School). The approach in this well-illustrated and
         well-researched study, which was one of the first to
         examine the Kansas City influence in jazz, is descrip-
         tive rather than analytical. A selected discography
         and bibliography are included.

2323.   Rust, Brian. *The Dance Bands*. London: Allan, 1972;
         New Rochelle, New York: Arlington House, 1974.

         Presents information on individuals and bands,
         British and American. The book, written by an out-
         standing discographer, is a detailed account of the
         contributions and historical significance of these
         artists and dance bands to jazz history.

2324.   Sargeant, Winthrop. *Jazz: Hot and Hybrid*. New York:
         Arrow, 1938; Rev. ed. New York: Dutton, 1946; London:
         Jazz Book Club, 1959; Reprint. New York: Da Capo,
         1975.

         Analyzes the musical ingredients of jazz. The author
         discusses African influences, jazz melodies, rhythms,
         scale structures, harmony, and other musical elements.
         A good bibliography and index are included. This often-
         quoted book ranks as one of the first serious attempts
         in jazz analysis.

2325.   Schafer, William J. *Brass Bands and New Orleans Jazz*.
        Baton Rouge: Louisiana State University Press, 1977.

        Presents the history of New Orleans brass street
        bands from the late nineteenth century to the present.
        The book is interesting although rather vague in some
        of its explanations. Included are photographs of New
        Orleans brass bands from the 1860's through the 1970's.

2326.   Schuller, Gunther. *Early Jazz: Its Roots and Musical
        Development*. New York: Oxford University Press, 1968.

        Discusses in depth the roots of jazz--its rhythm,
        melody, and harmony and their relationship to Africa.
        The bio-musical analyses and portraits of Louis
        Armstrong, Jelly Roll Morton, Bessie Smith, Fats
        Waller, and others are excellent. The analysis of
        the early style of Duke Ellington is equally good.
        A fine glossary of terms, selected discography, and
        index complete one of the best books on this subject.

2327.   Shapiro, Nat, and Nat Hentoff, eds. *Hear Me Talkin'
        To Ya: The Story of Jazz by the Men Who Made It*.
        New York: Rinehart, 1955. Reprint. New York: Dover,
        1966.

        Covers topics ranging from early New Orleans to the
        so-called West Coast School of Jazz. The book is
        unique in presenting views of numerous musicians on
        their own music as well as on the music of their
        peers.

2328.   Simon, George T. *The Big Bands*. New York: Macmillan,
        1967; Rev. ed. New York: Macmillan, 1971.

        Treats the big bands in four parts: the people
        associated with the bands; biographical sketches of
        seventy-two bands; individual musicians considered
        according to their functions; and interviews with
        seven musicians--Count Basie, Benny Goodman, Woody
        Herman, Harry James, Stan Kenton, Guy Lombardo, and
        Artie Shaw. The book is well illustrated and researched
        and contains a selected discography, name index, and
        foreword by Frank Sinatra.

2329.   Specht, Paul L. *How They Became Name Bands: The
        Modern Technique of a Dance Band Maestro*. New York:
        Fine Arts Publications, 1971.

        Provides good background information on people and
        bands involved in early radio broadcasts. The author

suggests how to build and retain a successful dance
band.

2330-2339. Deleted.

2340.   Stearns, Marshall W. *The Story of Jazz*. New York:
         Oxford University Press, 1956; London: Sidgwick &
         Jackson, 1957; Exp. ed. New York: New American
         Library, 1958. Reprinted through 1973.

         Traces the development of jazz from its West African
         roots through Bop. Although some of the author's con-
         clusions on West African roots are questionable and no
         musical analyses are included, this is one of the best
         books on the topic. The book does include information
         on the New Orleans background of jazz and the relation-
         ship of blues, work songs, spirituals, and ragtime to
         it. Stearns was one of the first authors to attempt
         to relate other Black American musical forms to the
         origin and development of jazz, and his study remains
         one of the more popular ones on the subject.

2341.   Tallant, Robert. *Voodoo in New Orleans*. New York:
         Macmillan, 1946. Reprint. New York: Collier Books,
         1962.

         Investigates the history of cult practices in New
         Orleans with a special attempt to connect them to
         jazz in that city.

2342.   Tanner, Paul, and Maurice Gerow. *A Study of Jazz*. 3rd
         ed. Dubuque, Iowa: W.C. Brown, 1977.

         Covers traditional jazz styles as well as jazz of
         the 1960's and 1970's. The book contains several
         musical examples and is unique in often listing stylis-
         tic characteristics. This is a good jazz history text
         for the general student and consequently is used widely.

2343.   Tirro, Frank. *Jazz: A History*. New York: W.W. Norton,
         1977.

         Overviews jazz history and attempts to elaborate on
         all the contributing elements in jazz, e.g., African
         and European influences, blues, spirituals, and ragtime.
         But there are serious omissions and weaknesses in this
         work--errors of fact as well as problems of conception
         in assessing correctly the African influences. Its
         major strengths are its scope--it covers jazz history
         through the late 1970's--and its several lists of
         reference materials. Examples are drawn from the jazz
         collection at the Smithsonian.

2344.   Ulanov, Barry. *A History of Jazz in America*. New
        York: Viking, 1952; London: Jazz Book Club, 1957;
        London: Hutchinson, 1958; Reprint. New York: Da Capo,
        1972.

        Covers the origins and development of jazz through
        the so-called cool era. Although the book contains a
        glossary of jazz terms and phrases as well as an index,
        it does not contain any musical analysis or examples.
        The book is clear and concise.

2345.   Williams, Martin. *Jazz Masters in Transition, 1957-69*.
        New York: Macmillan, 1970.

        Collects the author's previous writings on a myriad
        of topics concerning jazz change, development, innova-
        tions. Many jazz personalities are also featured in
        these eighty-seven perceptive critical articles.

2346.   Wilson, John S. *Jazz: The Transition Years, 1940-1960*.
        New York: Appleton-Century-Crofts, 1966.

        Surveys and analyzes jazz styles from 1940 to 1960.
        The author breaks down the jazz styles into five
        separate categories: Bop, i.e., the contributions of
        Roy Eldridge, Charles Parker, and Dizzy Gillespie;
        Cool, i.e., the music of Miles Davis, Stan Getz, and
        Gerry Mulligan; Return to the Roots, i.e., the music
        of Horace Silver and Ray Charles; Intellectualization,
        i.e., Kenton, Brubeck, and the Modern Jazz Quartet;
        and Reacceptance, i.e., musicians who revived tradi-
        tional jazz. The book is well-written and the author
        well-informed.

                            JAZZ ON FILM

2347.   Hippenmeyer, Jean Roland. *Jazz sur films, ou 55 années
        de rapports jazz-cinéma vis à trouvers plus de 800
        films tournés entre 1917 et 1972*. Yuerdon: Editions
        de la thiele, 1973.

        Contains a comprehensive filmography for the years
        1917 to 1972 as well as an introductory essay on jazz
        in motion pictures.

2348. Meeker, David. *Jazz in the Movies: A Tentative Index
        to the Work of Jazz Musicians for the Cinema.* London:
        British Film Institute, 1972.

        Identifies 709 films about jazz and blues including
        those in which jazz and blues artists appear as well
        as feature films of famous jazz musicians. The entries
        are annotated.

2349. Whannel, Paddy. *Jazz on Film.* London: British Film
        Institute, 1961.

        Lists sixty-one feature-length films and shorts,
        with annotations on the jazz musicians featured.

E.   TECHNICAL MATERIALS

ARRANGING AND COMPOSING

2350.   Alexander, Van. *First Chart*. New York: Criterion,
        1971.

Acquaints the arranger with the fundamentals of
scoring. In addition to information on instrumentation and voicings, the book contains charts for
analysis as well as information on the contemporary
rhythm section.

2351.   Baker, David N. *Arranging and Composing for the Small
        Ensemble: Jazz/R&B/Jazz-Rock*. Chicago: Maher, 1970.

Addresses the needs of the person interested in
writing for small combinations, that is, from three
to ten pieces. The book includes excerpts from small
group arrangements, complete scores of recorded and
published arrangements, musical examples, recommended
recordings, and suggested outside reading. Also included is an explanation of the nomenclature used in
the book with written examples of chords using the
nomenclature. This is an excellent book, comprehensive
in its treatment of arranging and composing, and highly
recommended.

2352.   Dellaera, Angelo. *Creative Arranging: Complete Guide
        to Professional Arranging*. New York: Charles Colin,
        1966.

Covers concepts pertinent to small and large group
arranging. The first part of this book deals with
visual representation of sound. In addition, the
author includes a series of interesting transposition
exercises for each instrument.

2353.   Ellis, Norman. *Instrumentation and Arranging for the
          Radio and Dance Orchestra*. New York: Roell, 1936.

          Treats such topics as harmony and voicings, form,
          and instrumental combinations. Some of the author's
          views on scoring, voicing, and arranging have been
          updated by other jazz arrangers.

2354.   Garcia, Russell. *The Professional Arranger-Composer*.
          New York: Criterion, 1968.

          Lists the ranges of instruments and then discusses
          topics such as dance band harmony, voicing form, dance
          band styles, and harmonic progression. This thorough
          book is one of the most popular ones on this topic.

2355.   Lapnam, Claude. *Scoring for the Modern Dance Band*.
          New York: Pitman, 1937.

          Presents information on dance band concepts--
          arranging, harmony, voicings, and instrumentation.
          Though not an in-depth discussion and now outdated,
          the book is informative about then-acceptable dance
          band techniques. Some examples are included.

2356.   Mancini, Henry. *Sounds and Scores: A Practical Guide
          to Professional Orchestration*. Northridge, California:
          Northridge Music, 1962.

          Covers the gamut on arranging orchestration for jazz
          and non-jazz groups. The chapters on harmony, voicings,
          and instrument combinations are particularly good.
          The book, well written and concise, includes musical
          examples, many of which reflect Mancini's unique personal
          style.

2357.   Murphy, Lyle. *Swing Arranging Method*. New York:
          Robbins Music, 1937.

          Treats the basics of harmony and scoring as well as
          the concepts and philosophies used by Swing bands.
          Much more attention is given to swing techniques for
          big bands than for small groups.

2358.   Russo, William. *Jazz Composition and Orchestration*.
          Chicago: University of Chicago Press, 1968.

          Expands on the author's earlier work. Musical
          examples in this volume, however, are drawn from
          Russo's work with several jazz groups whereas examples
          in the first book were written specifically for it.

2359.   ———. *Composing for the Jazz Orchestra*. Chicago:
         University of Chicago Press, 1961.

     Discusses chord symbols, types of chords, harmonic
     considerations, voicing, and writing for particular
     instruments and ensembles as well as other pertinent
     information about jazz composition.

2360.   Sebesky, Don. *The Contemporary Arranger*. Sherman
         Oaks, California: Alfred Publishing, 1974.

     Designed to eliminate many of the problems confronting
     the arranger who wants to write for the record industry.
     The book is unique in illustrating through scored and
     recorded examples those procedures that have proven
     most (and least) successful. Many of the examples are
     drawn from actual arrangements written for or recorded
     by several of today's leading artists.

                  ANALYSIS, EAR TRAINING, HARMONY,
                  SCALES, PATTERNS, AND THEORY

2361.   Aebersold, Jamey. *A New Approach to Jazz Improvisa-*
         tion. Vol. 3. New Albany, Indiana: Aebersold, 1969.

     Recommended for the student who has mastered the
     basic fundamentals of jazz improvisation, i.e., chord
     structures and scales. This volume, which deals with
     the $II - V_7 - I$ progression, contains eight recorded
     tracks: $II - V_7 - I$ all major keys; $II - V_7$ random pro-
     gressions; $V_7 + 9/I$ all major keys; $\emptyset V_7 - I_9/I$ all major
     keys; and F blues with an eight-bar bridge. The book
     also contains the needed scales and chords for each
     tune as well as twenty written patterns that can be
     played with the various tracks on the records. In
     short, the author provides the rhythm section and the
     student provides the improvisation. A good purchase
     for the intermediate level jazz improviser.

2362.   Baker, David. *A New Approach to Ear Training for*
         Jazz Musicians. Lebanon, Indiana: Studio P/R, 1975.

     This text and cassette tape contain a comprehensive,
     sequentially arranged list of chords and scales for
     use by all instruments. In addition, there are several
     ear training exercises and a discography which lists
     scales that the soloists use in their improvisations.

The method is excellent for the intermediate or
advanced performer who is serious about ear training
in jazz.

2363. ————. *Advanced Ear Training for Jazz Musicians.*
       Lebanon, Indiana: Studio 224, 1977.

       Covers the scales used in jazz and includes a
       cassette tape. Excellent for ear training.

2364. ————. *Techniques of Improvisation.* 4 vols. Chicago:
       Maher, 1971.

       Deals with the method for developing improvisational
       technique, II-V$_7$ progressions, turnbacks, and cycles.

2365. Berle, Annie. *Complete Handbook for Jazz Improvisa-
       tion.* New York: Amsco, 1972.

       Treats the basics of jazz theory from chords and
       patterns to progressions in a clear and concise manner.

2366. Bower, Bugs. *Complete Chords and Progressions for
       All Instruments.* New York: Charles Colin, 1952.

       Covers in Part I such three- and four-part chords
       as major, minor, harmonic minor scales, augmented,
       wholetone scales, and chord variations. Part II
       covers five- to seven-part chords such as dominant
       ninth, major seventh with added ninth, dominant eleventh,
       and thirteenth chords. This text is complete, with
       arpeggio exercises included.

2367. Branch, Harold. *Improvising 2-Bar Jazz Licks.* West
       Babylon, New York: Harold Branch, 1979.

       Based on harmony (C, D, E^b, F, G, A, B^b) with over
       fifty improvised licks included. The licks are pre-
       ceded by an outline of the major scale, chord, passing
       tones, and charging tones. For treble clef instruments,
       however, they can be transposed.

2368. Carubia, Mike. *The Sound of Improvisation.* Sherman
       Oaks, California: Alfred Music, 1975.

       Designed to instruct individuals, combos, jazz bands,
       and concert bands in a comprehensive method of im-
       provisation. A play-along cassette features the Thad
       Jones-Mel Lewis rhythm section while the tunes feature
       II - V$_7$ progressions and require some knowledge of major,
       minor and mixolydian scales. Good for high school and
       early college students.

2369.   Cassarino, Ray. *Chord Construction and Analysis:*
         Elements of Jazz and Pop I--Music Theory for the
         Contemporary Musician. New York: Consolidated
         Publishers, 1978.

         Explains how the combination of certain materials
         evolve from the major scales and are paired off to
         form various possibilities. A thorough presentation.

2370.   Deutsch, Maury. *Lexicon of Symmetric Scales and Tonal*
         Patterns. New York: Charles Colin, 1962.

         Contains a wealth of information on scales and
         melodic patterns designed to expand one's harmonic
         facility. Scales are treated in such categories as
         polyharmonic, polytonality, polyrhythm, micro-frequency,
         and polymodality. The book is well organized and
         scholarly.

2371.   Dunbar, Ted. *A System for Tonal Convergence for*
         Improvisors, Composers, and Arrangers. Kendall
         Park, New Jersey: Dunte, 1977.

         Presents an invention of twenty-four scales, including
         pentatonic, major, augmented, diminished, blues, and
         angular. All have from one to three tritones that
         cause them to gravitate toward one tonality--F major.
         However, they may be used to gravitate to any chord
         or tonality. In addition, each scale produces chords
         which may be used as collated motion to produce a
         desired chord or tonality. This method is good for
         teaching modulation, cross-scale chord substitution,
         a chromatic approach to any tonality or chord, and new
         scale color sources for improvisations to move from
         chord to chord.

2372.   Ellis, Don. *Quarter Tones.* Plainview, New York:
         Harold Branch, 1975.

         Discusses a comprehensive method covering the theory
         and application of quarter tones geared to the advanced
         student of harmony or improvisation.

2373.   Fisher, Clare. *Harmonic Exercises for Piano.* New
         York: Warner, 1973.

         Contains fifteen types of harmonic exercises for
         piano that are designed to be performed in several
         different keys. The book is intended for the advanced
         jazz theory student interested in new voicings and
         harmonic sequences.

2374. Haerle, Dan. *Scales for Jazz Improvisation*. Lebanon, Indiana: Studio P/R, 1975.

Covers the scales used in jazz improvisation. Scales are presented in bass and treble clefs. The text treats modes generated by the major scale (e.g., Ionian, Dorian, Phrygian); modes generated by the ascending melodic minor scale (e.g., Lydian augmented scale); and symmetric altered scales as well as miscellaneous scales.

2375. Kotwica, Raymond S., amd Joseph Viola. *Chord Studies for Trumpet*. Boston: Berklee, 1978.

Presents studies on chordal structures in all twelve diatonic keys and studies on chordal sequences containing some rhythm problems over various chord changes. Transcribed from *The Technique of the Saxophone*, this book includes major and minor, seventh and diminished seventh chords. The book is thorough and good for students who want to learn the whole range of chord structures and functions.

2376. Kynaston, Trent, and Robert J. Ricci. *Jazz Improvisation*. Englewood Cliffs, New Jersey: Prentice-Hall, 1978.

Designed for both the classical musician entering the world of jazz and the jazz musician seeking a detailed harmonic and melodic approach to improvisation. The book covers jazz chords and chord charts, jazz scales and scale charts, chord-function-scale charts, patterns, progressions, and more. The book is well written and geared to the student with some knowledge of the basics in music.

2377. La Porta, John. *Tonal Organization of Improvisational Techniques*. Delevan, New York: Kendor Music, 1976.

Offers a comprehensive jazz improvisation method for all levels of study, from beginning to advanced, written for C treble, C bass, and E^b and B^b instruments, with a supplemental piano "comping" book and four twelve-inch LP records. The text is well organized and logically presented, and the method is thorough.

2378. Markewich, Reese, M.D. *Inside Outside*. New York: Markewich, 1967.

Presents harmonic substitutions used in jazz and pop music with examples drawn from transcribed solos

by selected jazz artists. The author also suggests
new chord possibilities as a means of harmonizing some
standard jazz tunes. This well-illustrated book is
recommended for advanced improvisers familiar with
chord structure and voicings.

2379. Mehegan, John. *Jazz Improvisation*. 4 vols. New York:
Watson-Guptill, 1958-1965.

The first volume, *Tonal and Rhythmic Principles*,
covers the basic elements of improvisation. The second
volume, *Jazz Rhythm and the Improvised Line*, covers
the historical development of the improvised line of
jazz rhythm in five lessons with twenty-nine transcriptions of solos from Bessie Smith to Oscar Peterson.
The third volume, *Swing and the Early Progressive
Piano Styles*, analyzes the jazz styles of Teddy Wilson,
Art Tatum, Bud Powell, George Shearing, and Horace
Silver. The fourth volume, *Contemporary Piano Styles*,
presents illustrations of modern jazz technical approaches as contained in the compositions of Oscar
Peterson and several other contemporary artists.

2380. Pass, Joe. *Joe Pass Guitar Chords*. New York: Warner,
1975.

Teaches how different chords are voiced as well as
how they function individually and in chord progressions.
A good text for intermediate and advanced guitarists.

2381. Phillips, Alan. *Jazz Improvisation and Harmony*. New
York: Robbins Music, 1973.

Explains methods for creating and developing individual styles of playing, moving from elementary
improvisational and harmonic concepts to the advanced
levels. The text treats such topics as scales, basic
chords, modes and ragas, the complete fifteenth chord,
mystic chords, harmonizing with the isolated minor's
scale, and polytonality. This book is useful for
musicians, arrangers, composers, and students of all
instruments and musical forms.

2382. Ricker, Ramon. *Pentatonic Scales for Jazz Improvisations*. Lebanon, Indiana: Studio P/R, 1975.

Acquaints the advanced high school or college improviser with the vast resource of melodic material
available through the use of pentatonic scales. This
is not a complete method of improvisation but does
cover such topics as application of pentatonic scales

to various chord types, altered pentatonics, improvised
solos, and II-V-I exercises.

2383.   ———. *Technique Development in Fourths for Jazz
          Improvisations*. Lebanon, Indiana: Studio P/R, 1976.

          Designed for the advanced player, the musician who
          wishes to add to his improvisational skills. The
          book covers such topics as application of fourths to
          chord changes, contains a short discography of per-
          formers using fourths in their improvisations, and
          gives exercises.

2384.   ———. *The Ramon Ricker Improvisation Series*. 5 vols.
          Lebanon, Indiana: Studio P/R, 1979.

          Presents blues in all keys for all instruments.
          Volume 1 covers the beginning improviser; volume 2,
          the developing improviser; volume 3, all blues; volume
          4, II-V-I progressions; volume 5, Jerome Kern's great
          jazz songs. Each volume is accompanied by a rhythm
          section.

2385.   Rizzo, Phil. *Scale Variations*. Palisades, California:
          Palisades Publishing, 1960.

          Helps students learn how to practice and embellish
          scales for jazz improvisation. The book is somewhat
          outdated because it does not contain exercises on the
          modes and scales used in jazz since 1960.

2386.   ———. *Ear Training Based on 12 Tones*. Palisades,
          California: Palisades Publishing, 1978.

          Based on the use of the chromatic scale using a
          stationary "do" system, this programmed text contains
          material designed to be studied over a four-year
          period. The materials are to be sung and are designed
          for the beginning jazz student with an untrained ear.
          They provide good ear training for all music students.

2387.   ———. *Spread Chord Voicing*. Palisades, California:
          Palisades Publishing, 1978.

          Presents a wealth of information for beginning ar-
          rangers, composers, and pianists. Topics covered are:
          jazz piano fundamentals, basic chord symbols, enrich-
          ment and enlargement of given chord symbols, principles
          of voice leading, comping rhythms, and common substitu-
          tions. Though short, the book is well organized and
          informative.

2388. Smith, Hale, ed. *Progressive Jazz Patterns*. New York:
       Charles Colin, 1976.

       Gives examples in C-major jazz phrases set to chords
       in root and positions and all their inversions. The
       text also contains blank paper for the students to
       write out their solos.

2389. Spera, Dominic. *Learning Unlimited Jazz Improvisation:
       Making the Changes*. Milwaukee: Hal Leonard, 1977.

       Fully covers II-V7 patterns, instrumental and vocal.
       There are also brief sections on tempo, the language
       of jazz, and more. A cassette is included.

2390. Stanton, Kenneth. *Introduction to Jazz Theory*. Boston:
       Crescendo, 1971.

       Discusses the entire range of jazz theory, progressing
       from the basics (e.g., chord structures) to progressions
       and substitutions.

2391. Stuart, Walter. *Encyclopedia of Chords*. New York:
       Charles Colin, 1966.

       Deals comprehensively with chords in chromatic order,
       beginning on C.

2392. ————. *Jazz Scales*. New York: Charles Colin, 1974.

       Contains twelve jazz versions of each major and
       minor scale for all treble instruments.

2393. ————. *Create Your Own Jazz Phrases*. New York:
       Charles Colin, 1978.

       Coordinates chord symbols with one- and two-measure
       phrases. This is a step-by-step approach for all in-
       struments that does require some musical knowledge.

2394. Tilles, Bob. *Practical Improvisation*. Rockville
       Centre, New York: Belwin Mills, 1967.

       Treats a wide range of topics pertinent to jazz im-
       provisation, from intervals to the cycle of fourths.
       The author presents some particularly interesting ideas
       concerning how to compromise blues using major, minor,
       augmented fifth, dominant seventh, and diminished
       seventh chords.

2395. Tillis, Frederick. *Jazz Theory and Improvisation*.
       New York: Charles Hansen, 1975.

       Presents materials ranging from basic harmonic con-
       cept language to II/V7 progressions; substitute chords;
       and quartal and secundal harmony. All musical examples
       are written for the piano.

2396. Ulrich, John J. *Chord and Scales*. New York: Jazz
       City Workshop, 1975.

       Discusses the fundamentals of harmony needed for
       piano comping and improvisations. The text covers
       chord types, spellings, voice leading, chord pro-
       gressions, and much more. Recommended for pianists
       as well as other musicians.

2397. Volpe, Harry, and Jimmy Dale. *Jazz Improvisation on
       1000 Chords*. 3 vols. New York: Clef Music, 1974.

       Deals with both beginning and advanced levels and
       covers the entire range of chords and chord functions.
       For each of the one thousand chords presented there
       are from three to five inversions, patterns, scales,
       functions, and guitar fingerings given. Recommended
       for all musicians.

2398. White, Leon. *Modern Improvising: A Guide to Jazz Scale
       Soloing*. Studio City, California: Professional
       Music Products, 1978.

       Introduces the student with some musical background
       to the sounds of modern improvising through the study
       of the sources, organization, and application of various
       scales. The author offers some interesting ideas on
       improvising in jazz and on the act of melody improvising
       and argues that modes are a complicated and unnecessary
       approach to learning jazz. Numerous exercises and
       explanations are included.

2399. Wilson, Phil, and Joseph Viola. *Chord Studies for
       Trombone*. Boston: Berklee, 1978.

       Transcribed from *The Technique of the Saxophone*.
       Like *Chord Studies for Trumpet*, studies chordal struc-
       tures and chordal sequences with rhythm problems over
       chord changes. This text fully covers chord structures
       and functions.

ALL-PURPOSE IMPROVISATIONAL
AND JAZZ EDUCATION MATERIALS

2400. Aebersold, Jamey. *A New Approach to Jazz Improvisation.* 5 vols. New Albany, Indiana: Aebersold,
1972-1978.

Volume 1--*A New Approach to Jazz Improvisation*--
contains ten recorded tracks to practice improvisation.
Chord/scale progressions for each track are provided
for all instruments, and scales are written in the
staff for each chord symbol. Volume 2--*Nothin' But
Blues*--contains eleven different blues and is a
natural follow-up to volume 1. Chords and scales are
written in the staff for each recorded track. Volume
4--*Movin' On*--is advanced level. This set contains
nine original songs by Aebersold and Dan Haerle. Each
tune has the melody and the chord/scale progression
written out for all instruments. Volume 5--*Time to
Play Music*--has eight intermediate-level songs written
in the style of the great standards. Suggestions for
improvising on each tune and a scale syllabus are
provided.

2401. Applebaum, Stan. *Encyclopedia of Progressive Duets.*
New York: Charles Colin, 1973.

Treats progressive duets for treble clef instruments, with chord symbols and different tempo markings
included, in the first section. The second section,
"Duets in the Modern Jazz Idiom," contains ten original
duets by Irving Bush. The third section, "Duet Inven-
tions," has works compiled and edited by Constance
Weldon, with several duets in keys that have no more
than three flats. These duets, as those in the previous section, might be more helpful to pop rather
than jazz performers.

2402. Baker, David N. *Jazz Improvisation: A Comprehensive
Method of Study for All Players.* Chicago: Maher,
1969.

Discusses the technical problems in jazz improvisation. This is a well-organized manual useful for
both student and teacher.

2403. ————. *Improvisational Patterns: The Bebop Era.*
Vol. 1. New York: Charles Colin, 1978.

Covers daily jazz calisthenics for all treble clef

instruments (e.g., eight, nine, and ten note scales and major scales with added notes); also II, V_7 patterns covering two measures (beginning on different notes of the II and V_7 chords). A scale syllabus is included.

2404. ———. *Improvisational Patterns: The Bebop Era.* Vol. 2. New York: Charles Colin, 1979.

Presents exercises for all treble clef instruments designed to develop facility with the eight, nine, and ten note scales which gained ascendency during the Bebop era in the music of Parker, Gillespie, and Powell.

2405. ———. *Improvisational Patterns: The Bebop Era.* Vol. 3. New York: Charles Colin, 1979.

Deals with more daily jazz calisthenics as well as such other topics as tonic function patterns, special cycle patterns, turn back patterns, a seventh scale sequence, and some modal lines based on blues for treble clef instruments.

2406. ———. *Improvisational Patterns: The Contemporary Era.* Vol. 4. New York: Charles Colin, 1979.

Based on the belief, as are other volumes in this series of pattern books, that "the great body of improvisational materials is of high specificity with regard to its time and place within the jazz continuum." Covers such topics as pentatonics, fourths, fourths in various combinations, modal patterns, Coltrane changes, and II-V_7 progressions. Highly recommended.

2407. Bowers, Bugs. *Ad Lib.* New York: Charles Colin, 1953.

Approaches improvisation in an interesting and useful manner. The author first presents a tune, then writes out the chord and scale formation of each passage of the melody. He combines chord and scale forms before proceeding to the next tune.

2408. Brown, Marshall. *Duets in Jazz Phrasing.* New York: Charles Colin, 1961.

Covers numerous topics such as the shake, natural fall-off, bend, and false fingering. Good for young beginning players working on jazz phrasing on treble clef instruments.

2409. Coker, Jerry. *Improvising Jazz*. Englewood Cliffs,
       New Jersey: Prentice-Hall, 1964.

       Gives the beginning performer an insight into the
       logical development of jazz improvisation in a
       thorough, step-by-step approach.

2410. ————; Jimmy Casale; Gary Campbell; and Jerry Greene.
       Patterns for Jazz. Lebanon, Indiana: Studio P/R,
       1970.

       Contains a total of 326 patterns constructed for
       use in major through chromatic scales. This book is
       designed for performers.

2411. Dentato, Johnny. *Today's New Jazz Educator*. New
       York: Camerica Music, 1978.

       Presents original and mostly traditional jazz
       versions of such compositions as "Bill Bailey," "The
       Entertainer," "Maple Leaf Rag," and "Sensation Rag."

2412. Eisenhauer, William. *Contemporary Concepts for Stage
       Band*. New York: Bourne, 1974.

       Teaches sight reading in the jazz medium. The book
       contains patterns that illustrate articulation phrasing
       and much more that is useful. Good for beginning
       jazz students.

2413. Giuffre, Jimmy. *Jazz Phrasing and Interpretation:
       For C Instruments*. New York: Associated Music, 1969.

       Acquaints students either in classroom or private
       use with principles of jazz phrasing which they can
       apply to actual pieces in performance. The author
       examines each area of phrasing, catching some general
       practices, then examines specific exercises (e.g.,
       uneven eights, slide-slur, short pickup), pointing
       out what is needed to make a jazz passage. Good ap-
       proach to the topic.

2414. La Porta, John. *Developing Sight Reading Skills in
       the Jazz Idiom*. Boston: Berklee, 1967.

       Offers a programmed method for C instruments designed
       to aid students in improving their abilities to sight
       read in developing their musical conception of the
       stage band idiom as well as in developing their aware-
       ness of solo, duet, and group techniques. Each example
       is composed of one or two musical ideas and/or rhythmic

units of stage band music. The units are repeated and
varied melodically.

2415. ————. *A Guide to Jazz Phrasing and Improvisation.*
2 vols. Boston: Berklee, 1972.

Contains duets for C and E^b instruments representative
of a broad range of jazz performances from 1952 to 1972.
Each volume contains fourteen duets varying from intermediate to advanced levels along with a recording.
The second half of each composition is written as a
counterpoint to the first (A-section) so that two
students can play it as a duet. Individual students
can also play along with the recording.

2416. Levey, Joseph. *Basic Jazz Improvisation.* Delaware
Gap, Pennsylvania: Shawnee, 1971.

Covers different chord types geared to the beginning
improviser.

2417. Lindsay, Martin. *Teach Yourself Jazz.* London: English
University Press, 1958.

Comments generally on topics ranging from articulation to progressions. This do-it-yourself guide does
not treat any topic in depth.

2418. Matson, Rod. *Basic Jazz/Rock Improvisation for All
Treble Clef Instruments Including Guitar.* Westbury,
New York: Pro Art, 1974.

Surveys the fundamentals of music theory (scales,
key, intervals, chords) in the first part and offers a
step-by-step approach to the construction of original
improvised solos in the second.

2419. Most, Abe. *Jazz Improvisation for Treble Clef Instruments.* Sherman Oaks, California: Gwyn, 1975.

Contains twenty-five etudes broken down into jazz
phrases. At the beginning of each exercise is a
phrase or musical idea. The student is to learn the
exercise in all keys by using the cycle of fifths.

2420. ————. *Jazz Improvisations for Bass Clef Instruments.*
Sherman Oaks, California: Gwyn, 1976.

Serves as the counterpart to the treble edition.

2421. Mymit, Chuck. *A Beginner's Approach to Jazz Improvisa-
       tion.* New York: Chappel, 1973.

       Covers the study of all chords, a basic review of
       scales as well as II-V7 progressions, and the applica-
       tion of chord scales to tunes.

2422. Poole, Carl. *Jazz for Juniors: 15 Progressive Duets
       Designed to Develop Interpretation of Dance Music.*
       New York: Henry Adler, 1961.

       Designed for beginning jazz players with valuable
       tips on jazz articulation.

2423. Rothmans, Joel. *Reading with Jazz Interpretation.*
       New York: JR Publications, 1965.

       Aims at helping musicians attain the correct jazz
       articulation. Exercises are provided.

2424. Spear, Sammy; Robert Stein; and Nicholas Lamitola.
       *Basic Syncopation: A Practical Approach to Stage
       Band Reading, Interpretation and Articulation.*
       Westbury, New York: Pro Art, 1967.

       Provides lessons covering a wide range of reading,
       interpretation, and articulation for trumpet, saxophone,
       and trombone.

2425. Stuart, Walter. *Jazz Soloist: For All Instruments.*
       New York: Charles Colin, 1972.

       Discusses such topics for the jazz soloist as rhythm
       and transposition with exemplifying exercises included.
       An interesting book.

2426. ————. *Jazz Improvising for All Bass Instruments.*
       New York: Charles Colin, 1973.

       Explains specific components of jazz improvisation,
       along with exercises and chord symbols. Requires some
       knowledge of music.

2427. ————. *Rhythm and Syncopation in Modern Jazz.* New
       York: Charles Colin, 1974.

       Features only 4/4, 3/4, and 2/4.

2428. Shaw, Kirby. *Vocal Jazz Style.* Milwaukee: Hal Leonard,
       1975.

       Presents a good method for vocalist and instrumen-

talist. This book, designed primarily for reading
jazz articulations (e.g., accents, flips, fall-offs,
shakes), has clear explanations and illustrations.

2429. Wiskirchen, Rev. George. *Developmental Techniques for
       the School Dance Band Musician.* Boston: Berklee,
       1961.

Designed for beginning jazz instrumentalists or high
school jazz band directors. In one of the first books
written on this topic, the author offers good ideas
on the teaching of jazz articulation and phrasing and
includes appropriate exercises.

IMPROVISATIONAL MATERIALS

BRASS (TRUMPET AND TROMBONE)

2430. Aebersold, Jamey. *A New Approach to Jazz Improvisation.*
       Vols. 7 and 9. New Albany, Indiana: Aebersold, 1972-
       1978.

Contains eight jazz originals written by Miles Davis
in volume 7. The tunes are: "Four," "Tune Up," "Weird
Blues," "The Theme," "Solar," "Dig," "Milestones," and
"Serpent's Tooth." Volume 9 has eight jazz originals
by Woody Shaw: "Little Red's Fantasy," "Katrina
Ballerina," "Blues for Wood," "Moontrane," "In Case
You Haven't Heard," "Tomorrow's Destiny," "Beyond All
Limits," and "Beyond All Limits" (in a different tempo
and style). An LP is included.

2431. Alpert, Herb, and Hugh Masekela. *Herb Alpert and
       Masekela: Jazz Transcriptions for Flugle Horn,
       Trumpet and Small Ensemble.* New York: Almo, 1978.

Presents short bio-musical sketches on both performers along with such tunes as "African Summer," "Lobo,"
"I'll Be There for You," and "Skokiaan."

2432. Armstrong, Louis. *Jazz Giants--Louis Armstrong Dixie-
       land Style Trumpet.* New York: Charles Hansen, 1975.

Features over fifty transcribed solos of Louis Arm-
strong. Among them are "Tin Roof Blues," "High Society,"
"Doctor Jazz," "Copenhagen," "Chicago Breakdown," "New
Orleans Stomp," "Wolverine Blues," and "Milenberg Joys."

2433.   ———. *The Armstrong Treasury--Louis' Song Book/*
        Trumpet Edition. New York: Charles Hansen, 1976.

   Contains over thirty songs associated with Louis and
a special sixteen-page picture portfolio.

2434.   ———. *125 Jazz Breaks for Trumpet--Louis Armstrong*.
        New York: Charles Hansen, 1977.

   Compiles two-bar breaks in all keys from recordings
of Louis Armstrong.

2435.   ———. *Louis Armstrong's 44 Trumpet Solos and 125*
        Jazz Breaks. New York: Charles Hansen, 1976.

   Collects breaks and trumpet solos from the original
"Fifty Hot Choruses of Armstrong."

2436.   Baker, David. *Jazz Styles and Analysis: Trombone in*
        Recorded Solos, Transcribed and Annotated. Chicago:
        Downbeat Publishing, 1973.

   Includes transcribed solos and short biographies of
many jazz trombonists.

2437.   ———. *Dixieland Giants--Trombone*. New York: Charles
        Hansen, 1974.

   Offers twenty-five Dixieland standards arranged for
solo trombone and piano accompaniment.

2438.   ———. *Contemporary Techniques for the Trombone:*
        A Revolutionary Approach to the Problems of Music
        in the Twentieth Century. Vols. 1 and 2. New York:
        Charles Colin, 1974.

   Addresses itself to the teacher, student, and amateur
or professional trombonist interested in master techniques of trombone performance (jazz and non-jazz) in
twentieth-century music. The coverage ranges from
exercises to develop skills with angular lines to some
advanced concepts in jazz playing. The second volume
begins with polymetric music and continues with information on metric modulations. Profiles on two contemporary
trombonists (Jim Fulkerson and Stuart Dempster) and
suggested listening and study lists are included. These
are thorough volumes, recommended for serious trombonists.

2439.   Baron, Art. *Jazz Riffs for Trombone*. New York: Music
        Sales, 1978.

   Includes a discography and jazz riffs from easy to

advanced in the styles of such musicians as J.J. Johnson, Jim Robinson, and Roswell Rudd.

2440.   Carley, Dale. *Woody Shaw Jazz Trumpet Solos: Transcriptions from the Original Recordings.* New York: Almo, 1979.

Transcribes "In a Capricornian Way," "In Case You Haven't Heard," "Katrina Ballerina," "Little Red's Fantasy," "The Organ Grinder," "Rahsaan's Run," "Rosewood," "Stepping Stone," "There for Maxine," "To Kill a Brick," "Tomorrow's Destiny," "Woody I: On the Path," "Woody II: Other Paths," and "Woody III: New Offerings."

2441.   Candoli, Conte. *World's Greatest Jazz Solos: Trumpet.* New York: Almo, 1978.

Presents transcribed solos such as "Bernie's Tune," "Four," "Giant Steps," "Moody's Mood," "So What," "Oleo," and "Night in Tunisia" as well as short biographical sketches. This volume contains the same tunes as the other collections of world's greatest jazz solos.

2442.   Edmonds, Hank. *More of Miles Davis for All Instruments.* New York: Charles Colin, 1958.

Contains some tunes for piano-accordion-guitar and vibes (e.g., "Ruby and Garnet") and others for trumpet-tenor sax-clarinet (e.g., "Amethyst") or alto sax-bass sax and trombone.

2443.   Ferguson, Maynard. *The Jazz Styles of Maynard Ferguson.* New York: Warner, 1978.

Among the tunes transcribed for trumpet and piano included are "Chameleon," "Gospel John," "Maria," and "Primal Scream." A short biographical sketch is included.

2444.   Hirt, Al. *Jazz Giants--Al Hirt Trumpet.* New York: Charles Hansen, 1974.

Transcribes eight of Hirt's solos for trumpet and piano accompaniment: "Sugar Lips," "Cotton Candy," "Java," "Holiday for Trumpet," "When the Saints Go Marching In," "Easy Street," "Too Late," and "Carnival in Venice."

2445. Isacoff, Stuart. *Jazz Masters: Miles Davis*. New York: Consolidated Music, 1979.

    Presents solos transcribed for B♭ trumpet (with the exception of "I Waited for You," which begins with a piano arrangement). Chord symbols, indicating the basic changes, are given in the transposed key to relate to the melody line as written. Among the tunes included are "Dig," "Oleo," "Tune Up," and "Stella by Starlight."

2446. James, Harry. *Jazz Giants--Harry James Blues, Rhapsodies and Concerti*. New York: Charles Hansen, 1976.

    Contains the complete series of trumpet solos with piano accompaniment, including "Carnival in Venice," "Concerto in A-Minor," "Concerts in B♭-Minor," "Concerts for Trumpet," "Flight of the Bumblebee," "Trumpet Blues," "Cantabile," and "Trumpet Rhapsody."

2447. Kotwica, Raymond, and Joseph Viola. *Chord Studies for Trumpet*. Boston: Berklee, 1972.

    Based on source material taken from Viola's *Chord Studies for Saxophone*. The exercises have, however, been extensively revised to provide natural fingerings and phrasings for the trumpet. Each study begins with a major key and proceeds through minor, minor seventh, diminished seventh, and so on. The book also contains some exercises on chord sequences.

2448. Little, Lowell. *Know Your Saxophone*. Westbury, New York: Pro Art, 1975.

    Designed to provide the fundamentals and ear training necessary before one begins improvisation. This first volume was followed in 1976 and 1977 by *Know Your Clarinet, Know Your Trumpet,* and *Know Your Trombone*.

2449. McNeil, John. *Jazz Trumpet Techniques for Developing Articulation and Fast Fingers*. Lebanon, Indiana: Studio P/R, 1976.

    Discusses how to improve technique and articulation. Exercises, examples, and methods of practice designed to help the jazz performer are provided.

2450. Paparelli, Frank. *Dizzy Gillespie--A Jazz Master*. New York: MCA Music, 1961.

    Transcribes tunes such as "Bebop," "Blue 'n Boogie,"

"Dizzy Atmosphere," "52nd Street," and "Salt Peanuts" for B♭ and C instruments with piano accompaniment.

2451. Sloan, Ken. *28 Modern Jazz Trumpet Solos*. Lebanon, Indiana: Studio P/R, 1977.

Offers solos covering many styles and artists.

REEDS (CLARINET, FLUTE, AND SAXOPHONE)

2452. Aebersold, Jamey. *A New Approach to Jazz Improvisation*. Vols. 6, 8, and 13. New Albany, Indiana: Aebersold, 1972-1978.

Oriented to blues. Volume 6--*All Bird*--contains ten songs by Charles Parker. The recorded back-up rhythm section features Ron Carter (bass), Kenny Barron (piano), and Ben Riley (drums). The compositions are: "Now's the Time," "Billie's Bounce," "Yardbird Suite," "Confirmation," "Dewey Square," "Donna Lee," "My Little Suede Shoes," "Ormthology," "Scapple from the Apple," and "Thriving from a Riff." Volume 8 contains these nine originals by Sonny Rollins: "Doxy," "St. Thomas," "Blues Seve," "Valse Hot," "Tenor Madness," "Solid," "Pent Up House," "Airegin," and "Oleo." Volume 13 contains eight of Adderley's greatest hits. The tunes are: "Work Song," "Del Sasser," "Sack of Woe," "This Here," "Unit 7," "Jeannine," "Scotch and Water," and "Saudade." The rhythm section features Louis Hayes (drums), Sam Jones (bass), and Ronnie Matthews (piano). An LP is included.

2453. Bay, Mel. *Saxophone Improvising Workbook*. Pacific, Missouri: Mel Bay, 1979.

Studies the theory that guides improvisation in depth. Chordal, scales, and harmonic approaches are covered.

2454. Davis, Nathan. *Flute Improvisation*. New York: Armstrong, Edu-tainment, 1975.

Presents seventeen original flute solos representing various jazz styles as well as six exercises based on fourths, half-steps, and the diminished modal style of John Coltrane.

2455. Dentato, John. *How to Play Jazz Flute*. New York: Charles Hansen, 1975.

Includes sixteen jazz standards and originals, many

written with jazz variations as well as the original
version, with special tips and instructions on playing
jazz flute.

2456. ———. *How to Play Jazz Flute No. 2.* New York: Charles
Hansen, 1976.

Features eighteen jazz standards and originals arranged with the original melody and chord symbols,
plus a jazz variation.

2457. ———. *Jazz Flute for Christmas.* New York: Charles
Hansen, 1977.

Contains seventeen Christmas standards and carols
arranged with the original version facing a new jazz
version.

2458. Desmond, Paul. *Paul Desmond Jazz Saxophone Solos.*
New York: Almo, 1978.

Includes tunes like "Alianca," "Desmond Blues,"
"Late Lament," "Take Ten," and "Uberely." Chords in
parentheses are in concert key for accompaniment by C
instruments. A short bio-musical essay appears at the
beginning of the book.

2459. Gerard, Charley. *Jazz Riffs for Flute, Saxophone,
Trumpet and Other Treble Instruments.* New York: Music
Sales, 1978.

Offers riffs and patterns in the styles of Charlie
Parker and John Coltrane. Special sections cover minor,
major, II-V patterns, soul and rock, and whole-tone and
non-Western scales. Each riff is transposed four times.
Chord chart and discography are included.

2460. ———. *Improvising Jazz Sax.* New York: Consolidated
Music, 1977.

Focuses on tunes and exercises in the styles of
Charles Parker, John Coltrane, Johnny Hodges, and
Ornette Coleman. Turnbacks, chords, scales, pro-
gressions are covered, with all examples in C.

2461. Giordano, Jackie. *Jazz Flute--Godspell Selections.*
New York: Charles Hansen, 1977.

Contains nine compositions from "Godspell" arranged
as jazz versions with piano accompaniment.

2462.   Goldsen, Michael. *Charlie Parker Omnibook: For E^b In-
         struments*. New York: Atlantic Music, 1978.

         Transcribes numerous Parker solos (with chord symbols)
         that represent a cross section of his music. This
         very comprehensive text is a must for serious students
         of Parker or Bebop.

2463.   Goodman, Benny. *Jazz Giants--Clarinet Solos*. New
         York: Charles Hansen, 1975.

         Collects a variety of jazz tunes with piano accompani-
         ment such as "Rosette," "Why Don't You Do Right,"
         "Mahogany," "Hall Stomp," and "Bugle Call Rag."

2464.   ————, and Woody Herman. *Jazz Studies/Solos*. New
         York: Charles Hansen, 1974.

         Woody Herman deals in Part I with improvisation
         through chord studies in all keys. Part II consists
         of solos by Benny Goodman, including "King Porter
         Stomp" and "Tin Roof Blues." Part III provides the
         piano accompaniment to Part II.

2465.   Gornston, David. *Fun with Swing: For Clarinet, Trumpet,
         Vibes, Saxophone, Accordion, Piano, Violin and Theory
         Students*. New York: Sam Fox, 1978.

         Uses only three chords in three keys. For beginners,
         the book moves through phrasing to passing tones and
         first embellishments.

2466.   Harris, Eddie. *Jazz Cliche Capers*. Hollywood: Highland
         Music, 1978.

         Deals with jazz licks, or the short, popular phrases
         played by most soloists during several jazz eras. In
         the introduction, the author suggests eight ways modern
         jazz saxophonists play cliche effects. Recommended
         for all jazz saxophonists.

2467.   Herman, Woody. *Jazz Giants--Clarinet Solos*. New York:
         Charles Hansen, 1978.

         Features several compositions made famous by Herman,
         with piano accompaniment and chord symbols.

2468.   ————. *Sax Scales, Chords and Solos*. New York: Charles
         Hansen, 1974.

         Presents in forty-eight pages a complete method for

saxophonists interested in scales and other studies.
Six Woody Herman solos are included.

2469. Hodges, Johnny. *Six Originals*. New York: Charles
Hansen, 1973.

Provides five solos arranged for alto saxophone with
piano accompaniment. Included are "Spruce and Juice,"
"Two-Button Suit," "Butterfly Bounce," "Parachute
Jump," and "Uptown Blues."

2470. Jones, Quincy. *Quincy Jones Mellow Flute*. New York:
Charles Hansen, 1975.

Features the music of two of Quincy's albums with
chord symbols. The tunes include: "Along Came Betty,"
"Mellow Madness," "Boogie Joe the Grinder," "Is It
Love That We're Missin'," and "Soul Saga." A special
illustrated biography of Quincy is also included.

2471. Konitz, Lee. *Jazz Lines*. New York: William H. Bauer,
1959.

Consists of eleven tunes with chord symbols for B^b
instruments. Some of the tunes are written for two
instruments.

2472. Kupferman, Meyer. *Jazz Etudes for Clarinet*. New York:
Charles Hansen, 1977.

Contains such tunes for the advanced clarinetist as
"I Don't Care if the Sun Don't Shine," "Let's Get
Lost," "Stella by Starlight," "Penthouse Serenade," and
"Buttons and Bows."

2473. Laws, Hubert. *Flute Improvisation*. New York: Armstrong/
Edu - tainment, 1975.

Collects four of Laws's solos transcribed from some
of his most popular albums. The solos contain lip
trills, growls, pitch bonding, flutter tonguing, and
much more.

2474. McGhee, Andy. *Improvisation for Saxophone: The Scale/
Mode Approach*. Boston: Berklee, 1974.

Presents only the most commonly used and useful modal
scales.

2475. Miedema, Harry. *Jazz Styles and Analysis: Alto Sax*.
Chicago: Maher, 1975.

Approaches the history of the jazz alto saxophone through recorded solos that are transcribed and annotated. The book also includes profiles of each musician whose solo is transcribed. The coverage of alto saxophonists is wide and the transcriptions good.

2476.   Nash, Ted. *World's Greatest Jazz Solos: Saxophone.* New York: Almo, 1978.

Contains the same tunes included in the Lennie Niehaus collection for saxophone.

2477.   Niehaus, Lennie. *Jazz Conception for Saxophone.* Hollywood: TRY, 1964.

Focuses on rhythmic patterns for more advanced students. Twenty etudes in 3/4 and 5/4 meter cover several keys, with a phrasing section included.

2478.   ————. *Intermediate Jazz Conception for Saxophone.* Hollywood: TRY, 1966.

Stresses the fundamental rhythms, articulations, and phrasings commonly used by jazz groups. The book is divided into two sections--the first consists of twenty exercises on various rhythmic patterns; the second consists of twenty-five etudes which utilize all the material presented in the exercises. In both exercises and etudes, care is taken to phrase all the materials. This is a good book for students with some background in jazz.

2479.   ————. *Basic Jazz Conceptions for Saxophone.* Hollywood: TRY, 1964.

Designed for beginning students interested in jazz rhythms, articulations, and phrasings. A first section contains twelve exercises which emphasize various rhythmic patterns developed through a melodic song approach. The second section contains ten tunes which incorporate all of the material presented in the exercises. The author phrases all materials.

2480.   Paisner, Ben. *19 Swing Etudes for Saxophone, Clarinet, Xylophone, Violin or Guitar.* New York: Sam Fox, 1977.

Contains tunes with chord symbols and articulation markings.

2481. Progris, Jim. *Go for Baroque with That Jazz Feeling*. New York: Charles Hansen, 1974.

> Comprised of melodies from Bach, Schein, Handel, Corelli, Rameau, and others arranged with the original melody above a jazz interpretation. Instructions on jazz interpretation and articulation are outlined and chord symbols provided in this study book.

2482. Selden, Fred. *Far-Out Flute Solos*. New York: Charles Hansen, 1977.

> Presents thirty-two tunes with chord symbols above the solo lines.

2483. Sickler, Don, and Bobby Porcelli. *The Artistry of Joe Henderson*. New York: Big Three Corp., 1977.

> Consists of an innovative set of seven transcribed solos. All articulation and inflection markings are accurately notated and melodies included with a brief analysis of how the melodies are used in the solos.

2484. Snell, Howard. *Jazz Giants--Flute Yesterday and Today*. New York: Charles Hansen, 1975.

> Composed of solos with some exercises arranged for flute with chord symbols. The text includes examples of the music of Dave Brubeck, Duke Ellington, Horace Silver, Jelly Roll Morton, and others.

RHYTHM SECTION (BASS, DRUMS, GUITAR, PIANO, AND STRING INSTRUMENTS)

2485. Aebersold, Jamey. *A New Approach to Jazz Improvisation*. Vols. 11 and 12. New Albany, Indiana: Aebersold, 1972-1978.

> Volume 11--*Herbie Hancock*--contains eight of Hancock's greatest tunes. They are: "Maiden Voyage," "Cantaloupe Island," "Watermelon Man," "Dolphin Dance," "Jessica," "Eye of the Hurricane," "Toys," and "What If I Don't." The rhythm section features Ron Carter (bass), Kenny Barron (piano), and Billy Hart (drums). Volume 12--*Duke Ellington*--contains nine of Ellington's favorites: "Satin Doll," "Perdido," "Solitude," "Prelude to a Kiss," "Sophisticated Lady," "Mood Indigo," "I Let a Song Go Out of My Heart," "In a Sentimental Mood," and "'A' Train." The rhythm section features Ron Carter (bass), Kenny Barron (piano), and Ben Riley (drums).

2486. Adler, Wilfred, and Mel Bay. *Piano Improvisation*.
       Pacific, Missouri: Mel Bay, 1978.

       Designed to help the traditionally-trained pianist
       learn to improvise. This text, which is good for ad-
       vanced performers, contains materials in all keys and
       harmonic and melodic materials used in jazz in par-
       ticular.

2487. Ayeroff, Stan. *Django Reinhardt*. New York: Consolidated
       Music, 1978.

       Transcribes "In a Sentimental Mood," "After You've
       Gone," "Chasing a Rainbow," "Georgia on My Mind," and
       several others. The author also provides short state-
       ments on the solos transcribed, a biographical sketch
       of Reinhardt, and an interesting section on tools of
       the improviser.

2488. Baker, Mickey. *Jazz and Rhythm 'n' Blues Guitar*. New
       York: Amsco Music, 1969.

       Contains fourteen solo and rhythm duets in jazz and
       rhythm and blues styles for guitar. Requires good
       reading skills.

2489. Bay, Mel. *Rhythm Guitar Chord System*. Pacific,
       Missouri: Mel Bay, 1976.

       Covers the spectrum of chords the guitarist might
       encounter when performing jazz. Included are exercises
       on chord structures, patterns, and progressions. The
       system proceeds from the simple to the complex and is
       recommended for all guitarists.

2490. Boukas, Richard. *Jazz Riffs for Guitar*. New York:
       Music Sales, 1978.

       Presents guitar riffs in the styles of Django Rein-
       hardt, Charlie Christian, Joe Pass, Wes Montgomery,
       and Tal Farlow. Arranged in order of difficulty,
       each riff is presented with alternate fingerings for
       easy playing in difficult keys. A solo at the end of
       the book combines short and long phrases into a com-
       plete piece, and a discography is included.

2491. Branch, Harold. *Practical Cha-Cha and Merengue Figures*.
       Plainview, New York: Harold Branch, 1976.

       Designed to acquaint one with rhythms that are not
       commonly used in jazz. The book is also designed to

provide some insight into the structure of Latin musical styles. The exercises are in three-part harmony and are organized by chord progressions.

2492. Bredice, Vincent. *Guitar Improvisation*. Pacific, Missouri: Mel Bay, 1976.

Includes a wide range of information on guitar improvisation, for example, the harmonic aspects of bass line construction. While this book is geared to the beginning student, it should be supplemented with other materials.

2493. ———, and Charles Hansen. *Basic Impulse Bass Guitar*. New York: Charles Hansen, 1975.

Aimed at the beginning electric bassist. The text covers the basics, such as chord structures and progressions.

2494. Butler, Artie. *Creative Keyboard Sounds*. Sherman Oaks, California: Gwyn, 1976.

Acquaints keyboard players with basic rock, boogaloo, gospel, Latin rock. Exercises and explanations for each style are included.

2495. Capuano, Ed. *Improvising Jazz Guitar*. Fairfield, New Jersey: Aquarius, 1978.

Begins with jazz theory and proceeds through scales, modes, jazz chord progressions, and use of major and minor arpeggios. Helpful finger charts are included.

2496. Carrol, Frank. *Easy Electric Bass*. New York: Warner, 1978.

Contains some valuable information on how to build a bass line. In addition, the author includes etudes and boogaloo patterns covering all major and most minor keys.

2497. Carter, Rich. *Jazz Guitar Masterpieces*. Studio City, California: Professional Music Products, 1978.

Comprised of transcriptions of several outstanding guitar soloists along with the discography from which the transcriptions were made.

2498. ———, ed. *The Lee Ritenour Book*. Studio City, California: Professional Music Products, 1979.

Presents songs illustrative of the many and diverse

facets of Ritenour's music. In some cases the second
guitar, piano, and bass parts are included. Among the
tunes selected are "Sugar Leaf Express," "What Do You
Want," and "The Captain's Journey."

2499.   Carter, Ron. *Building a Jazz Bassline.* New York:
        Charles Hansen, 1971.

        Shows the student how to build a bass line through
        knowledge of chord structures and harmony. The informa-
        tion proceeds from the simple to the complex.

2500.   ———, and Charles Hansen. *Comprehensive Bass Method.*
        New York: Charles Hansen, 1977.

        Offers materials ranging from chord functions to
        progressions useful for both acoustical and electric
        bassists. The book also has several exercises for each
        position discussed. Good for all bassists.

2501.   Chesky, David. *Advanced Jazz/Rock Rhythms: For All
        Treble Clef Instruments.* New York: Charles Colin,
        1978.

        Encompasses contemporary jazz-rock rhythmic and
        melodic devices.

2502.   Clayton, John. *Big Band Bass.* Lebanon, Indiana:
        Studio P/R, 1978.

        Discusses the essentials for becoming a big band
        bassist. The text includes information on building
        bass lines, chord function, and much more. An excellent
        and comprehensive text for both double and electric
        basses.

2503.   Colin, Charles, and Bugs Bower. *Rhythms Complete.*
        Vol. 1. New York: Charles Colin, 1975.

        Represents the entire range of rhythmic problems in
        238 melodies. For treble clef instruments only, but good
        for improving sight reading for all musicians.

2504.   ———. *Rhythms: For All Instruments.* Vol. 2. New
        York: Charles Colin, 1976.

        Designed to improve sight reading. The studies cover
        a myriad of rhythmic problems.

2505.   Cusatis, Joe. *Rudimental Patterns for the Modern
        Drummer.* Melville, New York: Belwin/Mills, 1968.

Covers the basic patterns and techniques necessary to
become a good drummer. The book is good for beginning
drummers regardless of style preference.

2506. Davis, Richard. *Walking On Chords for String Bass and
        Tuba*. New York: Sympatico Musico, 1977.

Contains a series of twenty etudes designed to teach
the student to play walking bass lines and chord
changes. Tuba players will have to perform the etudes
an octave lower.

2507. Dawson, Alan, and Don DeMichael. *A Manual for the
        Modern Drummer*. Boston: Berklee, 1975.

Geared to the beginning or intermediate drummer able
to read music. The text is divided into three sections:
fundamentals of drum-set playing, dance band drumming,
and jazz. Also included are chapters on playing drum
solos and transcribed solo excerpts of famous jazz
drummers.

2508. de Mause, Alan. *How to Play Jazz Guitar: For Group or
        Individual Instruction*. New York: Acorn Music, 1978.

Progresses from learning, singing, and playing each
jazz style to jazz rhythm, harmony, structure, basic
improvisation, and dynamics. Treatment of these topics
is not too thorough, and to use this book effectively,
the student should be familiar with the first four frets
on the guitar (first position).

2509. Denatato, Johnny. *The All New Louis Bellson Drummer's
        Guide*. New York: Camerica, 1979.

Contains notated rhythms, including salsa, rock, jazz,
reggae, and batucada.

2510. Dennis, Matt, and Mel Bay. *Introduction to the Blues*.
        Pacific, Missouri: Mel Bay, 1978.

Covers blues chords, inversions, progressions, and
melodies. This is a good first book for the beginning
pianist.

2511. Dewitt, John, and Charles Hansen. *Rhythmic Figures for
        Bassists*. 2 vols. New York: Charles Hansen, 1977.

Designed to acquaint the intermediate to advanced
bassist with contemporary bass lines. The bass lines
in both volumes proceed from the simple to the complex.

Also included is information on fills, double stop
patterns, and transcribed solos. Good illustrations
are also provided.

2512.   Dobbins, Bill. *The Contemporary Jazz Pianist*. 2 vols.
Jamestown, Rhode Island: GAMT Music Press, 1978.

Treats comprehensively the entire range of jazz piano
playing. The materials cover topics from the basics of
improvisation to a wide variety of scales (modes, progressions, and substitution and much more).

2513.   Drew, Lucas. *Basic Electric Bass*. New York: Sam Fox,
1977.

Includes several solos and duets for electric bass.
The solos, though not complex, lend themselves to
harmonic analysis.

2514.   Dunbar, Ted. *New Approaches to Jazz Guitar*. Kendall
Park, New Jersey: Dante, 1977.

Contains excellent theory and techniques on guitar
improvisation. A sequential guide to learning chords
is provided as well as some pertinent information on
voicings and altered scales. One tune is used to
illustrate the thirteen exercises.

2515.   Edison, Roger. *Jazz Guitar: A Systematic Approach to
Chord Progressions*. Sherman Oaks, California: Alfred
Publishing, 1978.

Discusses holding the pick, reading chord diagrams,
the cycle of fifths, chord substitution, and jazz
progressions.

2516.   Filiberto, Roger. *Play Electric Bass from Chord
Symbols*. Pacific, Missouri: Mel Bay, 1978.

Suggests a detailed method for reading chord symbols.
The explanations are clear and concise.

2517.   Fisher, Clare. *Harmonic Exercises for Piano*. New
York: Warner, 1975.

Presents fifteen types of harmonic exercises for
piano. The book is designed to help the advanced
pianist with new chord voicings and harmonic sequences.

2518. Fowler, William. *Guitar Patterns for Improvisation*.
Chicago: Downbeat Publishing, 1974.

Deals with the guitar fingerboard as well as chords,
structures, progressions, and melodic materials.

2519. Friedman, David. *Vibraphone Technique: Dampening and
Pedaling*. Boston: Berklee, 1977.

Emphasizes mallet-dampening and pedaling skills used
in jazz playing, although techniques presented are
appropriate for all vibraphonists. There are twenty-
seven related etudes.

2520. Greene, Ted. *Jazz Guitar: Single Note Soloing*. Vols.
1 and 2. Westlake Village, California: Dale Zdenek,
1978.

Covers the basics of chord structures, progressions,
etc. in the first volume. Volume 2 is more advanced,
covering playing through changes, chromatic tones,
basing solos on a given melody, and altered scales.

2521. Haerle, Dan. *Jazz Improvisation for Keyboard Players*.
3 vols. Lebanon, Indiana: Studio P/R, 1977.

Volume 1--*Basic Concepts*--deals with creating melodies
using the left hand, pianistic approaches to improvising,
and chord progressions. Volume 2--*Intermediate Concepts*--
deals with developing melodies, further use of the left
hand, and scale choices for improvisation. Volume 3--
Advanced Concepts--deals with advanced factors affecting
scale choice and approaches to harmonic conception.
A useful, well-presented series.

2522. Hammick, Valda. *Electric Bass Technique*. Hollywood,
California: Solena, 1977.

Thoroughly covers left hand technique, ranging from
fingering position to bass patterns. The most advanced
text on the subject.

2523. Harley, James. *Instant Blues*. New York: Placeback,
1973.

Offers a precise approach designed to help the
beginning guitarist. The text covers the basics of
blues chords, scales, and progressions.

2524. Harvey, Eddie. *Jazz Piano*. London: English Universi-
       ties Press, 1976.

       Concerns the principles of jazz piano improvisations.
       Included are several compositions by modern jazz com-
       posers and many musical examples.

2525. Kaye, Carol. *Contemporary Bass Lines*. New York:
       Warner, 1976.

       Contains bass lines indicative of several styles of
       rock that can be analyzed for their rhythmic and har-
       monic content. The bass patterns might be useful for
       jazz bassists playing the fusion type of jazz.

2526. Kerper, Mitch. *Jazz Riffs for Piano*. New York: Mitch
       Sales, 1978.

       Consists of riffs and phrases in the styles of Bud
       Powell, Herbie Hancock, and McCoy Tyner for the inter-
       mediate jazz pianist. A series of solos combines short
       and long riffs into complete pieces. Arrangement is
       from simple to moderately complex, and a discography
       is included in this extremely useful and practical book.

2527. Kessel, Barney. *The Guitar*. Lebanon, Indiana: Studio
       P/R, 1975.

       Helps guitarists with varying degrees of experience.
       The book covers topics from fingering patterns to chord
       progressions and substitutions. This is primarily an
       all-purpose, how-to book.

2528. Kriss, Eric. *How to Play Blues Piano*. New York: Music
       Sales, 1975.

       Designed for the young beginner, with information
       on blues chords, blues progressions, blues tonalities,
       slides, and much more.

2529. Kroepel, Bob, and Mel Bay. *Piano Rhythm Patterns*.
       Pacific, Missouri: Mel Bay, 1978.

       Contains a wide variety of accompaniment patterns
       for the left hand in jazz, gospel, and rhythm and
       blues styles.

2530. La Porta, John. *Functional Piano for the Improviser*.
       DeLavan, New York: Kendor Music, 1969.

       Based on learning the harmonic rhythm of a tune
       through its application and analysis at the keyboard.

Seventy-two tunes with voicings for all chords are included for this purpose. Very thorough.

2531. Leavitt, William G. *Melodic Rhythms for Guitar*. Boston: Berklee, 1975.

Presents forty-two exercises and ninety-two harmonized etudes, with chord symbols given for each example. The text is geared to the guitarist with some knowledge of the basics of music and is particularly good for sight reading and jazz patterns.

2532. Lee, Ronny, and Charles Hansen. *Jazz Guitar*. 2 vols. New York: Charles Hansen, 1975.

Includes ten theory lessons, assignments, and jazz solo lessons in volume 1. Volume 2 contains forty-two jazz solo lessons, several musical examples, and some information on voicings.

2533. Lucas, Paul. *Jazz Improvisation for the Rock/Blues Guitarist*. Lebanon, Indiana: Studio P/R, 1978.

Puts forth a comprehensive method, from the basics to chord voicings, blues progressions, and blues scales.

2534. Mance, Junior, and Charles Hansen. *How to Play Blues Piano*. New York: Charles Hansen, 1975.

Introduces the beginning jazz student to piano blues techniques and the basic sounds of the blues.

2535. McGuire, Edward F. *Guitar Fingerboard Harmony*. Pacific, Missouri: Mel Bay, 1978.

Emphasizes chord formations, voicings, progressions, and tonal functions.

2536. Mehegan, John. *Swing and Early Progressive Piano Styles*. New York: Watson-Guptill, 1964.

Analyzes the music of Teddy Wilson, Art Tatum, Bud Powell, George Shearing, and Horace Silver in a continuation of his previous books.

2537. Menke, Tony. *Rock Blues Guitar Groove*. Pacific, Missouri: Mel Bay, 1974.

Helps young bassists incorporate rhythmic patterns into their bass lines and improvisations.

2538.   Montgomery, Monk. *The Monk Montgomery Electric Bass
        Method*. Lebanon, Indiana: Studio P/R, 1978.

        Provides a complete method, from the basics to
        challenging solo ensemble work. The information on
        bass lines and bass patterns is especially helpful.

2539.   Niehaus, Lennie. *World's Greatest Jazz Solos: Piano*.
        New York: Almo, 1978.

        Contains transcriptions for piano of several solos
        from great artists. Included are: "Four" (Miles Davis);
        "Giant Steps" (J. Coltrane); "Maiden Voyage" (H. Han-
        cock); "Monk's Dream" (T. Monk); "Oleo" (S. Rollins);
        and "Yardbird Suite" (C. Parker). Also included are
        short bio-musical sketches of the composers.

2540.   Nunes, Warren. *Jazz Guitar Series*. 5 vols. New York:
        Charles Hansen, 1976.

        Covers the entire range of guitar playing, from the
        basics of chord construction to chord progressions,
        substitutions, fingering patterns, and much more.
        Volume 1 covers rhythm and background chords; volume 2
        covers the blues; volume 3, guitar solos; volume 4,
        solo patterns; and volume 5, jazz guitar portfolio.

2541.   Pass, Joe. *Joe Pass Guitar Chords*. New York: Warner,
        1976.

        Shows how different chords are voiced, how they
        function in progressions, and how they function in
        relation to other chords. The author classifies the
        chords into six major categories. All chord voicings
        are written in fret and musical notation.

2542.   ———. *The Joe Pass Guitar Method*. New York: Theodore
        Press, 1977.

        Discusses chord structures, patterns, progressions,
        and substitutions.

2543.   Payne, Ron. *Basic Blues for Piano*. New York: Almo,
        1978.

        Contains information on blues chords, blues pro-
        gressions, riffs, bass line construction, syncopation
        studies, and glissandi as well as several exercises.
        The musical examples are recorded.

2544.   Peterson, Oscar. *Jazz Exercises and Pieces for the*

Young Pianist. No. 1, No. 2, and No. 3. New York: Charles Hansen, 1975.

Offers excellent original exercises and tunes to strengthen the fingers and teach vocabulary, phrasing, and technique to the young jazz pianist.

2545.   Progris, James. *Basic Electric Bass.* 5 vols. New York: Sam Fox, 1974-1978.

The first four volumes cover the spectrum of bass playing, including chord structure, chord functions, walking bass patterns, and etudes. The fifth volume consists of 140 basic rhythmic patterns, chord progressions, walking jazz patterns, and etudes at an advanced level. The text also covers rhythms not commonly used in jazz; e.g., 6/4, 7/4, 7/8, 9/8.

2546.   Rector, Johnny. *Guitar Chord Progressions.* Pacific, Missouri: Mel Bay, 1978.

Serves as more than an encyclopedia for guitar voicings, with information on chord progressions, extensions, alterations, and substitutions. Good musical examples are provided for each chord discussed.

2547.   Reid, Rufus. *The Evolving Bassist.* Chicago: Myriad, 1974.

Geared toward developing a total musical concept for the double bass and for the four and six stringed electric bass. Good for classical and jazz bassists.

2548.   ————. *Evolving Upward Bass Book II.* Chicago: Myriad, 1974.

Deals with patterns and technique in continuation of the first book. The book includes fifteen etudes that are used to perform blues lines and standard jazz progressions.

2549.   Reinhardt, Django. *The Genius of Django Reinhardt.* New York: Jewel Music, 1978.

Presents a short biographical sketch, plus a rare picture of the Django Reinhardt Quintet. Among the tunes included are "Anounman," "Belleville," "Daphne," "Minor Swing," "Swing 42," "Tears," and several others.

2550.   Roberts, Howard. *Super Chops: Jazz Guitar Techniques in 20 Weeks*. North Hollywood: Playback Music, 1978.

    Gives the improvising guitarist a regimented program of weekly programmed project lessons. The author recommends fifty minutes per day and six days per week of practice. Previous musical background is necessary.

2551.   ———. *Howard Roberts' Guitar Manual Sight Reading*. North Hollywood: Playback Music, 1972.

    Covers such subjects as sight reading on single and combined strings, linear reading, and ledger lines. Helpful in developing an awareness of problems confronting guitarists.

2552.   ———, and James Stewart. *The Howard Roberts Guitar Book*. North Hollywood: Playback Music, 1971.

    Contains five sections dealing with topics ranging from the fingerboard and licking to improvising, comping, and chord solo playing. Requires some knowledge of music.

2553.   Roth, Arlen. *How to Play Blues Guitar*. New York: Music Sales, 1978.

    Introduces blues basics, rhythm and lead guitar techniques, scales, patterns, and fingerings. All musical examples are written in both musical notation and guitar tablature.

2554.   Sandole, Adolph. *Jazz Piano Left Hand*. New York: Sandole, 1978.

    Deals usefully with comping, varying chords, and progressions, along with several musical examples.

2555.   Schwartz, S. *Jazz Patterns Made Easier. Jazz Beginnings Made Easier. Jazz Improvisation Made Easier. Boogie Basics Theory. Jazz Instructor (step by step). Erroll Garner Jazz Stylings. Midnight Sun. Fats Waller Jazz Stylings. Country Blues*. New York: Charles Hansen, 1974-1977.

    Presents detailed lessons for the average pianist on blues, the walking bass, the voicing of chords, improvisation, syncopation, suspensions, inner voices, and more. Also included are numerous arrangements of popular songs in jazz style as well as pieces which illustrate jazz style and concepts.

2556.   Smith, Johnny. *The Johnny Smith Approach to the*
          Guitar. 2 vols. Pacific, Missouri: Mel Bay, 1976.

          Focuses on the harmonic aspects of guitar playing.
          The explanations of chord symbols and types, voicing
          alternatives, tonal perspectives, progressions, and
          other supporting materials are excellent.

2557.   Southern, Jeri. *Interpreting Popular Music at the*
          Keyboard. Lebanon, Indiana: Studio P/R, 1978.

          Discusses how to transform printed symbols into
          contemporary sounds, moving from the simple to the
          more complex application of chords. This is primarily
          a piano voicing text not for beginners.

2558.   Spera, Dominic. *Blues and the Basics.* Milwaukee:
          Hal Leonard, 1973.

          Teaches heterogeneous classroom improvisational
          techniques for each instrument in the rhythm section
          as well as for B^b, C, and E^b instruments. Proceeds
          from the simple to the complex. Includes cassette tape.

2559.   Storeman, Win. *Jazz Piano: Ragtime to Rock Jazz.*
          New York: Arco, 1975.

          Covers the basics of several jazz styles with several
          musical examples for intermediate-level pianists.

2560.   Strum, Harvey, and Harold Branch. *Improvising Jazz and*
          Blues Guitar. Plainview, New York: Harold Branch,
          1977.

          Deals with blues fundamentals for beginning improvisa-
          tional instruction. The students write out and play
          their improvisations to gain skill in reading and
          notating music.

2561.   Tarto, Joe. *Basic Rhythms and the Art of Jazz Improvisa-*
          tion. New York: Charles Colin, 1973.

          Instructs beginning players in performing syncopated
          rhythms for jazz band reading and improvisation.
          Exercises do not contain separate parts for treble clef
          instruments but are designed for one or more players.

2562.   Ulano, Sam. *Simplified Coordination System.* New York:
          Almo, 1974.

          Provides information on the essential coordination
          skills needed for contemporary drumming. This intermediate-

level text concentrates on developing hand independence in six different stages: jazz, Latin, rock,
double bass drum reading, two lines, and polyrhythms.

2563. Wright, Eugene. *Jazz Giants/Modern Music for Bass*.
       New York: Charles Hansen, 1977.

       Contains twenty-seven compositions arranged for
       piano and bass with chord symbols. Recommended for
       the advanced bassist.

F. ANTHOLOGIES-COLLECTIONS
(RECORDINGS)

Art of the Jam Session: Montreux '77--O. Peterson, Gillespie,
C. Terry, Lockjaw Davis, NHOP, Milt Jackson, Ray Brown,
Monty Alexander, Ronnie Scott, Pass, Basie, Al Grey, Vic
Dickenson, Sims, Eldridge, Benny Carter. 8-Pablo L. 2620106.

The Bass--Blanton, Pettiford, Brown, Mingus, Chambers, Lafaro,
Hinton, Duvivier, Garrison, Grimes, Haden, Sirone, Workman,
Carter, Clarke, Davis, Izenson, McBee. 3-Impulse 9284.

Big Bands' Greatest Hits, Vol. 2--Hampton, Spivak, Brown,
Ellington, Thornhill, Kyser, Pastor, Bradley, Busse,
Martin, Noble, James, Kaye, Gray, Herman, Lombardo.
(8-72) Col. CG-31213; CGA-31213.

Black Giants--J.J. Johnson, J. Lewis, M. Davis, Silver, Monk,
Mingus, Bud Powell, Hawkins, C. Terry, Blakey, R. Lewis,
Armstrong, Ellington, Gillespie, Garner, Q. Jones, Basie,
Tatum, Coltrane, C. Adderley. 2-Col. PG-33402.

Brass Fever--Rosolino, Winding, G. Brown, Bohanon, Brashear,
Marcus (arr). Impulse 9308 (Q).

Charlie Parker Memorial--D. Gordon, Konitz, Hayes, E. Jeffer-
son, Dorham, Ray Nance, H. McGhee, Red Rodney, Philly Joe
Jones, Muhal R. Abrams. 2-Chess 60002.

Charlie Parker, 10th Memorial Concert--Gillespie, Konitz,
Moody, Eldridge, Hawkins, Cave Lambert, Billy Taylor,
Dorham, Kenny Barron Trio. 5510; 8T5510.

CTI Summer Jazz in the Hollywood Bowl--Deodato, Hammond, Bob
James, Ron Carter, DeJohnette, Benson, Airto, Crawford,
Farrell, Turrentine, G. Washington, Hubbard, Laws, Milt
Jackson. (Rec. 7/72)--Live One CTI 7076; 8-7076; C-7076.
Live Two CTI 7077; 8-7077; C-7077. Live Three CTI 7078;
8-7078; C-7078 (W.E. Phillips).

Decade of Jazz, 1959-69. Vol. 3--J. Smith, Quebec, Burrell,
D. Byrd, Morgan, Dolphy, Silver, Turrentine, O. Coleman,
Donaldson. Impulse 99.

Definitive Jazz Scene, Vol. 1 (9-64). Vol. 2--Charles, Scott,
    Hampton, Nelson, J.J. Johnson, Coltrane, Tyner, Albam,
    Flanagan. (3-65) Impulse 100. Vol. 3--Coltrane, Shepp,
    Nelson, Tyner, Hamilton, Russian, Jazz Quartet, Scott E.
    Jones. (1-66) Impulse 9101.

The Drums--Blakey, Roach, Clarke, Philly Joe Jones, Sid
    Catlett, Jo Jones, Connie Kay, Haynes, Richmond, Bellson,
    Manne, Hamilton, Purdie, E. Jones, Rashied Ali, Milford
    Graves, Baby Dodds, J. Chambers, Beaver Harris, N. Connors,
    E. Blackwell, Sunny Murray, Mouzon, Paul Motian, B. Alt-
    schul. 3-Impulse 9272.

Encyclopedia of Jazz in the 70's--Leonard Feather presents
    L.L. Smith, Manne, Tapscott, Gil Evans, Barbieri, Dank-
    worth, Cleo Laine, Akiyoshi and Tabackin, Amram, Simone,
    Groove Holmes, Rich, Jazz Piano Quartet, O. Nelson,
    B. Mitchell, Ellington. 2-RCA APL2-1984.

Greatest Jazz Concert in the World--*Ellington & Orchestra*--
    Fitzgerald, Peterson, Benny Carter, Hawkins, Z. Sims,
    C. Terry, T-Bone Walker. (JATP) 4-Pablo 2625704 S25704.

Guitar Players Main 410

Impulsively--Barbieri, Jarrett, White, Mel Brown, Klemmer,
    Saracho, Haden, Redman, Marion Brown, Sun Ra, J. Coltrane,
    Rivers. 2-Impulse 9266 (Q); 8027-9266H.

Jam Sessions at Montreux '77--Basie, Gillespie, Milt Jackson,
    Ray Brown, O. Peterson, Benny Carter, Sims, Lockjaw Davis,
    C. Terry, Faddis, Eldridge, Al Grey, Vic Dickenson.
    NHOP 2-Pablo L. 2620105; S20105; K201105.

Jazz for a Sunday Afternoon, Vols. 1/2--Adams, Corea, R. Davis,
    Gillespie, E. Jones, M. Lewis, Nance/Adams, G. Brown,
    Corea, R. Davis, Gillespie, Lewis. (4-68) 2-Solid 18027/8.
    Vol. 3--Bryant, H. Edison. Solid 18037.

A Jazz Piano Anthology--Blake, J.P. Johnson, Waller, Yancey,
    Hines, Tatum, Wilson, Ammons, M.L. Lewis, P. Johnson,
    M.L. Williams, Basie, Ellington, Monk, Powell, Garner,
    J. Lewis, Silver, B. Evans, C. Taylor, and others.
    2-Col PG-32355.

Jazz Years--25th Anniversary--Rogers, Tristano, Charles,
    Giuffre, M. Jackson, Modern Jazz Quartet, Blakey, Newman,
    Mingus, Coltrane, Coleman, Mitchell-Ruff Trio, Allison,
    B. and G. Lewis, Crawford, Lloyd, Hubbard, Kirk, Mann,
    Lateef, McCann and Harris. 2-At. 2-316; TP-2-316;
    CS-2-316.

Master Jazz Piano--Hines, S. White, C. Jackson, C. Hopkins,
    McShann. Mas. J. 8105. Vol. 3--T. Wilson, Hines, Hearn,
    S. White, Dunham. Mas. J. 8105. Vol. 4--McShann, Hines,
    Hearn, Smalls, C. Jackson. Mas. J. 8129.

Masters of the Modern Piano--Bud Powell, Cecil Taylor, Mary
    Lou Williams, Paul Bley, Wynton Kelly, Bill Evans. (Rec.
    '55-'66) 2-Verve 2514; 8T2-2514; CT-2-2514.

Montreux Collection--Basie, J. Griffin, M. Jackson, Eldridge,
    J. Pass, O. Peterson, E. Peterson, E. Fitzgerald, Gillespie,
    and others. (Rec. '75) 2-Pablo 2625707; S25707.

New American Music, Vol. 1--G. Evans, Milford Graves, M.L.
    Williams, S. Rivers, S. Murray. Folk. 33901.

Piano Giants--Ellington, Hines, Tatum, Garner, Monk, Powell,
    Tristano, Haig, Shearing, Lewis, Silver, Hawes, Timmons,
    Peterson, Newborn, Jamal, Garland, Kelly, Hancock,
    Zawinul, Corea, Jarrett, Tyner. 2-Prest. 24052.

Prestige Giants, Vol. 1--Davis, Monk, Dolphy, Rollins, MJQ,
    Parker, Coltrane, Allison, Lateef, Mingus. 2-Prest. PRP-1.
    Vol. 2--Davis, Coltrane, Mulligan, Brown, Getz, Moody,
    Pleasure, Ammons and Marmarosa, Santamaria, McDuff.
    2-Prest. PRP-2.

Progressives--McLaughlin, Mahavishnu Orchestra, Santana, Bill
    Evans, O. Coleman, Dailey, Jarrett, Weather Report, Soft
    Machine, Mingus, D. Ellis, P. Winter, M. Ferguson.
    2-Col. CG-31574; CGA-31574.

Ragtime Special--Max Morath, Muggsy Spanier, The Ragtimers,
    and others. 2-Camd. ADL2-0778.

The Saxophone--Hawkins, Carter, Byas, Stitt, Rollins, Hodges,
    Webster, Coltrane, Shepp, Young, Parker, Dolphy, Coleman,
    Sanders, Simmons, Gilmore, Ayler, Klemmer, Brown, Redman,
    Rivers, Barbieri. 3-Impulse 9253.

Soul-Jazz Giants--Ammons, W. Jackson, L. Davis, Scott,
    G. Holmes, McDuff. Prest. S-7791.

Time Is Running Out--Ellis, Ritenour, Brashear, Bohanon,
    Jackson (arr.). Impulse 9319; 8027-931H.

Three Giants--Gillespie, Coltrane, Rollins. (Rec. '52, '53,
    '57, '60) 2-Trip 5038; 8T-5038.

Trumpet Tribute--Fats Navarro, Clifford Brown, Booker Little,
    Kenny Dorham, Woody Shaw, Bill Hardman, Walter Kelly,
    Blue Mitchell, Lonnie Smith, Peck Morrison, Walter Perkins.
    2-Trip 5036; 8T-5036.

25 Years of Prestige--Tristano, Konitz, Getz, Winding, Navarro, Grey, Joe Holiday, Leo Parker, Miles Davis, King Pleasure, Monk, Rollins, Coltrane, Golson, Garland, Eddie "Lockjaw" Davis, Dolphy, Burrell, Ammons, Dexter Gordon. 2-Prest. 24046.

When the Saints Go Marching In--Fountain, Hirt, Girard, Almerico. (6-72) 2-Camd. CXS-9018.

Wildflowers: New York Loft Jazz--Kalaparusha, Ken McIntyre, S. Murray, Rivers, Anthony Braxton, Marion Brown, Leo Smith, Randy Weston, Michael Gregory Jackson, Dave Burrell, Ahmed Abdullah, Andrew Cyrille, Hamiet Bluiett, Julius Hemphill, Jimmy Lyons, Oliver Lake, David Murray, Sunny Murray, Roscoe Mitchell. (Rec. 5/76)

ADDENDUM

History of Jazz Series (Folkways Records)

A ten-volume series that covers the historical development of jazz from its beginnings to the early thirties. Most valuable for many of the rare early recordings that are now out of print. The series includes the following: Vol. 1, The South; Vol. 2, The Blues; Vol. 3, New Orleans; Vol. 4, Jazz Singers; Vol. 5, Chicago, No. 1; Vol. 6, Chicago, No. 2; Vol. 7, New York; Vol. 8, Big Bands before 1935; Vol. 9, Piano; and Vol. 10, Boogie Woogie.

Smithsonian Collection of Jazz (Smithsonian Institution)

An excellent collection of jazz recordings in chronological order. The collection includes an excellent booklet on jazz styles, artists, and recordings. Particularly strong on jazz since Bop.

G. JAZZ RESEARCH LIBRARIES

Berklee College of Music--Library
    1140 Boylston Street
    Boston, Massachusetts 02215

    Subjects: Some jazz and rock.

Detroit Public Library--Music and Performing Arts Department
    5201 Woodward Avenue
    Detroit, Michigan 48201

    Special Collections: E. Azalia Hackley Collection (Blacks
    in the Performing Arts). Contains some materials of
    potential interest to jazz scholars.

Indiana University--Black Music Center--Library
    244 Sycamore Hall
    Bloomington, Indiana 47401

New Orleans Jazz Club--New Orleans Jazz Museum--Library
    340 Bourbon Street
    New Orleans, Louisiana 70116

    Subjects: Jazz, Swing, ragtime, boogie woogie, Bop,
    minstrelsy, progressive jazz.

    Special Collections: Music of Africa, Haiti, and early
    Louisiana.

    Holdings: 600 books; 20 bound periodical volumes, 5
    vertical file drawers of archival material dealing with
    jazz and its pre-history; photographs, tapes, sheet music,
    and records.

New Orleans Public Library--Art and Music Division
    219 Loyola Avenue
    New Orleans, Louisiana 70140

    Special Collections: Souchan Jazz Collection (Recordings);

New Orleans Public Library (cont'd)

early U.S. sheet music; Fischer Collection of early vocal recordings.

Holdings: 28,000 books; 1212 bound periodical volumes; 4 vertical file drawers of film catalogs; 4 vertical file drawers of pamphlets; 45,276 mounted pictures; 19,273 phonograph records; 800 framed art prints.

New York Public Library--Arthur Alfonso Schomburg Collection
515 Lenox Avenue
New York, New York 10037

Special Collections: International in scope and interest. Includes more than 58,000 volumes (all areas of Black music) along with phonograph records, tape recordings, promos, posters, paintings, sculptures, clippings, periodicals, pamphlets, sheet music, and newspapers as well as large holdings of manuscript and archival records. Much of the collection is of jazz.

Rutgers, The State University of New Jersey--Institute of Jazz Studies
Newark, New Jersey 07102

Holdings: 6000 books; 5000 bound periodical volumes; records and collections, manuscripts, piano rolls, photographs, jazz magazines, music, instruments, and sculptures.

Library open to public by appointment only.

Tulane University of Louisiana--Archive of New Orleans Jazz
Howard-Tilton Memorial Library
New Orleans, Louisiana 70118

Subjects: New Orleans jazz, with related background material and a limited amount of material pertaining to later developments in jazz.

Special Collections: Nick La Rocca Collection (2644 items); Al Rose Collection (902 items); John Robichaux Collection (7219 items); Herbert A. Otto Collection (20 tapes).

Holdings: 971 books; 6 reels of microfilm; 32 motion picture reels; 7415 periodicals; 5456 photographs; 56 piano rolls; 8617 records; 2046 reels of tape recorded music and interviews.

Open to researchers.

U.S. Navy--School of Music--Reference Library
    NAVPHI Base, Little Creek
    Norfolk, Virginia 23521

    Subjects: Analysis, conducting, composition, counterpoint,
    harmony, instruments, jazz, military music, and theory of
    music.

University of Miami--School of Music--Albert Pick Music
        Library
    Coral Gables, Florida 33124

    Subjects: Music scores and recordings.

    Special Collections: Autographed recordings (composers and
    performers); ethnic recordings, especially African, Latin
    American, American Indian, and jazz.

    Holdings: 12,000 music scores and 8000 phonograph records.

Yale University--James Weldon Johnson Collection
    120 High Street
    New Haven, Connecticut 06520

    Special Collections: Founded by Carl Van Vechten in 1961.
    Concentrates on the achievements of Blacks in the United
    States in the twentieth century in the fine arts. It
    contains extensive holdings of original recordings of
    Black performers, e.g., Bessie Smith, Clara Smith, and
    W.C. Handy. Also included are some original manuscripts
    of Black musicians.

INDEX TO SECTION I:
JAZZ AND ITS GENRES

INDEX TO SECTION II:
REFERENCE MATERIALS